A SHORT TIME
FOR
INSANITY

A SHORT TIME FOR INSANITY

An Autobiography

William A. Wellman

HAWTHORN BOOKS, INC.
Publishers / New York

To Mommy and our seven kids and their kids, both here and en route, with profound apologies for some of the language and some of the things you didn't know about your daffy old man.

FOREWORD

As a breed, the men who have devoted their lives to directing movies share many admirable human qualities—strength of character, quickness of mind, a sense of humor about themselves, and a wry sense of perspective about their work. I've never met a veteran of this craft who was pompous or self-important or—at the other end of the spectrum—falsely modest or self-pitying. Among their minor, but no less revealing, virtues is a reluctance—not shared by their class enemies, actors and producers—to write their autobiographies. On those rare occasions when they overcome that reluctance, however, another of their excellent qualities comes into play; they do the job themselves, without ghostly assistance and, generally speaking, with a cheerful willingness to name the names of those who did them dirt, or who managed to embarrass themselves in the author's presence; to admit their own mistakes and foolishnesses; to generally offer a true portrait of the way things really were, the way things really got done in Hollywood during the time of it's—and their—greatness. In this connection one thinks of the autobiographies of Frank Capra, King Vidor, Joseph von Sternberg, Raoul Walsh and, of course, the splendid volume you now hold in your hand.

William A. Wellman likes to grouse that people are always complimenting him on *The Best Years of Our Lives* (William Wyler) of *Some Like It Hot* (Billy Wilder). Doubtless these gentlemen receive kind words for *his* pictures—films like *Public Enemy, Wild Boys of the Road, A Star Is Born, Beau Geste, The Ox-Bow Incident, The Story of G.I. Joe*—and one likes to imagine that all the WWs follow the sensible policy of the late John

Ford, who was always being complimented for Howard Hawks' *Red River,* and who was always pleased to accept the kindness of strangers with the modest admission that, yes, he'd always liked that one himself. These confusions prove nothing except that, until the recent advent of the film scholar, the film student and, less grandly, the film freak, people were a little vague about the names of the great directors, principally because they were a little vague as to just what directors did and why they were important. I suppose that's why I've been asked to introduce a man who seems to me to need no introduction, a man who has been a presence in my life—because of his movies—literally for as long as I can remember, some thirty or thirty-five years before I began to enjoy the pleasure of his company.

For me, Bill Wellman is a significant historical figure, as are most of his colleagues. And it seems to me he—they—should be so regarded by just about everyone. For the films they made during our formative years had as much to do with the creation of a generation's sensibility—moral as well as aesthetic—as anything the politicians of their time did, and far more than any writers or painters or social scientists did. These people, of course, are inveterate tooters of their own horns; if anything, we know too much about them.

What we know about directors, on the other hand, is an amalgam of legend, rumor, bad journalism, and old press agentry. It is mainly through a close study of their films that one has, until recently, gained an accurate impression of men like Bill Wellman —and even that, of course, has been blurred by the fact that they didn't always choose their own projects, didn't always work closely with the screenwriter, often saw their visions unconsciously reshaped by an actor's presence or quite consciously jiggered by a meddlesome producer. This being so, it is pleasant to observe, having read *A Short Time for Insanity,* how much of the true, one and only Bill Wellman did find its way onto the screens of our childhood. The reader will quickly perceive, for example, how central the gift for telling a story is to Bill. And telling it briskly, efficiently, humorously, even nuttily. One hates to attribute to a man who abhors pretention, literary or otherwise, a sense of the absurd. But it is present here, as well as in comedies like *Nothing Sacred* and *Roxie Hart,* and even in pictures like Buffalo Bill (the wonderful shooting gallery sequence)—inextricably linked with his basic storytelling gift.

Other aspects of the man's basic vision are clearly present, both in his films and in this book—his infinite curiosity (he once told me that his main goal as a director was to attempt every kind of film there was); the simple, basic toughness that prevented him from suffering fools gladly, and led to his nickname, "Wild Bill"; the understated, quickly revealed, quickly covered up sentiment for old times and lost friends; a somber, brooding awareness —also not lingered over—of the world's thoughtless brutality.

I mention all these matters here not because I always observed them in Bill's movies when I first saw them, but because, even looking at them now, my critical gear all tuned up so it can click off terrific perceptions by the minute, I tend—like anyone else— to get caught up in the spell of his storytelling and to forget all about themes and techniques and all the other stuff that gave Bill's best films a resonance that continues to rumble down the years. I mention these matters also because, if you're not careful, his autobiography will sweep you along like one of his movies, hustling you from funny story to crazy interlude to poignant shred of memory without giving you time to think a great deal about the man who wrote it, except to think—quite correctly— that he's a very considerable work in his own right.

I'm not going to spoil his story by rehearsing the tale of how a nice middle-class youth from New England managed to become, in about a decade, a high school dropout, a World War One flying hero with the French air force, a screen actor (briefly), and, finally, a director—in the process winning, for his first major production, *Wings,* the first Academy Award ever given for best picture of the year. Nor can I begin to tell, with his mixture of humor and exasperation, of his early marital (and mother-in-law) misadventures. Nor can I speak, with his mixture of love and gratitude, of the last four decades of what appears to be a perfect marriage with his beloved Dottie, and his joy in his role as the father of seven children and grandfather of their numerous off-spring. All of that awaits the reader who can possess himself in patience for just a couple of minutes more.

I simply want to point out that such obvious matters as the motive for writing his book, and the structure and style he chose for it, are true measures of the man. He wrote the book something like a decade ago, as a way of keeping his mind occupied and as a distraction from the pain that was the result of a severe back operation—that was, in turn, supposed to cure a spine broken in a World War One plane crash. He did it—as the length of time between the completion of the manuscript and his offering it for publication attests—not because he wanted to impose himself and his life on strangers, not because he thought he was an important fellow we were all just dying to know better (though, indeed, some of us were), but because there was nothing else he could do. There were literally no other distractions available to him—and Bill is one of the most energetic people I've ever met. He drives himself and everybody else crazy if he doesn't have something to do. The book, then, was a last resort for him—not the first thought of an egocentric old gentleman nodding off in his retirement. But even in his constricted circumstances it was not enough for Bill to do one of those name-dropping, and-then-I-made Holly-wood autobiographies. (Indeed, the names mentioned most frequently and with the most affection herein are not household names in any household but the Wellmans'.)

No, what he did was to construct a free-association autobiography in which he tried to recreate the hallucinatory workings of his mind as he fought the pain—and the drugs that were supposed to relieve that pain—during his long struggle back from his closest brush with mortality. Technically, it was a bold experiment for a man who had never written a book before. But it worked. It worked because his struggle to free himself from drug dependency through his own unaided efforts is dramatic and inspiring, and in itself a good example of the kind of tough, courageous man he is, and because it provides a compelling and suspenseful framework for his life story, gives it a broad contemporary relevance that should commend *A Short Time for Insanity* even to those who care little for film history. Most important, it works because the form suits the man so well. On nothing stronger than aspirin, Bill Wellman is a free-form conversationalist, a man whose mind just naturally perceives relationships between ideas and incidents the rest of us don't notice. It's part of what makes him so much fun to be with, part of what makes him seem forever young.

What I've been saying here is that Bill Wellman is an American original, a spiky, self-reliant character, whose particular pleasure is to invent his own highly individualistic solutions to the problems of life and art and to not give a damn whether or not anyone else approves of them. It's my powerful feeling that we don't make men like him anymore and that most of our problems in this country stem from that sad fact. He's going to snort when he reads this, but I love him. He has been a valuable example to me and, with this book, I think he's about to become a valuable example for a lot of other people. If he doesn't, that's their problem—and we're in worse shape than I thought we were.

—RICHARD SCHICKEL

December 12, 1973

ONE

The wedding was made more picturesque by the presence as an usher, of her handsome cousin William A. Wellman, in the light blue uniform of the French Air Corps. He was home from service in the Lafayette Flying Corps to recuperate from injuries suffered when his plane was shot down.

Samuel Williston, *Life and Law*

Sounds rather intriguing, doesn't it? Kinda romantic. A great introduction for the hero in a movie—movies, that big nest of hits and flops, with so many little broken dreams wiggling out from it, from which come the few hitters and many floppers; some to their big Bel Air swimming-pooled estates, some to their poolless homes, some to their rooms, their bars, their dames. All will be back tomorrow, the hitters fighting to stay on top, the floppers fighting to *get* on top. And through it all occasionally stumbles a bum, with a crown on his head.

I am that bum, that twenty-one-year-old blue-uniformed usher. Frankly I can't remember a thing about the wedding. I know it's true because my Uncle Sam wrote about it. I know it's true because he is a great and loved man. A famed teacher of law. A man who has devoted all his enormous talent and long life for the good of others. A gentleman. He is now one hundred and bedridden and doesn't know where he is or who he is—or who anyone is. He is dead, but he still breathes.

I am alive—a few hours ago in my backyard, if you can call six acres a backyard, I reached for a flower and I got stuck; I couldn't move. I knew something was all gone, and I was terrified. After sixty-five years of fighting and flying and directing and living and marrying, I get it reaching for a flower.

They ambulanced me out of the estate, yelling like a banshee Indian—I don't remember much of it, just the big-eyed, frightened stare of the youngest of my brood of seven, Maggie, a freckle-faced, red-haired little girl of eight. She knew something had happened to her crazy old man, and she was terrified because she loved him very much.

The first day was an abandoned day. It never happened. The second, they let me become normal only long enough to take X rays. The blood pressures and the blood tests and the urinalysis and the other isisis they did when I was out. The X rays they saved for me when I was in. Have you ever been X-rayed, with a back that was either broken or had a few crushed disks, or maybe just a pinched nerve or two, or maybe it just had something that they didn't know anything about? Whatever it was, it hurt like hell, and I was only comfortable when lying on my right side, as quiet and motionless as a very old, very frightened possum.

I have seen guys kill cattle in a slaughterhouse. They are tender compared to the nurse and the X-ray expert, whatever the hell his title is, that worked me over. Reminded me of a wrestling match. At this stage of the match the heavy was on; and I, the nice clean-living young fella, was getting the bejesus kicked out of him. The boos of the crowd became the groans and cries of me. After dozens of chiropractic yanks at the neck, the skull, the shoulders, the upper back, the lower back, the middle back, the left leg, the right leg, the old possum became a tiger. I zapped the nurse in the hind end, threw a punch at the exponent of the X ray, and passed out. Immediately a false rumor was circulated through the hospital that I was a son of a bitch.

The next day was the day of judgment. In the morning new specialists took a crack at me. They hit everything and

4

finally arrived at my rectum, searching I suppose for my prostate, and when they found out that I had one and that it didn't explode on contact, another guy came in and started to feel my scrotum. This was too much. I complained in four-letter words, and the false rumor started circulating again. I was then served with a couple of capsules. I asked the doctor what they were, and he smilingly told me they were called green hornets; he had a swell sense of humor. They were striking-looking things, half deep brown and half kelly green. Nothing soft- or gentle-looking about them; on the contrary rather on the severe side, but effective; you know, like an athletic girl—these were the babies that contained, among other things, codeine—they numbed the pain and the brain. From now on you were to be half nuts most of the time. Shouldn't be anything unusual for you; after all you have directed some three hundred actors and actresses, give or take a few, from Dustin Farnum to Robert Mitchum, and that is liable to make anyone a little balmy.

Drugs can excuse you for going nuts—for the writing not to be in continuity—but mixed up as is your thinking during this grisly period of your illness—mixed up, full of codeine—with a little extra additive. Codeine—it kills your pain and strangles your bowels, until it would take an act of God to make them move. An act of God or the skill of a Spud Taylor. My first movement was a rip-roaring passing of a rack of pool balls, from the one to the fifteen, wild as hell, and in every pocket on the table.

A little later, Mommy, that's my wife, and Bill, my oldest boy, came in to hear the results of all the tests and the momentous decision of the great medical brains that had been cake-walking through my structure. I recognized them, but in an out-of-focus kind of way. I wanted to say something nice to Mommy, but it wouldn't form. It didn't have to. She kissed me, and I went to sleep again. Sometime later I started to drift back and heard the murmur of many voices and suddenly, above it all, Mommy's, clear as a crack of a whip, asking in that demanding tone, "Isn't there some other doctor in Los Angeles whose opinion you all would respect?" There was absolute quiet for long enough to make me think I had gone again when suddenly one name rang out—McKeever—and then I knew that there was something really wrong with my back, and I was terrified. I left them for a while. Or did I? Sometimes they were there, and then seemed to fade out slowly like the end of a picture, only there wasn't any music.

This was a hell of a time to think of my inability to remember names. I squawked about it once to Spud Taylor; we were playing golf one midsummer's day in San Fernando Valley. A midsummer's day in the San Fernando Valley is like a Turkish bath with no cold wet towel; Spud at the time was the president of the club, and since we both broke 80, we had exciting matches together, played to win with a few bucks on the side.

The day was so hot that the president and his guest were just about the only golfers goofy enough to play. We were sweating *up* one of the fairways, after a couple of good drives, and for some inexplicable reason I started to complain to Spud about my great talent for forgetting names. Friend or foe, relative or neighbor, or even sometimes my kids. In fact, I once forgot my own name; I was a little loaded, but not enough to excuse this boring habit. I explained to Spud that this was not a result of fast living, crashes, crack-ups, mental lapses, or senectitude, but a horrible whammy that I had been forced to live with all of my life. If I had a buck for every time I had to resort to "whatever happened to what's-his-name," I would be a very wealthy sexagenarian (a man between sixty and seventy years). Why they stick that three-letter word in is something I never will understand. Maybe it's just as a reminder, a bit of a word to dream by, or a punishment.

We climbed on in silence. I looked at Spud, and he seemed to be away, way off. I wondered whether it was the reminder, the dream, or the punishment, when he snapped out of it.

Spud had started out to be a brain surgeon. If I remember correctly, when he went to Mayos to further his studies, he suddenly realized that the most neglected, most important, and perhaps the most painful part of the human body was the rectum. Despite its location, Spud made the change and became not only the best, but literally a magician of the prat; and because of his choice, many of my friends and hosts of others sit comfortably. Spud has a very sly sense of humor and a very wide open boyish smile. Makes you want to smile too. But when he turned to me, he was dead serious. He asked me if I was through squawking. I said I was, and then he said he wanted to tell me a little story. Something that had happened to him just three days ago.

Spud's office had a big reception room, and when you came in for your appointment, there were usually some others there awaiting their turn. At first it was a little embarrassing, until you got it through your thick head that they all were brothers under the skin. Of course sitting down in a nonchalant manner was sometimes pretty hard to do. Once I groaned, and the guy sitting opposite me smiled and applauded softly. The secretary sat inside a windowed little room with a corridor running down to Spud's office; to the right of Spud's office was another corridor that led to two undressing rooms on either side of his chamber of horrors, in which was a contraption he called a table. It was the goddamnedest table I had ever seen, much less been on. One lay on it on his or her tummy, and Spud pressed a lever, and oh so gently your position was changed. You ended up, head pointing to the floor, and your rear pointing at Spud, who stood, by the way, very erectly. You get the picture?

Three days ago, a middle-aged lady came into Spud's office. The secretary had left to run an errand leaving him all alone in his office going over some overdue bills. Madame X, seeing no secretary, catching a quick shot of Spud, breezed right down the corridor and entered his office unannounced. Spud, taken aback, could not think of her name. She talked as if she was a returnee, and after a few minutes of quiet but dull repartee, she excused herself and departed down the corridor leading to the ladies' undressing room. Spud heard the familiar dropping sounds of a female get-ready, and then the footsteps in the chamber of horrors and the faint sounds of Madame X mounting the table. He was bitched, buggered, and bewildered; but he stuck to his guns and found himself standing erect, rubber-fingered, foot on pedal, and ready. He pushed. She changed position. He looked. Immediately he knew her name, her age, how many children she had, her prescribed diet, her whole history, her aggregate. He asked me if I had any complaints now.

We had arrived at my ball. I took out my four wood and laid it on the green. I looked at him and said—none!

The murmur of voices almost brought me around again, almost but not quite. I opened my eyes and looked at the spot on the wall that a picture of the Christ had occupied. Thank God it was gone. The landscape was there, with its soothing green fields and comfortable trees and soft sky.

I suppose the rumor was abroad again, but I think the sister, to whom I had complained, understood me. When you lie in one position for days, the slightest move hurts like hell, you get a bedsore on your hip, and your field of vision is very limited. Mine zeroed in on a print of the Christ. The face only slightly resembled the fine paintings that I had seen and used in many of my pictures. This one was completely negative, not a line in its face. The eyes were big and lifeless. There was a curl to the hair as if just dressed, the eyebrows were tapered, and the eyelashes looked like Mae West's. I made up my mind then that this was the work of a fairy. I tried not to look at it, but this was the only place I could look! I was surrounded. Being an Episcopalian in a Catholic hospital, in my conscious moments I tried to be on my best behavior, but this was a challenge that was beginning to weaken me.

I am a Bostonian born in Brookline, Massachusetts, and reared for most of my boyhood in Newton Highlands, a suburb of Boston. Crystal Lake was a block away. They cut ice there in the winter and stored it in the big icehouse on the other side of the lake. The railroad track ran right alongside of it. In the winter we skated, in the summer we swam, in the fall we gathered chestnuts that fell from the big proud trees that lined the lake. Have you ever tasted roasted chestnuts? Not the big ones. The medium size. Not the ones you get in New York. The Boston chestnuts. You've heard that expression "sweet as a nut"? Could well have been "sweet as a Crystal Lake chestnut." Funny how few things you really remember with mouth-watering relish—Boston baked beans, fish balls (not cakes, balls), steamed clams, and chestnuts. Steaks and chops and roast beef you get anywhere, and they're good anywhere, but nowhere can you get these savorous four—the beans, the balls, the clams, and the nuts—except in Boston, and they're very inexpensive dishes. You can feast on them if you're broke. Which by the way we were a great deal of the time.

My dad was what we call an inner and outer. One month we would eat the beans and the balls and the nuts, not just one night of the week but two or three, and if things got really rugged, we had beans every night. You got full of them and you'd want something different, but somehow you never got sick of them, and after a few nonbean nights we would ask Mother for some more Boston baked beans. These we would get and with them often a change in our financial status. The old boy would come home from his brokerage office with his pockets bulging and his breath an alcoholic haze. We had the best from then on until his luck suddenly vanished and we went back to beans, balls, clams, and nuts.

A wonderful thing about being half screwy under so-called sedation is that you think only of the highlights. A night bright as day from a majestic full moon. It's the moon that you see. The source of all the breathless beauty that surrounds you—just as the reverse is true. A presidential parade with its thousands of onlookers and the accustomed waving smile of the president. Some silly idiot with ears like a donkey is smiling too, but a few of his teeth are missing and he is right in the foreground. And he is the one you see.

My mother is now ninety-three years young. She is a little

bitty gal, a little too heavy, but sharp as a tack and fairly active. Her maiden name was Celia McCarthy. She was a beautiful woman and loved and understood my rather unreliable father. She had but two children, my older brother by sixteen months and me, the problem child. She still has her cocktail before lunch, another before dinner, and a spot of bourbon on retiring. She smokes a pack a day and can beat the hell out of anyone playing bridge. A few months ago she fell downstairs—rolled all the way to the floor below—result, no broken bones, a slight shock, and multiple black and blue spots, some located, in brilliant technicolor, where a mirror was needed to view. I called and asked her why the acrobatics at her age, and she told me very simply that the reason for her present good condition was that when she felt herself going she relaxed completely and had the fastest, bumpiest tour down a staircase that has ever been accomplished by an old bag completely sober. This gives you a small idea of my mother. A little old lady who has loved but one man all her life. Who lived with him and loved with him through every joy and sorrow, through every strength and through every weakness. Before World War I she became the probation officer of the city of Newton. This she did for her love and understanding of all boys, especially the "wandering" ones, as she called them. She hated the word "delinquent." She worked for nothing. My brother and I went to Newton High School, a distance of about two miles from our home, to and from. En route we passed through a section called Kerry Cross, full of Irishers. They didn't know my mother's maiden name was McCarthy, and I doubt if it would have made any difference.

They leveled on us as being of the upper crust. A masterpiece of misunderstanding. In other words they gave us the business. My mother told me a few years ago that she remembered a stretch that I went through with a black eye, for four months. It was a wandering black eye. The moment the right became normal I got it in the left. My brother, being shorter than I and

much heavier, lowered his head like a goat, but he had marbles on the top of his skull that I think are still there.

I wonder what else they put in with this codeine. What
started all this Crystal Lake folklore? I remember—the pansy
Christ.

Someone was working on me again, but the hands seemed
different. They were working in a place that hurt. In fact they
seemed to follow the hurt all the way down to the bottom of my
right foot. They were strong yet gentle, and suddenly they left
me and then I heard the voice of the hands, McKeever: "Mrs.
Wellman, if I were Bill, I wouldn't let them operate on me until I got down on my hands and knees and crawled." That
brought me around just enough to thank him and ask him to
do me a great favor: get me the hell out of here. He just
looked at me with a patient understanding smile and told me
to be a good little boy and take it easy. The way he said it I
knew he wasn't kidding. I made up my mind to behave myself,
and as I started to drift away, far, far off, I heard Mommy can-
celing the operating room and then just the faint touch of her
soft warm lips and I was gone. It took this kind of a serious
few weeks in a hospital full of uncertain days, hours when
you didn't know where you were or, for that matter, didn't
care; when just a kiss from the one you loved meant more
than medicine or doctors or nurses or pain. It meant life.

I dreamed of my dog. That is, the dog of my kid days.
The dog of my life. The president was then Mr. Taft, so we
called the pup Taffy. Mother gave it to us both on Christmas
Day. A round furred bundle of black and white. He was just
about everything. A little spitz, a dash of Eskimo, and a touch
of collie; with brains and guts and a love for me that was
eternal. My brother spent most of his time working in the tool
shed with a jigsaw making wonderful things. I spent all my
time out of doors, skating in the winter, tapping the maple trees
for their sweet syrup, baseball in the spring and summer and
swimming, football in the fall and chestnuts, and Taffy be-

came mine. When Christmas came again, my brother's present to me was his half of the dog. I slept outside in a sleeping porch. Didn't have to, but I liked it. Taffy slept with me. Sometimes we got rained on. That Christmas night we got snowed on. I woke up the next morning, and there he was beside me, sound asleep with his old head sticking out of the snow like an ink spot on a marshmallow. She came in again—that is, into my subconscious —she and that unpleasant German nurse who had the 7:00 A.M. to 3:00 P.M. stretch of taking care of me. The three words "taking care of" she reduced to one, "scrubbing." This was the washingest dame that ever soaped a diaper, soaked a panty, or hung out my jockey strap that had just finished its third successive trip through the washing machine. It wasn't that dirty, just protected things that she apparently was allergic to.

She took all this out on me, and each morning I was scrubbed back to reality by an oozy washcloth, full of too much soap and too little hot water. This morning I rebelled. I told her that I was going to stay dirty for two days. She told me that she had her orders. I told her I wasn't interested in her orders. She told me that the doctor was. I told her I wasn't interested in the doctor. She told me it was the rule of the hospital, and I told her it wouldn't hurt the Catholics to have one dirty Protestant lying in its hospital and that furthermore if we didn't stop this "I told her, she told me" business, I'd bite her and that I wouldn't be choosy where. She left me alone, and the sister entered to pay her respects. I had a hunch that she had heard this delightful pleasantry and might be on the side of the oppressed, so I took a chance and again explained my revulsion to the picture of the Christ and why I had asked for the fields, the trees, and the sky. She didn't answer right away, and I began to wonder if I had unknowingly committed some horrible sin against the church, when from left field she said, "Mr. Wellman, you were a flier, weren't you? A pursuit pilot?" I said yes. A long, long time ago. She just looked at me and with a faint little smile on her face left the room. That night they gave me my jolt, and I went to sleep—no, it's not that easy; you don't go to sleep, you sort of go through a series of quick dissolves, in and out. Then in again, then out again; in and out like a cuckoo until finally, the outs win.

It only lasted about three hours. I came to and asked my nurse for my ration of green hornets. She said patiently that there was another hour to go. She was the nurse that had the eleven to seven shift. A big gal, quiet as a mouse, and knew her business. I liked her and wondered how I could get her switched to the scrubbing shift without making trouble. I wouldn't mind being washed by her. She came over and gave me a cooling dermassage treatment, and I lasted the hour out. Then I got my reward, and just before leaving for my few hours in wonderland, she told me that tomorrow I could hang my feet over the bed for a few minutes. Big deal. But it was a start for home.

I aimed carefully, zeroed in on the shining bald head two stories down, and let the stink bomb go. My aim was perfect. There was an odorous splash, and my education, scholastically speaking, was finished. The head belonged to the principal of the high school.

The hodgepodge of things you think of. How fast they come and go. My first crack at making a living: Green Seal chocolates, carton belting, wool. Never sold a box of chocolates or a foot of belting or a pound of wool or whatever the hell it is you sell wool in or of or by. Sorting soles, the kind you wear on your shoes. Rights and lefts and just so many. Then you tie 'em up and start all over. All day long. Every day. Six days a week. Rights and lefts, tie 'em up. Start all over again. My brain got tired, and I ended up scaling lefts and rights at the most insufferable foreman that ever lived. I walked out amid the cheers of my downtrodden comrades. This unusual sound of happiness brought another mirth-loving boss storming in. Silence snapped to attention as did I, thumb to nose, and once again the rumor started. This time in a shoe factory.

Another jarring night full of pain and an indescribable restlessness. I was turning, getting off the right hip, and it hurt. It was kinda like a golfer moving his head. I took divots too far ahead or too far behind the ball. Big divots of pain. My thinking was as screwed up as an overproducered director.

How cruel a boy can be to his dog. A dog brimming over with the only genuine, unswerving, unending love that he will ever have.

I taught Taffy many tricks. He learned easily and quickly. One was to sit up on his haunches in a puddle of water, cold water, not just for a minute or two, but until he began to lose his balance and sway, and if he put his paws down to steady himself, the ordeal would start all over again. I can remember him looking up at me with his pleading dark brown eyes that seemed to talk, and you can imagine him saying, "For Christ sake, what the hell!" When I thought he'd been up there long enough, I would call him and he would come tearing to me; I would hold my arms outstretched, and when he got within jumping distance, he would take off and hit me on the chest with all his fifty pounds. Sometimes I stayed erect, sometimes we would go down together and roll in the grass, or in the snow, or in the water of the ocean or of a lake, or the pulled-down freshly washed clothes on a clothesline, and once amid the debris of a fragile armless Victorian chair. A much treasured family heirloom.

Sex entered into our relationship.

It was at Camp Passaconaway on Bear Island in the middle of Lake Winnipesaukee. My dad was having one of his good periods and sent my brother and me there for a wonderful summer of almost everything we loved—baseball, swimming, tennis, good food, but no girls. This was a problem. Plenty of girls on the mainland but none on the island. Occasionally we were taken to the mainland for supplies, and during the hour or two we had there, some of us used to rustle up girls. Have you ever rustled up a girl and come out with a little knickknack, in fact two little knickknacks? This my pal what's-his-name and I had the great good fortune to accomplish; and an accomplishment it was, in every sense of the word, but the trips were too few and the time too short, so we made dates at night. It was very simple. All we had to do was go to bed with our swimming trunks on, wait until the breathing became heavy and the snoring opened up, steal out the back of the tent, circle the whole camp and start running to the opposite end of the island three miles away, and then swim a good mile and a half to the mainland, landing at a point just below where one of our little knickknacks lived. This has happened before. Guys have made their way to dames through rain and snow and wind, by land and by air and by God, but very few have done it this way and with a dog right alongside of you. Stealing out of the tent with you, running to the other side of the island with you, swimming the lake beside you, noiselessly, understandingly, politely, and always disappearing at the right moment and not coming back until his master was crawling into the drink for the long swim back to the island and the long, long *walk* home. Happy but pooped—that is, all but Taffy. He just stayed at our heels, his long red tongue out a mile, panting like a guy about to have a heart attack, but I was wise to him. I knew he was faking. He wasn't tired. He was just envious. I told my buddy that this was really something. Two great little gals, eager and willing. This could go on all summer long. Maybe our batting average would take a tumble, but hell it's a long walk and a long swim. That's bound to make you a little tired. And what about Taffy? He's doing all the work and getting no play. Then I got an inspiration. These little gals would understand. They wouldn't think this was foolish, so we decided to ask them to search the mainland for a female dog in heat. Any dog except some little bitty thing. Just measure her for size. I looked back at Taffy. He looked up at me. His tongue went in and his tail began to wag. Not from side to side, but in a circle.

You know, it *happened*. Several trips later, when we splashed ashore, there she was. A beautiful little collie dog, and when Taffy saw her, no dog has ever shaked himself loose of a fur full of water as fast as he did. He came out of this spasm of shaking looking like a well-laundered young prince. They met. She coy. He with that goddamned tail going in rhythmic circles, and he hypnotized her. Believe it or not, that John Barrymore of dogdom sauntered off into the woods not turning around once. She seemed glued to the spot, her eyes never leaving him, when suddenly she just sort of opened up, like a beautiful flower, and ran after him as graceful as a little doe. They disappeared into the quiet of the forest. He was gone for three days.

I woke up in pain but laughing. My nurse asked me what was so funny. I told her I had just remembered how I got a dame for my dog. She gave me my green hornets, patted my head, and went back to her chair and made an entry in the nurse's report. She shook her head, a worried little shake, and I went back to sleep.

It wasn't really sleep. It was more like a stupor. The pain was there but sort of far away. Different thoughts kept whizzing by: Taffy, pictures, the bad ones, mistakes, money, mothers-in-law, a Russian girl, fights, Zanuck, an old Essex, Lefty Flynn, Catalina (the old Catalina), a crash dive in a sub, the first time I walked a wing, Teddy Roosevelt, breaking seventy, a dogfight over Lunéville, chocolate ice-cream sodas, Wilson Mizner, my trust in Boston, being confirmed, the tragedy of Ernie Pyle, of Bill Fields, of Gregory La Cava, of Gene Fowler, of Tommy Hitchcock, the Butterick Lumber Company. All quick unfinished bombs.

I came to, and it was early morning. The sun was out, but not for me. I hurt badly. I looked for my hated picture of the Christ, but I had forgotten that the sister had changed it. The fields, the trees, the sky, were there, and standing to one side of it was my benefactress, looking down at me with that faint wistful smile on her face. The sun became brighter. She pointed at the picture and said one simple little word: "Better?" I told her it was much better and thanked her. As she started for the door, I said I hoped she understood. She said she did now. That in my business she imagined things could be a little unusual to the layman. I agreed. She continued that perhaps sometimes our artists became a little confused. I told her that was true but that it was also true that some businessmen and doctors and plumbers were a little confused. She stood there in the doorway for just a moment, wonderful little figure in black and white, and then said sadly: "And so is the whole world." Then she was gone. No, she didn't go, she just vanished. I lay there for a quiet moment trying not to think of what I knew was coming, but I couldn't stop it. What a pity that she was a nun—don't misunderstand me, not being a Catholic, and in my way of thinking, what a helluva mother she would have made.

I drifted off, thank God, as my German pal began to deflea me and I found myself crawling through a little opening at one end of a freight car in the yard of the Butterick Lumber Company in Waltham, Massachusetts, in the middle of the winter. Chee-rist, it was cold.

Another guy crawled in the opening at the other end, and we started to disembowel the car of its pine flooring.

This we started on our bellies and ended up in the early morning standing erect. From this painful job one was promoted to that of the lumper. He was the guy that carried the lumber from the jerk inside to the jerk that was piling. The piler started in reverse from the ones in the freight car. They worked down. He worked up. As they became lower, he became higher until he towered over the lumpers, the loaders, the tallymen, the trucks, and the busy whore in the shingle shed.

I became a piler because I was a helluva lumper. I was a big success in the lumberyard. I didn't have to use my brain, and I didn't have to be nice and polite to some druggist or mill superintendent, hoping the son of a bitch would buy a couple of boxes of Green Seal chocolates or a few pounds of wool. For what? Hoping he would in turn sell it, and I could again make the same boring trip and say the same monotonous crap and achieve the same piddling result. Maybe that was why I got married so many times. Sick to death of a new girl every night. The same boring trip, the same monotonous crap, the same result, and then that embarrassing "how to get rid of her. . . ."

The ordinary air sneaked in on the gas in the balloon, and it burst.

It was summer and I was hot and sweaty. Why the hell didn't my German keeper bathe me. This would be the time, but she had to do it when it was cool in the early morning; when you could sleep a little, in peace and quiet, just a very little.

My house was on fire. They told me when I was having a meeting on the next picture I was going to make. The comptroller had just given me an envelope with my first check on my share of *The High and the Mighty*. I stuffed it in my pocket and ran for my car. When I got home, it was all over but the limp hoses, the sweating firemen, the backing-out apparatus, and the smell. I have smelled smells before, but never one so enduring. Months later, it would suddenly creep through the house and as suddenly fade away. That's it, that's what I was, a smell. Sometimes fresh and sometimes sour. Mommy's hair was always sweet, long and sweet, and soft and safe, and a nice place to go to sleep in.

It was close to Christmas, and Mommy had been wrapping gifts. She wrapped them so beautifully that it seemed a pity to unwrap them. The fire started in our bedroom, devoured that and its roof, and all the presents, and finished in the dressing rooms. Dottie lost everything, either by fire or by damage. I lost less, because I had room for a Menjou wardrobe, but not the appetite. I lost my three suits including a tuxedo, two pair of gray slacks, five sports shirts, three ties including a black four-in-hand, four pair of gray socks and one black pair, two pair of shoes including pumps, three pair of well-broken-in, comfortable, well-worn, old, wonderful desert boots and two jockey straps, and some pictures. One of Tom Hitchcock, one of me in front of a Nieuport I flew at the front, and one of a German Rumpler Tom and I brought down. These were gone—forever.

How screwy can you get? Lumber, to limp hoses, to Mommy's hair, and all in but a few minutes. There's a Tinker to Evers to Chance for you, and now one from left field. Acute fibrositis. That's what the man said I had. Not gout, not just fibrositis; acute fibrositis—inflammation of the joints. Inflammation could be spelled with four letters—pain. My fibrositis was the wandering type from left knee to right ankle, then a short stretch at the left elbow, like a sparrow in a country lane. The shoulders are the vacation spots. It hit every joint but one. That one is off limits. Why can't it affect that joint? It couldn't do any harm. At my time of life it might do some good. At least it could awaken it, and I would once more know it was still there and alive—maybe just faintly breathing, but alive.

You gotta say something for this codeine dope dict. You're never bored for the lack of things to think about. It's just hard sometimes to bring them to a conclusion—like that Christmas in 1917. Lunéville, Escadrille N. 87. All Frenchmen except two Americans—Hitchcock, eighteen years old, and me an old twenty-one. There was snow on the ground. Landing a Nieuport under ideal conditions is rough. No breaks— no nothing—just flying by the seat of your pants. We were on the first patrol.

A mechanic for some reason or other was out in the middle of the field. What the hell he was doing out there I never found out. Suddenly an Albatros dived on the field from nowhere—one of those sneak shooting-up missions. You don't have much time to do anything except run for the trenches leading to the machine gun emplacements. I picked mine and made it in nothing flat. Some of the mechanics were wheeling two of the Nieuports out of the hangar on the double to rev them up, and with one of the planes was a pilot getting on his gear, readying himself to be a hero. To my disappointment, I saw that the other plane was mine; with the big Black Cat insignia and the bigger Number 3. I was to be a hero but not out of choice. I started out of the coziness of the trench and saw the Albatros making a pass at the poor sap of a mechanic who was running like a scared rabbit, but straight ahead, never changing his direction, just giving the Hun a perfect target which he took full advantage of. A sudden burst and the rabbit rolled to the ground. He didn't fall; it was more an acrobatic roll and then a couple of fish-out-of-water flops, and he just relaxed. This changed my attitude. We were sitting ducks if he made another pass, and nobody ever took off as fast as I did. If I got in the air, I had a fair chance. I got up, but he didn't come back and I didn't find him. It was a helluva victory. One poor goddamned mechanic, and the German went home—mission accomplished. I often wondered what kind of a man that German flier was. He took a chance. He had us cold, and he took it all out on one stumblebum in the middle of a snow-packed runway. As the French say, *C'est la guerre.* That seemed to excuse everything.

The codeine was working but in a nasty way. Everything that was flashing through my mind was unpleasant. Years ago at a golf course, a pal of mine wanted to play the whiskey route. We both had finished eighteen holes, and I had played badly and was through. He went on alone carrying his bag, and I took off for the nineteenth hole. There I played very well. He was playing the first, second, eighth, and ninth holes. After a few belts and feeling better, I went out to watch him come in. The ninth hole ran parallel to the first, and from the clubhouse you can see them both from tee to green. I walked down to the first tee, looking toward the ninth tee, when suddenly I saw him; a good drive down the first fairway. There he was, lying way out there, all alone. A heart-attacked red-shirted golfer—a little bleed on a huge green giant.

I came to, it was naked weather, and I was perspiring; no, that is too polite a term for it—I was sweating. I got my four-hour allowance of green hornets and evaporated. Mr. Codeine changed my modus operandi, and I started to think of someone lovely, delicate, and adorable—Mommy. The look on her little face as she ran down the driveway, treading her way among the snakelike hoses, inactive now, but still gasping for the water that had been turned off. Her thunderstruck gaze was riveted on the upper story. Our wing of the house. Our room of joy and sorrow, but always of love. It was black and gone, and the big homey living room below it was a hippopotamic shower. The piano was waterlogged. The huge braided rug was soggy, soaked, and stinking. The room looked bony. I walked out of what was once a door, and she saw me. She didn't do what they do in the movies, run into my arms sobbing, just stood there looking at me as if everything was all right, and then with a little shrug of her little shoulders she walked past me into what a few hours ago had been her dream motherland.

Pat, the oldest, a stewardess with TWA, was on flight; Bill, the next and the oldest boy, was at college; so Mommy and I and Kitty, Cissy, Mike, and Maggie moved to the Bel Air Hotel. Tim, the second oldest boy, stayed in the house. He had his bear dogs to take care of.

That night, late, after all the kids were alseep, Mommy and I went to bed. Our room had twin beds. I have never slept with anyone. As a matter of fact I never was a good sleeper. I am one of those roaming guys in a bed. Asleep or awake, I am constantly turning, twisting, itching, scratching, or passing wind, trying to cover it with a cough but never able to synchronize the two. Finally I quieted down. Mommy started to cry, a muffled soft little sobbing. I knew she thought I was asleep; I didn't let her know I wasn't.

I became alive again, and it was dark. What night it was, I don't know, but my favorite big night nurse was there, and she gave me an alcohol rub, then divvied out the hornets. As they were taking effect, I thought of a funny incident with the insurance adjuster, when he was listing our losses, to reach an evaluation on all the destroyed or damaged articles.

I refused to go through my dressing room. Too many wonderful memories up in smoke. Too many pictures of old flying pals: Tommy Hitchcock, Jules Baylies, Dave Putnam, Reggie Sinclair, Dave Judd, Staff Brown—all gone. Forever. Made me sick. These were real friends. Four of them Staff, Tom, Jules, and Dave, dead. Jules, Staff, and Dave in my war. Tom in the second. I don't think I ever passed through my dressing room that I didn't look at Tom's picture.

We trained together at Avord. Went through acrobatics together at Pau. Ended up together at the front at Lunéville in the Alsace-Lorraine. Flew patrols together, shot up enemy airdromes together, shot down a German Rumpler and a Fokker together. Lived together. Dropped President Wilson's message to Congress on America's entrance into the war, translated in German, in the front-line trenches together. Went to Paris together. Hell, we did everything together, and on two occasions he saved my life. Tom was a ten-goal polo player. Tom was a ten-goaler in everything.

It is very difficult to write what you really think of a great friend if it be a man. It is easy to say you love a woman; there is so much of her to love and so many inducements. She is so full of confusion and neatness, kindness and hostility, joy and sorrow, hunger and diets and of course sex; but how the hell do you say I love a man? Today.

Mommy volunteered for the job of going through my burned-out dressing room with the keeper of the bees. There had been a radio and a pair of Bushnell Triple Tested 6×25 Field $11.0''$ field glasses and several other expensive items such as rifles, revolvers, books, etc. All burned, some beyond recognition. They arrived at some sort of a price, including shirts, suits, neckties, underwear, and an item I added, two jockey straps, used. For some unknown reason these two items became of great importance to me. Gone was the sorrow of all my lost treasures. The present had swallowed up the past. What was I to get for my two old friends, the two jailers of my most precious jewels? Seventy-five cents. Not seventy-five cents apiece, but seventy-five cents for the two.

A few minutes later, they started going through what was gone in my wife's dressing room. My lovely little wife had been a hoarder of brassieres. This was unknown to me, in fact, unknown to herself. She had just naturally saved brassieres. Those from her years of dancing and her years of just liking a new brassiere as the styles changed or the occasion demanded. As a result of this very normal female procedure, sixty-five bras. Know what the going price on burned bras is, old burned bras, new burned bras, fakey burned bras? Three dollars and fifty cents a burned bra.

Gentlemen, may this world-shattering sense of values put you where you belong—get lost.

I became very restless. It was dark, and although my nurse told me it was warm in the room, I was cold. I was cold, and the bedsore on my right hip was giving me trouble. I asked for the green hornets, but it was not time for them. The guy next door was having his fun too. I could hear him groaning. It fascinated me because of the rhythm. I timed it. One every five seconds on the nose. This man's agony became a metronomic marking of time. The sheep jumping over the fence. One man's misery became another man's contentment. I was lulled to sleep.

The green hornets were driving my subconscious nuts. Awake or asleep, it made no difference; I was like a leaf in the wind, way up in the sky. Living in the past or just the immediate present. Worrying about how tough it was going to be, if I ever got over this radiculitis, to break myself of whatever habit I might be forming. I spoke to one of my medical brains about this, but he laughed it off. This worried me all the more, for this was the guy who told me (laughingly) that my ailment, in the syllabub of the medical profession, was often called "window pain." When I asked for an explanation of that rather harmless-sounding simile, he said that some few times patients suffering with my affliction took the easy way out, and jumped out of the window. I assured him that this I would gladly do if I could jump and if the window was on the bottom floor. He told me not to worry, that there were ways of bringing one back to normalcy, quickly and easily and comfortably. I didn't believe a word he said, but bravely decided to go along with him. Live my life as it came; go nuts and end up as a gateman at the 20th Century–Fox Studios, on the night shift, so I could tip my hat politely to all the producers as they left the studios to go to their homes and rest their exhausted brains?

Most producers have always reminded me of the guy in the old Hertz commercial, only they come gliding down and land in an old jalopy, painted taxicab yellow, with a not-too-well-cured skunk's tail flying from the antenna.

The Butterick Lumber Company slid in again; winter and winter in Waltham can be all kinds of winter. A chinook had struck. The high-piled snow was melting fast, making ice ball throwing the game of the day.

I was a piler by then and was finishing a pile about a good story high. A couple of ice bombs had swished by my head, and I had swished a couple myself. No direct hits but a few near-misses. Playful stuff. Fleming, the yard boss, came strutting through the yard, yelling at anyone he could pick a reason to yell at. His yells were of the four-letter variety; in fact he was one of those guys that couldn't speak a sentence without saying shit or Christ or son of a bitch. His vocabulary was rather cramped.

He was my height, but much stockier, about one eighty on the hoof. He had the evilest face I have ever seen, with a broken nose that was his own personal brand of toughness. The old-timers ignored him, but obeyed him. The young fellas were all scared of him. All but me. Don't think I was particularly brave, just very observing.

One day he bawled out a big kid who had just signed on as a lumper. It was a few minutes before closing time, and the big kid was pooped. He was lumping for me, and after he had passed up his boards he leaned against the pile and lit himself a cigarette. Fleming saw him and started to work on him. Nobody was ever blasted as was he. Blasphemy that seemed not only unending but never repetitious. It was the work of a master, and when Fleming ran out of four-letter words aimed at the kid, he changed directions and aimed his profanity at the kid's father and eventually, without losing a breath, at his mother.

This was too much for the kid to take. He threw his cigarette away, and as he was about to take a step toward Fleming, Fleming turned and sauntered off. I was looking at him as he did this, and I caught a flash of fear in the big mouth's ugly face. I had a hunch that the owner of the yard and his son, two real tough guys, weren't in love with Fleming either; and since I needed some sort of recognition for advancement, I thought this could be the time. I aimed an ice bomb at Mr. Fleming and hit him right on top of his foul noggin. It didn't knock him down, but he lost a few steps and then took on everyone in the yard. He said that if the dirty son of a bitch who threw that would come down, he'd kick the shit out of him.

For a second it flashed through my mind that I hoped I hadn't misjudged that flash of fear on Fleming's face, but it was too late; I had already committed myself and had yelled to him that I was the dirty son of a bitch that had nailed him, and down I climbed.

He stood there waiting for me, but he wasn't saying anything. This was disconcerting. Everyone in the yard was watching. Guys on high, in trucks, in freight cars, on the ground, from the bleachers to the box seats. My big moment had arrived, and to use Mr. Fleming's language, I kicked the shit out of him. The next day I was promoted to tallyman, an observing hero.

They say fighting is not the way to settle things, that nobody ever really wins. I wonder. Sometimes you win a friend.

Zanuck and I had a fight in Canada once. We were on our way to a hunting trip in true Zanuck fashion. The correct guns, clothes, guides, booze, dames, and horses. Fifty of them; that is fifty of the horses.

Our hunting companions were Brick Enright, John Adolphi, and Grant Withers. Brick and John were Zanuck's guests, Withers was mine. All three are now dead.

My thoughts started to quarrel with themselves. A dogfight of reflections. The hens won.

I raise hens. Twenty-four Rhode Island reds to be exact. The rooster is out. Long gone because of the neighbors. They objected to his clarion call in the early mornings, thereby putting an end to a fantastic sex orgy of the greatest bank-walking rooster that ever took charge of twenty-four dames. I at times was very envious of that strutting, capable guy. Twenty-four gals literally fought over him, and the winner always, and I mean always, was rewarded. The deed accomplished, a shake of his shoulders, an enormous flutter of his feathers, and he was ready again. What a man.

There was of course a bitch among the twenty-four, an egg-eating hen.

I did my best to catch this dame eating an egg, but never succeeded. Finally I caught a suspect, isolated her for a few days, and watched what she did to her eggs. The rooster did not go along with this kind of treatment. It was not democratic, and the economic grievance of said hen was entirely uncalled-for. I know that he thought I had deprived her of her right of property; that I had broken the law, the law of eminent domain. Each hen that I caught to put to the test was taken against his very loudly voiced squawks and well-timed charges. On one occasion, I got mad and teed off on him as you would a football. He landed hard on his feathered butt, a good twenty-five feet away, and the rest of his complaining was done by sulking and clucking. I had dishonored him in front of his harem, and he never forgave me for it.

When I finally caught the culprit and chopped off her head, the rooster went into semiretirement. It lasted a few hours.

26

I love babies, but when they use them to sell toilet paper, it makes me sick. The ad of the lovely sleeping little girl who can be expected to live until 2036. Her life expectancy is seventy-three years. A little boy's is sixty-seven years. I am sixty-seven. The shadows are falling. Where did all this come from—from the green hornets, and I need two of them right now.

It seems to me that I haven't seen anybody for days. That is, anybody who wasn't dressed in white. I haven't even seen my sister friend. I wonder how she really feels. My nurse, who is a Catholic, says that all nuns are mothers to everybody. Maybe I'm dumb, but I have the lovely little mother I want, and I don't want any other. I'm a little screwed up on this one, and I am not going to try and work it out. For my money, it's all right just as it is. *C'est la guerre.*

David Selznick was a good Hertz man; he always landed in a Rolls Royce. L. B. Mayer was a Hispano Suiza man; so was Goldwyn. Zanuck was a Thunderbird, a green Thunderbird—and Jack Warner, what kind of a Hertz man would he be? It seems that every year he is honored as a man of the year for something or other, and this little butter-up is too unimportant for one so famous, so the hell with him. When he comes down, there won't be any car there. It will make a very pleasant sound effect.

After the row we two had in Vancouver, Zanuck thrust my return ticket at me and said I was through with the trip. I agreed heartily, adding sarcastically that it was not right for a director to take a punch at his producer, but that I would be glad to do it all over again; whereupon the melee started once more with Adolphi, Enright, and Withers grabbing us; and, somehow in the fracas, poor old John Adolphi got nailed on the nose. It floored him, and it looked for a moment as if he might have been badly hurt. This broke it up and as we were staging this picnic in the lobby of the hotel, someone wisely suggested that we go to our room before the mounties arrived.

I went to mine, Zanuck to his, and all night long Adolphi was trying to bring two knuckleheads together. I refused to have anything to do with Zanuck, even though we had been very successful together, with pictures like *Public Enemy, Wild Boys of the Road, So Big,* etc. I was as fond of him as a director can be fond of a producer, and I imagine he had the same feeling toward me.

I admired him for his guts and the quality he had of grabbing a headline and generating the speed and enthusiasm all down the line to make a good picture quickly—at this, he was a master and the hardest-working little guy you have ever seen in all your life. We had good moments and bad, but there was one thing you could count on. When you wanted an answer, you got it right then and there; if he shook hands on a deal, it was a deal, period.

Later on when I worked for him again, I got him to let me make *The Ox-Bow Incident.* I had bought the property from Harold Hurley, a producer at Paramount Studios, after he had gotten into some sort of a beef with the big boys and was relieved of his job. Things apparently had collapsed all around him, and I offered him five hundred bucks more than he had paid for the book. This he gladly accepted, and then I went to all the producers for whom I had worked and got turned down. Zanuck was the only one with guts to do an out-of-the-ordinary story for the prestige rather than the dough.

Zanuck was in the army during the war, and this was the time of *The Ox-Bow Incident.* He was stationed in London, and the studio head was Bill Goetz. The production head, Bill Koenig, and Lew Schrieber did the dirty work.

I had the green light on *The Ox-Bow* and was working hard and fast to get it rolling before some of the principals might be called into service. The budget had been completed, and the estimated cost determined. That was it. When the unholy three heard the amount, they decided that it was a bad deal at the time and so prepared a cable to Zanuck, informing him in no uncertain terms their opinions on the project. All emphatic nos. Goetz, being a fair and decent executive and an unusual one, called me in to his office and let me read the verdict and asked me if I wished to add my point of view. I thanked him and said I did, and I wrote, "This is to remind you of our handshake; regards, Bill Wellman." That's all. Next day they got word back. "Let Wellman go ahead." It was all just that simple.

Kind of nice, huh? When the picture was first released in this country, it fell flat on its face.

One of the important dailies, the *Hollywood Reporter,* had this to say in its criticism of the picture: "not even a B-type Western." Them's harsh words, and they can break your heart when everybody else seems to agree with them.

They released it abroad, and it was over there that it became popular. So much so that they rereleased it here; and on the second time around, it got some acclaim and incidentally a little money. Whatever it got I was proud of it, and so was Zanuck; if it hadn't been for him, I would never have been able to make the picture.

The direct antithesis was an epic I made for Warners, mistitled *The Lafayette Escadrille.* It was a story I wrote myself called "C'est la Guerre," the most widely used French expression during World War I. It was the echo of tragedy.

I was in the Lafayette Flying Corps, an outgrowth of the Lafayette Escadrille, which was composed of the first group of Americans who volunteered to fly for France. The excitement that this generated brought a lot more crazy American kids who wanted to fly, and they were formed into the Lafayette Flying Corps. After their training was complete and they had their wings, they were sent to Le Plessis Belleville. There to wait until a flier was killed, wounded, missing, or whatever, in any of the sixty-odd fighting escadrilles all along the front. If your number was up, you were sent to his escadrille to replace him.

I was sent to N. 87, the *chat noir* escadrille at Lunéville in the Alsace-Lorraine. Tom Hitchcock later joined me there. All the other fliers were Frenchmen who I'm sure had never met an American before, much less tried to understand one.

This is sort of a thumbnail sketch of "C'est la Guerre."

The hero was part real, part fiction. He was patterned after a pal of mine. We went to war together, and we had a great many of the experiences, good and bad, that I used in the story. It was a tragedy about a young American flier and a little *fille de nuit*. The central theme of the love story had, revolving around it, the entire training of young fliers who learned to fly in a Blériot, with no instructor, except on the ground, no parachutes, Nieuports and Spads, vacillating guns and luck, good or bad.

Let's call him Joe, and the little French girl Joan: they met in Paris in the house where she plied her trade. She was his girl as long as he paid for it.

He was living in a little hotel awaiting the papers that would make him officially a member of the Lafayette Flying Corps and send him to Avord in the south of France, to start his basic training.

He had plenty of money, so all of his time was spent with Joan until his orders came through. Suddenly they realized they were in love.

He had five days more, before taking off for Avord, and months of training, with no leaves to look forward to, so she ran away from the panel den, and they found a small studio in a garret across the river, and moved in to hide, be alone, be happy.

She spoke but little English, he but little French, yet they understood each other completely; and with the help of a French-English dictionary, they came to a perfect understanding. She couldn't at first believe his falling in love with her. Her past would always, she thought, come between them, but he made her understand that he was not the slightest bit interested in what she had been, or done, before they met, only what happened from then on. He meant it, and they were in happy land.

His money was almost all gone, not enough left to take care of her while he was away, and so she became a conductress, a beautiful little black-clothed conductress, working for just enough to keep herself going, while her man was getting ready to fight for her country. Makes it a pretty rock-ribbed kind of love, and so he left, and she was alone and respectable and deeply in love.

While we were sweating it out at Avord, he would get letters from her, and since I was his pal, he used to ask me to help him translate them. From a pocket dictionary, sitting outside a hangar or in a deserted barrack or in the can, I heard a beautiful love.

Joe missed her so badly that finally he went nuts, hit a drill instructor, who happened to be a *sous-lieutenant,* and was put in the jug to await court-martial.

We all heard what Joe could get. Devils Island or worse for hitting an officer in wartime, so we broke into the jail one night, overpowered the two *polius* on guard, and got him out, and while we were about it, we released everybody else.

We got him over the wall, and then he was on his own.

He was off to Paris and his Joan, but he was still in the uniform of the *élève pilote*—army shoes, puttees of blue, tan military trousers, leather coat, and the French blue cap. They would pick him up very quickly, because there were not many of those on the loose.

On his way to the railroad station, he picked a fight with a *poilu* on a lonely road. He needed the uniform and his papers. Unfortunately he picked on a savate champion, and it became a bloody battle. Joe finally knocked him out, was terribly hurt himself, but he changed his clothes, sneaked on a troop train to Paris, and got there.

When he arrived in Paris, he took a taxi to their garret hideaway and stumbled up the stairs, crashed through the locked door, and collapsed on the floor. It was early in the afternoon, and Joan was still at work.

When she came home, she found him there unconscious; and with the help of an old *réforme* who was the concierge of the apartment, they got him washed up and in bed, and the concierge brought a doctor friend of his who understood. They patched Joe up, got some hot soup down him, and he smiled again, this time into his loved one's face.

He was a pretty sick boy for a couple of weeks, but with the loving attention that he got from his little girl in the night and the old concierge in the daytime, he recovered with nothing to show for it but an ugly scar shooting out from his right eye —and a terrible loneliness. Joan worked during the day. They still had to eat, and he couldn't go outside. He was literally a prisoner of love.

He studied French and read the Paris newspapers. Day in and day out; *Je suis, tu es, il est, nous sommes, vous êtes, ils sont, elles sont,* newspapers, and Joan at night, and ecstasy. Some nights they would steal outside and sneak along the Seine, hand in hand. Joe had by now a heavy beard and looked just like a *poilu,* but it was dangerous and they didn't go too often.

One day he kicked boredom in the butt, tossed the French grammar under the bed, threw caution to the winds, and side-streeted his way to Joan's former house of employment.

Madam was glad to see him. Happy that Joan was happy, but a little puzzled; and when he explanied his loneliness, how impossible it was to get an answer to their predicament, hiding in a room all day and all night, every day and every night, she gave him a job as a pimp, or as she said, a trumpeter of love. Made it sound kinda nice.

His territory was between the Folies Bergère and 23, rue X. You never spoke of them as houses of ill repute, just as a number on a street. A little more homey.

She explained to him that as long as he stayed within the confines of his territory, inside his new home, inside the Folies or inside certain taxicabs, she could guarantee his safety. This meant that Joan would have to move back to her former home, this time as a beautiful young woman in love, employed elsewhere.

32

The shoe was on the other foot. Joan worked all day. Joe worked all night. Now she was the lonely one and even though they lived in the back of the house, the alley side, the sounds of revelry surrounded her. Sounds that she used to live by became part of her sentence. A punishment for what she had been before. A reminder of the greatness of her man and the fullness of their love, for neither one of them ever spoke of the closeness of the old life.

To him this was a chance for them to get out. Maybe through the South Americans that played in the orchestra. Maybe through some of his friends, like me or Duke Sinclair or Jim Hall. He was around now and active. He would find a way to get to South America, to get married, to get for them what he used to call the throw-out-your-chest kind of happiness. She understood and was very patient.

Madam dressed her new protégé as a wealthy South American. The shave, the haircut, the clothes, and the false papers did the trick. From the left side, he looked like a very handsome South American playboy, but when he turned and you saw the right side of his face, with its angry deep scar jutting down from the eye, the playboy was erased.

Joe did well as a procurer but failed in every attempt to get him and his loved one out of France. Only once did he think he had things arranged, but America's entrance into the war wiped that out completely. He was once more a prisoner. This time at a number on a street.

Came months of procuring, dodging the military police, living for the few wonderful hours he and Joan had together. An hour that came just before she went to work and after he had returned from work, and the hour when she returned from work and just before he went to work. Those too-short hours spent with her and those long, never-ending ones spent waiting for her.

Then came the general, an American general, who wanted to be a playboy, and Joe spotted him and made contact.

On their way to the number on the street, Joe took the big gamble and told him everything. The general never said a word, just listened.

Joe begged him to give him another chance. Make him his driver, anything as a stepping-stone to becoming a flier again. Anything that would give him the chance to become a man again.

When they arrived at 23, rue X, the general remained seated. Joe got out, came around, and opened the door to let him out. He still didn't move, just sat there thinking. Then very quietly told Joe to get back in, he wanted to go to his hotel.

All the way to the hotel not a word was spoken.

Joe began to figure what he would do if the general intended to turn him in. It wasn't his place to say anything more. He had declared himself. It was up to the general now.

They drew up to the hotel. The general got out, hesitated for a moment, and then turned to Joe, still inside the cab. He thanked him—for what, Joe didn't know. Then his manner changed, and in almost a command he ordered Joe to report to him at 10:30 in the morning, suite 302. Then he was gone.

Joe hurried home. It was early morning, and Joan was fast asleep. He wanted to awaken her to tell the big news, but she looked so peaceful, so beautiful, that he just sat there looking at her. She stirred a little, awakened slowly; and when she saw him gazing down at her, she reached for him and they kissed, a long, lingering, lovely kiss.

Then he told her everything. This might well be their big chance. The chance to get away from "the number on the street."

Wherever he might go, she would follow him; others have done it. All over France, there were the camp followers. Women fighting to be with their men, sacrificing everything for a few precious moments. She would join this legion of the dedicated. Somehow they must always be together, forever.

Then he told Joan how the general had thanked him. Out of a clear sky he thanked me. For what?

Joan looked at him almost like a mother about to give her young son a little lesson in life.

"He thanked you because you made him think or maybe because you made him, how you say, remember?"

It suddenly became very quiet. For just a moment there was no noise. He took her in his arms. There were tears in her eyes, but they were not for the general.

Joe became the general's private driver. He was skillful and trustworthy. In a few months he got what he was after. He was sent to Issoudun and started his training to become a flier.

Months later he had received his wings and was commissioned a second lieutenant. (I was in Paris when he hit town, a full-fledged *pilote* and on his way to the front.)

Joan never gave up her job, a job that in a small way helped her country. She worked and prayed and waited.

I was there when they met. Words can't describe it. Neither one said a word, just melted into each other's arms. An immense sigh came from his lips; from hers, a little purr. They walked away arm in arm, oblivious of everything and everybody around them, including me. I watched them as they disappeared from view, a bright new knight and his lady fair, a conductress all in black. It seemed almost like gazing into a crystal ball, and it frightened me.

I was there when they were married, in a little bitty church on the outskirts of Paris. The church organ played softly; and in the distance, the way-off distance, the organ of war was playing its tune of insanity.

I saw her once during the ceremony turn a frightened look at a faraway rumble and then saw her look at him, a look of love and worry and hope, and her faint "I do," a whispered two-word prayer.

They spent the afternoon in the Bois de Boulogne lying on the grass, with the sun on their faces and the clouds in the sky.

He gave her his identification bracelet and shortened the links so that it would fit her tiny little wrist. Second Lieutenant

Joe S. Smith, AEF Squadron 94—she read this aloud in her broken English, sealed by a kiss. Two lost souls in love. An ex-pimp and an ex-whore. The next morning, Joe flew out of Le Plessis Belleville, bound for Squadron 94 in the Champagne sector. She was there all alone to watch her life fly away, never to return, for he became lost and strayed into Germany and was brought down by two eager Fokkers.

When she read of his death in the Paris paper, just a name in a too-long list of casualties, she jumped into the Seine River and drowned her sorrow and her life, and only a friend and a general knew who it was that was dragged from the dirty waters clothed in black with an identification bracelet on her small, cold, chalk-white wrist that read: Second Lieutenant Joe S. Smith, AEF Squadron 94. Whom the gods love die young.

That was the story of the picture that was made called *C'est la Guerre* and changed to *The Lafayette Escadrille,* with a made-over happy ending that brought the hero back to his lady's ever-loving arms and fell flat on its ass, artistically, financially, and spiritually—it was produced by Warner Brothers.

A bad picture is like a frightful birthmark on your face —it never leaves you, first run, second run, reruns, TV prime time, late time, lousy time; it's always there for people to stare at unbelievingly or turn away from or worse still turn off, or should that be better still? It's your eternal badge of embarrassment.

A new ailment has become attached to me. It is called teno-synanitis of the left patella, which means I have a hell of a sore knee. Needless to say I am getting a little bored by all these different itises that are attaching themselves to me and especially this one, because I am just beginning to stagger into the can, and I have to march in like a marine before they will let me out of this den of suffering and back to my lovely home and my adorable family. However, I always have the green hornets every four hours!

I began to think of coons. My boy Timmy hunts bears. Has dogs trained just for bears and as a side delicacy coons. No deer or cats, just bears or coons.

If one of the dogs forgets and goes for a deer, he gets the business and in no uncertain terms—in short he gets the bejesus kicked out of him. If he persists in his love of the deer, they break him either by hanging him from a tree, with a cute little deer's head dangling by him until gamey, or the scoundrel is nailed inside a large wine barrel with a three-day dead dear as copilot and unceremoniously rolled down a lovely sylvan hillside. This breaks the dog, and he never deers again.

I know a couple of couples that would be infinitely happier if they took a variation of this shock treatment. Might make them make up their minds and do their wonderful kids a massive favor.

That's one thing about being sick. You can always fix everyone else up, and it always starts with that old bromide, "They don't know how lucky they are," and the funny thing is that before I became sick I didn't know either.

Oh well, back to the coon. . . .

Next door to us lives a remarkable family—the Landises—Mother adorable, Father a great guy, and three wonderful boys, Bill, Tom, and Hughie. Tom, the middle one, is my Tim's pal—they are identical, not much for clothes, shaving, school, company, neckties, overcoats, or bedtime. They like woods, mountains, bears, coons, water (in its place), cake, one girl apiece, and dogs. They were both born a hundred years too late. They should be discovering the West.

The father, among other things, is vice-president of Western Airlines, for my dough a hell of an airline: courteous, careful, and capable.

I must not be going to die. Maybe I will be crippled—walk like a guy with a wooden leg or, when spoken to, turn like a clown with a stiff neck—but whatever be my fate, at the moment I have become argumentative and what better subject could I pick than Western Airlines. There are so many of them, Eastern, Northern, Southern, South-Eastern, United, National, TWA, American, Pan American, it goes on and on and on, and out of this fantastic cluster of airlines my attendant nurse, the German one, must have a favorite that is not mine, and I can get into an argument with her, prove my point, win a victory for Western, and put her in her place. So here goes.

"Nurse, what airline do you like?"

"I don't like any of them. I do my traveling by train or bus."

"Oh-hhh."

I knew I should have kept my big mouth shut. Now she might come over and wash me. I have a hunch that when she gets me clean enough, she is going to attack me. Won't do her any good, for my sex flew out of the window days ago and is now perched high in a pine tree overlooking Big Bear Lake, away from the smog and leering at the girls as they go water-skiing by with the wind blowing their hair and beating against their young, firm, eager breasts.

I guess at this point in my sickness you can't have sex unless you think about it, and I just haven't been thinking about it. Must be the green hornets. They lull your pain, relax you, and put you to sleep, *all over,* and the only thing that occasionally awakens is your brain, and then it's goofy and all the things you think about are like firecrackers, alive with a loud bang and then dead with a spitting sputter.

If you did have it, how would you use it here? There's no sex in a hospital anyway. There are a lot of results of sex. Beautiful little bundles of love and a few ugly packages of unmentionables, but sex in a Catholic hospital? It would be kinda rugged, wouldn't it?

The coon again. It would be very unusual if I could start one train of thought, go through with it without being side-tracked.

Tom and Tim decided to tame a coon. Coons can be made into very lovable pets; it is understandable if only because of their hands—not paws, hands. They can do everything with their hands that we can do with ours. Pick up anything, tear anything, push and pull anything, and even pick their noses. How human can you get?

So they disappeared into the hills for an hour and came back with a beaut. A big rough tough male with as pretty a coat as ever graced a cute co-ed.

Since they had not built a cage and runway for him, they dumped him in the Landises' cellar for safekeeping. They gave him free run of a cellar, a neighborhood new and strange and unexplored.

Mr. Landis and the two older boys, Bill and Tom, went to their grapefruit ranch just outside Indio for the weekend.

This left Mother and the youngest, Hughie, alone in their big house. Hughie had just gotten over the flu and was not quite up to snuff, and Mrs. Landis had an evening to herself to spend in leisure, early to bed with a good book and a period of aloneness, which all loving wives look forward to occasionally but seldom get.

It was all still through the house and nothing stirred, not even a husband. Mother was safe and comfortable in bed and reading with no interruption, when suddenly the toilet flushed.

Hughie's room was on the other side of the huge roof-ceilinged living room, on the ground floor. Mother's was on the second floor.

This did not bother her, for little boys have to go to the ducky, sometimes constantly, but when it happened again too quickly, Mother was up like a shot and tearing downstairs, across the huge living room where noises had a habit of bouncing off the walls. It happened again as she came nearer to his door. Softly she opened it, and there lay Hughie sound asleep like a little angel. Mother quickly closed the door and with a proud little smile on her face, thought that her well-trained son had accomplished his feat fast asleep. Suddenly, as she crossed the room of echoes, the toilet flushed again.

This time she knew it was not Hughie, and she got scared.

39

She thought the sound came from the cellar; and being a gal of nerve, she took her husband's shotgun out of the closet, and though unloaded it gave her the necessary strength to open the cellar door, switch on the light, and steal down the stairs. Suddenly, the toilet went off again. She hesitated and then realized that no burglar would be using the bathroom to lure her downstairs, so boldly she went the rest of the way, peered around a little hallway, and there was the open-doored bathroom and the toilet flushed again and Rastus sitting there. But he wasn't doing anything, just flushing.

Since that was Mother's introduction to a coon and since a coon has a very fierce look and a strange ghostly chatter, Mother took off, and all through the night Rastus flushed the toilet and Mother wished that Father and the boys were home, and the bed got very big and very lonesome.

Rastus faded out, and my annuities came on stage.

Years ago, in 1927 or '28, after I made *Wings,* I started to make big money, and the taxes were very, very small. It hurts to even write this.

My brother, an immensely successful and wealthy man, laid it on the line for me. He told me that since I had no business sense whatsoever and since I added with my fingers and since I only had ten, he thought it would be an excellent idea if I invested my money in annuities, and he gave me the names of three of the leaders.

I took his advice and kept sticking it in until well after fifty—and because of that can sit back and watch the world roll by. Which it is doing entirely too fast for my sense of well-being.

I am now sixty-seven and of course have become a person that they, the insurance companies, could well do without.

One of my annuities paid off when I was fifty, so I collected and immediately put it back in the other two.

They were called the five optional affairs and so good that they have not been writing them for years. In other words, I have two of the big companies firmly grasped down where the hair is short.

One of the companies pays through the nose with no outward signs of emotion one way or another, but the other grumbles. They are lousy losers. It is done very carefully by an occasional letter asking very cleverly if I am dead.

At first this surprised me but didn't bother me particularly; but after the third, which I read a little hungover, I blew my top.

I sat me down and composed a masterpiece of complaint, resentment, and indignation. I compared their method as against that of their competitor. I cried long and hard and then thought it over for a minute and strangely enough it started to tickle my sense of humor. Someone wishing so hard that I would die and they would make themselves another buck or two. So—I tore it up and wrote them the shortest letter possible. It had two words: "Not yet!" and I signed my name.

Zanuck was on again. It was amazing how this little guy kept creeping back from the past, and I enjoyed his company in retrospect much more than I had in reality.

We were again in the hotel in Vancouver and poor old Adolphi was still wet-nursing us both, trying to avoid something that had already happened.

I was in bed in my room. Zanuck across the hall in his, and Adolphi was still going from one to the other trying to bring two bullheads together. As for me, nothing doing. I was leaving in the morning, to hell with Zanuck, when suddenly he appeared at the door. I got out of bed in a hurry expecting a rerun of our fuss in the lobby, but the little giant came forward with his hand outstretched, and we shook and Adolphi started to cry. That was the end of that little goodie.

For four days we piddled around Vancouver, outfitting ourselves for the big hunt. Warm clothing, rifles, ammunition, sleeping bags, blankets, the works, and then we were on our way. A long train ride to somewhere where the guides and the horses awaited us—the base.

When we arrived, we spent two days riding and getting to know our respectives guides. Each hunter had his own.

Hours were spent at a range shooting so that we all didn't start out trigger-happy.

In the evenings Grant Withers and I tried our best to get used to the rum that the guides drank. It was tough work but zesty, and Zanuck did not like our wholehearted approach to the job, but he didn't raise any stink over it, so Grant and I carried on manfully, tapering off about three in the morning of the day the big caravan was to start the mighty hunt.

We were going after moose, caribou, Rocky Mountain sheep, goats, and grizzly. There were fifty horses in the train, those to be ridden and those that packed the food, medicines, salt to cure our trophies, tents, kitchenware, etc. It was a helluva setup. Typically Zanuck.

As we sat on our horses waiting for Zanuck, who had just received a call from California, I looked blurrily at Withers as I told him I felt so lousy that I was going on the wagon. The guide's rum had done the trick, I was sick, real sick, but not sick enough to hear Zanuck saying that I didn't have the guts to quit. That did it. I quit and on a trip that got tougher each day. I lost weight, couldn't eat, and for a few days thought I was going to die and wished that I would.

Zanuck and I had not been too cozy since our argument in Vancouver. In fact that was a week ago, and since that time neither one of us had said a word to each other. A nice congenial way to start a hunting trip.

We were off. For days we just traveled, uphill and downhill. Fording rivers, climbing mountains leading the horses. It was too tough for them with anyone on their backs, so we led them. My horse laughed at me, the great Western director.

Three days we spent going through the game reserve. No shooting, and we saw moose and caribou by the hundreds. All the game we were going to break our backs to get went waltzing by us with complete abandon. It was a very important experience.

Finally we got through the reserve, and as it was late afternoon, we—or rather Zanuck—decided to camp by a river for the night.

We pitched our tents, the fire was started, and the cook (we had a cook) started to prepare dinner; for the first time since we left our base, I was hungry. Hungry and I wanted a drink. Even the guides' rum would have tasted like nectar. I ate heartily, but I didn't drink, and I hated Zanuck for it, especially when I saw him pick up his ears when first I was asked if I wanted mine straight or with mountain water.

After the meal, Zanuck excused himself and went on a talky walk with the head guide. Going to lay out the big attack on the moose, and we the soldiers sat around waiting for our orders. They came, with map and explanations all done with great Zanuck enthusiasm, which at this particular moment of my nonalcoholic life bored the hell out of me.

Boiled down, it amounted to this: We were a party of five. Three were to go around the sunny easy side of a range of mountains where undoubtedly moose and caribou by the herds were just breathlessly waiting to be picked off by these rugged Hollywood hunters. The other two were to go around the tough side, and if you have ever heard a Zanuck description of a tough side, you know it would end up leathery. He had a knack of calling a spade a spade, a dame a dame, a flop a flop, or a success a personal stroke of genuis. The two on the tough side were to be primarily concerned with grizzly. We were all to meet three days later at point X.

This sounded great to me. I had visions of an easy jaunt, down lovely valleys; pursuing some dumb moose and maybe even shooting one, and of course I could sneak a couple of snorts of my guide's bottle and maybe I would sleep a little. When you first go on the wagon, you don't sleep too well.

My pipedream was interrupted by a request from Zanuck. A request from Zanuck is like a "you wouldn't *mind* doing such and such" from some lieutenant colonel in the army or the air corps or wherever the hell there are lieutenant colonels.

Everybody "not-at-alled" Zanuck but me. I was too busy trying to figure out why I was out here. I had learned early to keep my work separate from my play, and here I was out in the wilds of Canada, with the producer I was making pictures for, and there wasn't a camera in sight, no dames, no golf course, no nothing, just Zanuck. I decided that I was off my rocker. He of course was going to take the grizzly route, and he requested the privilege of choosing his buddy.

I was smoking a pipe, a favorite pipe, when he chose me. I broke the stem, put my teeth right through the hard rubber.

All was quiet for a moment. I got up and asked him if he would take a little walk with me. I had a few things I would like to straighten out. He was very willing, so we strolled away as friendly as could be.

When we got out of earshot of the camp, we stopped. I reminded him that we had not spoken to each other for a week except for his jolt about my not having guts enough to go on the wagon; that he was a crack shot, could hit a dime as far as he could see it; that I would be perfectly willing to shoot with him in the air but that I had no desire to get drilled by mistake, especially in the wilds of the woods, where it was very cold lying on the ground without a sleeping bag. In short I was a little perturbed, and would he mind telling me why the hell he chose me to be his buddy-buddy?

He looked me straight in the eye and said very simply, because he knew I would stick with him.

I turned away from him. I thought for a minute that I was going to slobber. I said okay, let's go, and go we did.

From early morning till late at night we hunted. He followed a grizzly's tracks for two days. He sprained his ankle, and I got blood poisoning. We forded more goddamn rivers than you can shake a stick at. On one we lost the pack horse that had all the medicine and salt to cure our trophies with. We were snowbound for two days and ended up breaking trail for the horses, and we rode through a blizzard to get to point X, a week late, only to find that Adolphi, Enright, and Withers had gotten sick of the whole deal and had returned to the base, and all we had to show for it was one lousy caribou.

We stayed there for two long wonderful weeks of hard but successful hunting. Start out in early morning in the dark. Ride to the base of a mountain, leave the horses, and start climbing until you reach the top. Sounds simple, but for the untrained, it's rugged. You lose your breath, your footing, and your patience, and when you do arrive far above the clouds, you sit waiting for the sun to rise and the clouds to clear, and then you search the valleys with high-powered binoculars for game. And believe me, they were there. Great herds of moose and caribou. With the expert help of the guide, you pick out your trophy, and then the fun starts. With your gun cradled in your arms, you slide down the snow-covered mountain in the path made by the guide's backside. How fast you go I don't know, but it beats any roller coaster I've ever been on. During this pratoggan slide you must be careful not to let your heels dig in or your gun bang against a rock. If this happens, as it did once to me, you automatically become a superb tumbler—only you don't end up against a mattress, usually against a snow-covered boulder, and all your wind leaves you and you lie struggling like a poisoned beetle gasping for a breath of cold mountain air, and when you get it, it's like swallowing razor blades.

When you arrive at the bottom, you crawl to some hidden spot with the wind in your face, and you watch the unsuspecting moose stream by until your trophy arrives. I hit mine with four 30-30 slugs, and that great giant of the wilderness took off and ran for two miles before he gave up and died. We followed his blood-soaked trail for the two branch-slapping exhausting miles, and only the man-killing exertion made the prize worthwhile.

Now came another dainty morsel. The dismembering of the head and cape that eventually, for hundreds of dollars, will be mounted, hung in the playroom, and gape down benignly at all the silly people, drinking and hooting and babbling about nothing in particular, totally oblivious of this monarch of the wilds who once ruled his clean, carefree kingdom with no two parties, no long-winded politicians, no sex perverts, no delinquents, no Cosa Nostra, and no producers or agents or stars. Just a kingdom as uncontaminated as the snow on its towering mountaintops.

Zanuck and I hunted every minute of every day for the two weeks. He was crippled and so was I, but nothing stopped us. I didn't stop because he wouldn't and if that screwball could keep it up with an ankle that looked like a housemaid's knee, then I with my touch of blood poisoning had no real excuse to quit.

I didn't have the appetite for hunting that Zanuck did. We were allowed four Rocky Mountain goats, a sad-eyed animal that looks like a long tobacco-stained white-haired friend of anybody's. I got one, halfway up a mountain. He slid all the way down to the valley dead, and I slid all the way after him sad. When I arrived at the corpse and looked at the face that was going to join friend moose in the playroom, I got a real jolt, for it reminded me of a pal of mine who had been my assistant. The eyes were not closed; they were just gazing at me with a look of complete surprise. The same look that was on Charlie Barton's face when I tore into him once for some not-too-important mistake he had made. I didn't shoot another goat.

A few days later, I got a caribou. These animals are the most beautiful runners I have ever seen. They run very proudly with their fine heads arched back and their chests pushed out pointing, like an arrow.

The trophy of Canada is the Rocky Mountain sheep. I got a twelve-year-old in a little niche on top of a mountain.

There were twelve of them all eating the dead grass underneath the snow that they had uncovered. Their butts were to us —us being my guide and me. We crawled as close as we dared, hidden by some high snow-covered boulders. My guide pantomimed to me to aim for the fourth from the right. I did, he whistled, they turned like lightning and were off with the speed

46

of a Koufax-pitched baseball. I fired and hit, and my sheep jumped the highest, most graceful jump into oblivion that I have ever seen.

We got our two moose, two caribou, mule deer, a wolf, but no grizzly and were on our way home, sick of the grub we had to eat, too-fresh meat, no fresh vegetables, and of course no desserts.

Another blizzard hit us, and we rode through it for two long rugged days. Two hours of the first day were spent crossing a long lake. You couldn't see more than a horse-length ahead of you. The snow was not snow; it was gale-driven icicles, and you spent the whole long frightful hours hanging on with one hand and covering your face with the other.

Through all the good and the bad, the success and the failure of the whole goddamned trip, Zanuck rode like a knight in armor. Never a squawk, always bubbling over with enthusiasm, living for the next day. Planning some better way to get his kill. Some new tough place to seek it out, and when it was all over, I was thankful for the experience, if only to have been with one of the guttiest guys I have ever known—and I have known some real pros. Don't ever sell Darryl Francis Zanuck short, although he did me, years later, when he took credit for Cagney's squashing the grapefruit in Mae Clarke's face—it was like Babe Ruth striking out.

TWO

The big morning at the hospital finally arrived. I had awakened still lying on my bedsored right hip. The green hornets had worn off, and my German nurse was on duty, getting ready to vacuum me clean. I felt ugly, but much stronger than before. My trips from bedside had been more often and less faltering, but the doctors had not said when I could leave. I decided to make a supreme effort and help myself. My keeper, thinking I was still asleep, left the room momentarily, and I forced myself to a sitting position on the side of the bed, my feet touching the floor. I sat in this position, like a sprinter at the mark, waiting for the return of my four weeks' hate. Finally the big moment arrived, and she came back in the room. Just as she passed through the door I let out a bellow like a gung-ho marine and charged into the can, slamming the door shut behind me. It was a good thing that I did, for I very nearly nose-dived into the toilet. They couldn't get rid of me fast enough. I was on my way home.

I went to the hospital in an ambulance with the siren screaming like a ravished dame. I came home in an ambulance with the siren as silent as a little mouse.

As I came down the driveway, everything seemed so peaceful and quiet and graceful. The flight of the birds, the slight sway of the night-blooming jasmine in the soft warm breeze. It was even a smogless day, and the sky was blue and dotted with lovely white puffy little clouds. The smell was so fresh, no hospital smell, no smell of suffering.

The lovely little smile on Mommy's face. All through the

ride home, and now at home, that enchanting little smile said everything. How much she had missed me, how glad that I was home, how much she loved me. Even though I hurt like hell, life was still very sweet.

My bed, a three-quarter size, with a firm mattress. I had been sleeping in this baby for thirty-odd years, and I had grown accustomed to its feel, its sounds, and its warmth. I didn't realize, until safely back in it, how much I had missed it. I thought that maybe I should have named it, masculine of course, because Mommy's was feminine. I know because I used to crawl into it after Mommy had gone down to get the kids their breakfast. It was much warmer and softer than mine, and it smelled like a lady.

I went to sleep with the help of my two green hornets. I don't know how long I slept, but when I awoke (it was always a slow process this awakening, this throwing off the effects of my hornet friends), I saw Maggie, the youngest of my brood, gazing down at me. It was she who had seen me taken away weeks ago, and it was she who was the first to see her old man home. She threw her strong little arms around me and cried her welcome.

One by one they all trooped in—Big Bill with a "glad to have you back, Dad." Kitty who went all to pieces. Tim who almost kissed me, but drew back a little embarrassed—he was a man now; I had just lost a boy. Cissy who gushed over with happiness and relief and talk. Mike who gently lay down beside me and stroked my head with a sticky hand. I still had a boy. All but Patricia; she was an airline hostess for TWA and was on flight somewhere over Albuquerque. And of course Mommy bustling around noiselessly, getting everything ship-shape for my comfort and convenience and watching it all with the proudest, happiest look on her sweet face that I had ever seen. All mother.

It was a helluva homecoming, interrupted by the doctor. They all were shunted out, and I felt like bawling.

Weeks went by. Weeks of physiotherapy, traction, stretching, exercising, bedsores, indigestion, slumbering bowels, faltering trips to the bathroom, agony, green hornets, and unending love and understanding.

Nobody was allowed to see me for quite some time. This started the ugly rumor that I was in pretty bad shape and liable to black out any day.

Friends. How many do you think you have?

By friend, I mean a Tom Hitchcock, who by choice saved my life—not once, but twice. Or a George Chandler who would give me literally the shirt off his back. That's it for *me,* boy, just two, one of whom is dead. True, I probably have some few in the well-wisher class, not too many, just a few. Maybe it's because of me, because I am not a particularly lovable fellow. Maybe it's because of the fight you put up to get somewhere. Maybe it's because you have helped some people financially or maybe because in your job a crowd of people worked for you or with you or however you want to put it. The result, not many real friends. Try this on *your* piano—it's best late at night when it's quiet and everybody is sound asleep, everybody but you.

Two of the well-wishers crashed the gate. It was a hot humid afternoon, and I felt just like the weather. They were very polite and did their best to entertain me with *Hollywood Reporter*-type conversation. How this picture was doing. What that personality was thinking. How great I would be for a certain yarn. A couple of new dirty stories, and the lid fell. I couldn't take it any longer, so I feigned falling asleep. I did it beautifully because I am undoubtedly, or rather was, the best actor in Hollywood, even though I was a director.

Many times when stuck on how to handle a certain situation, a director might ask the help of the producer, the writer, his assistant, or his cameraman, and God forbid sometimes the actor or actress. This mistake I made once, and saw an actor make the big change to actor-director-producer-and-writer, everything but the financier. He eluded that one. I asked his advice at three o'clock on an afternoon. He gave it to me quickly, and I did it his way. I finished the day's shooting his way. He slept proudly that night dreaming of megaphones and Oscars. Looked at himself in his favorite full-size mirror next morning fully dressed and suddenly saw the great director smiling back at him. He took off his tie, rumpled his hair, turned up his coat collar. I had made the big mistake. I swore never to do it again, and I never have.

I had different techniques to gain time to gather my so-called directional forces together.

George Chandler was technique number one. George was not only my pal but a great actor as well. He had played everything for me, from the dumb messenger boy in *A Star Is Born* to the screwball husband of Ginger Rogers in *Roxie Hart*. George had been in close to forty of my pictures, and he developed a second sight of my moments of uncertainty. If he happened to be in the scene that was bothering me, he would find some way of buggering it up, forgetting his lines, sneezing, not once or twice, a seizure, or whispering while I was talking —then the roof blew off, and believe me I could blow it a mile. When I had put George and all his relatives and ancestors where they belonged, I called off work for ten minutes, stormed into my dressing-room office, slammed the door shut and sat down quietly, and always worked out my problem. It was like magic.

If George was not on the picture, I made a deal with my most trusted one. A property man, or assistant, or a cameraman. I gained the false reputation of always knowing what I wanted.

I heard my two well-wishers quietly leave my room, steal downstairs, and go out the front door. To get out to the street, they would have to walk up the driveway passing just under the window closest to my bed. I can just see them as they got outside, breathing a great sigh of relief as if just leaving a funeral parlor. I heard but two sentences clearly. Number one—"Cheerist, that poor bastard's dead and doesn't know it." Number two—"Oh, what the hell, he's lived a hell of a life, what the hell's he expect, to live forever?"

The repetitive hells didn't bother me as much as that horrible word *forever*. I hope to live as long as I can, provided of course that I can take care of myself. I have no desire to become a vegetable like my Uncle Sam was, and be a thing that has to be turned on and off like a mechanical gadget. Thing or not, that word "forever" frightens the hell out of me. Maybe it's because I never became completely blanketed by some religious theory or belief. This I have tried to do to the best of my ability, but it has never been all-embracing, never been able to erase that one ghastly word "forever"—for a limitless time, for endless ages, for eternity, FOREVER!

In a codeinic haze, I journeyed back to the early twenties. Location, the corner of Western Avenue and Sunset Boulevard. The place, the Fox Studios. The era, William and Dustin Farnum, Tom Mix and Buck Jones, Shirley Mason, Emmett Flynn, Theda Bara, Al St. John, Raoul Walsh, F. W. Murnau, Jack Ford, Victor McLaglen, Bernard Durning, to mention a few.

I had directed, or rather I had misdirected, one picture at the Goldwyn Studios, the title of which escapes me, thank God. Oh no, I just thought of it: *The Boob*. In it were George K. Arthur, Tony D'Algy, Charlie Murray, and a young star by the name of Lucille le Sueur, later to be known as Joan Crawford.

The brass took one look at my first directional blooper and bounced me right out of the studio, and fate demoted me to an assistant director once again. I got the demotion and a job with a stage director making his first attempt moviewise.

We went on location to Santa Barbara, and everything seemed as smooth as silk. I knew my job and did it well, helping on suggestions for setups only when asked. Naturally there was envy and some criticism on my part, but I kept it all inside and minded my own business.

After we had been working for about a week, the director asked me to come to his room that night. I had a hunch that something was wrong, and my hunch was right. He told me that I was doing a fine job but that because I had directed a picture and this being his first and since he was from the stage, he felt certain that people would give me the credit if the picture was successful; this he did not want. Furthermore he had already been in touch with the production office, and an old-time assistant was on the way up, even as I was getting my walking papers.

He did it nicely. I thought it was a lousy trick, but realized I could do nothing about it anyway, so I left without saying a word (something distinctly out of character) and have never spoken to him since, nor has he spoken to me. He because of shame, me because I'm a heathen.

When I got back to the studio, the production office offered me their condolences and since no other picture was about to start, fired me—or should I say let me go?

My let-go lasted for a year and a half. I went to studio after studio, climbed fences to get in, but no dice. It's the typical Hollywood story that happens so often it gets boring in its repetition. Give up the apartment for single room with bath, then room with bath down the hall, to damn near no room at all—when suddenly the savior appeared, walking down a street in Culver City, leading a mule. The main street, just in front of what was then the Ince Studios. I had just been eased out of the production office with not even a false promise of a job and was leaning against a tree—they had trees on streets in those days—about to take off on the long walk to Hollywood. I was so low that carfare meant another meal.

He was dressed like a cowboy—not the moving picture cowboy; the real thing. Old western hat, old western shirt. Old western tie. Old blue jeans. Run-down western boots. He looked like a half-breed. He gave me the once-over as he passed by, and I saluted him. This stopped him. He didn't say hello or what's your name, just said I looked kinda hungry. I was, and I said so. He told me to fall in and come to dinner. I fell in, he introduced me to Virgil (that's the mule), and we walked. We must have walked for a mile, side by side, not saying a word until I broke the silence by telling him he had a good mule. He said Virgil was a mighty fine mule, and I found out that this was a long speech for old Dan at this time of day.

Dan Dix was his name. Virgil was a trick mule, and Dan had trained him since he was a pup. At the moment, Virgil had a big part in a Will Rogers picture, and they had finished their day's work and were on their way home. His home was a shack on an acre of ground. Behind the shack was an immaculate-looking small white barn, spotless.

This was where Virgil lived. Dan lived in the shack. The shack had two rooms and a bath. One room was his bedroom, the other was the living room, dining room, and kitchen. There was a cluster of well-groomed apricot trees just in front of the shack. These trees meant a lot to Dan, as I was to find out very soon.

We went into the barn with Virgil and I saw a mule get the VIP treatment. The stall was spotless with fresh straw on the floor. He got a big helping of oats and then a binful of hay. While he was eating, Dan brushed him down, changed his water, hugged his head, and we went into the shack to get dinner.

He asked me to sit down, and he went to the kitchen side of the room and came back with a couple of glass tumblers, went over to a beautifully carved oak chest, which was padlocked, pulled out a bunch of keys from his pocket, and unlocked it. His back was to me, so I couldn't see what he was getting. It must have been something of great value; when he turned around, I saw it: a jug half full of an orange-colored liquid.

He filled both glasses and gave me mine, and we drank. My first mouthful damn near gagged me, but I didn't want to offend him, so I took another. This one wasn't so bad—in fact, it tasted pretty good, and it sure as hell warmed you up. He asked if I liked it, and I said yes after that first swallow. He told me that I would nuzzle up to it. We sat there drinking, and the world started to get rosier. I asked him what it was, and he told me it was apricot brandy. He made it himself from his own apricots, and it was the only liquor he drank. I saw his point.

Dan put the jug down on the table beside me after refilling our glasses; while he became busy getting dinner, he told me all about Virgil. He started right at the beginning. From the day he found him standing over his dead mother and wondering why she didn't get up and give him his dinner. All through his bottle-feeding days, the training, the circuses, the rodeos that Virgil starred in. The kings and queens that he had performed before. The money that they had made together, but not where it had all gone. It was like a proud father telling about a famous son.

We got loaded, had a great dinner, did a lot of talking, and when the evening was all over, two guys knew each other.

I came to dinner and stayed for six months. Six of the happiest months of my life. My luck changed, I got a job, and I fell in love with Virgil.

Dan had an old jalopy, which towed Virgil's carrier whenever they went on any locations. Since the Goldwyn Studios were within walking distance, Dan was not using the car and insisted that I take it to help me in my quest for a job. This made it very easy and got me back in time for a few belts of Dan's nectar before dinner.

On my second trip to Hollywood, I got a tip that Bernie Durning was looking for an assistant. Durning was the top director of melodramas, real blood-and-thunder action pictures, a big, handsome, hard-drinking, tough, lovable guy with a terrific temper. He was well over six feet, dressed immaculately, came from the actors' ranks, and was in love with and married to a little bitty gal named Shirley Mason, who was a star at the same studio, the Fox Studios at the corner of Sunset and Western.

I knew nobody that was acquainted with Durning, but I felt that if I could get to see him, I might sell myself, so I sent in my name and my reason for being there, and then I sat in the reception room for three days, sending in my name in the morning when I arrived and later in the afternoon just before takeoff time.

Sitting across the way from me the first day was a faultlessly groomed man, older than I, and from his looks an actor. I couldn't tell if he was French or just a very sauve-looking American. He was reading a book and sat there all day occasionally casting a look at the stony-faced cop who was the receptionist. When I gave the gorilla in blue my name and told him I wished to see Mr. Durning, he telephoned into the great director's office and snapped a "Mr. Durning isn't in yet" at me, and that was it. So I sat down to commence my long vigil.

Second day was just like the first. My friend was sitting in the same place but reading another book. I reported in and sat down to wait. My friend had a small leather case with him and when the noon hour came, he opened it, spread his handkerchief over his lap, and started eating a delicious-looking sandwich. I was young and always hungry and apparently looked it. Suddenly he just came over, sat beside me, took out another sandwich, and offered it to me. I should have said "no thank you," but I didn't. I took it, thanked him, and started to eat. He had coffee with two cups, and he passed me one—I took it, thanked him, and drank it.

We ate on silently, and when we finished, I told him how much I appreciated the luncheon, and he apologized for not having more. I apologized for eating half of his and then told him who I was and what I was doing there. He explained that he was doing the same thing only in a different field, acting, and then he told me his name: Adolphe Menjou.

We talked all afternoon, announced our presence again, to no avail, and left with a "see you tomorrow."

The third day started off just like the other two. Luncheon time came, and this time I had a couple of Dan's sandwiches with me and a small flask with a couple of belts of the apricot brandy in it. We had a cocktail before lunch, and Adolphe liked it, and he started telling me some stories. No one can tell a story like Menjou, in every dialect, and all new. I laughed myself sick, the cop got into the act and had himself a good time, and when it was over, he started trying to get us our interviews. He was not successful with Adolphe, but he pressed the magic button for me, and I was on my way to see the great Durning.

Durning had his office in one of the bungalows that dotted the studio. No one ever got to the bungalow from the reception desk as fast as I did. I made it in nothing flat. Arrived in front of his secretary from nowhere and was told to go right in, Mr.

Durning is waiting for you. How about that, waiting for me, what kind of a man is this?

As I came into his office, he got up from behind his desk. He got up but never seemed to stop getting up; he was so tall that he breathed different air. He finally arrived at about six foot seven, stuck his big paw out, and we shook hands. I was nuts about him right then.

He told me that the assistant director that had taken my place in the Goldwyn fiasco used to be with him, and he had recounted the whole deal to him. He thought it pretty shabby, but a knock is oftentimes a boost, so the only thing to do is forget it. I told him that I had forgotten it but not the director, nor would I ever forget the pompous little bastard as long as I lived. He gave me a funny little smile, and to this day I don't know whether he agreed with me or not.

He touched on the flop I had made and hoped that I realized that perhaps, because of it, I would be much better when the opportunity knocked again. I told him he could make book on that, and then we got down to business.

One more thing. He spoke of the success I had had flying at the front with Tommy Hitchcock. I told him you just couldn't miss with a man like Tommy, and then I realized for the first time how much my flying had meant to me, and I held my head high.

He picked up a script from his desk and showed me into an office in the same bungalow. Called in his secretary and introduced her to his new assistant. I almost fell on my face, acknowledged the introduction, and asked him when I start. He said you already have, slapped me on the back like a big bear, and started out. At the door he turned, closed it, and said, "By the way, there are two things that I insist upon. One—loyalty, of which I have no worry. Number two—dames in my pictures. No fooling around with any of them, at any time. On the set, on location, or in your stalking time." His number two rang out like an order from a rugged sergeant, and I knew he wasn't kid-

57

ding. Then in a somewhat more subdued tone of voice, he added a priceless bit of advice. He said if you take my tip you'd keep your chasing out of the business entirely. There are lots of happy hunting grounds all around, but you stay out of this fakey love nest.

With but one exception, I have not shot a gun off in this cinematic game preserve through all my ninety-odd pictures, and of course that one exception happened in one of Bernie's pictures.

She was a beautiful little thing. Came from my home city, Boston. Graduated from Wellesley College, which I had frequented successfully many times during my Newton High School days. She had the looks, the desire, the ability, and the personality. All she needed was the chance, and this I got her in one of Bernie's pictures. In return for which, she got me, and it was a very unfortunate get for me.

It was one of those "making up for lost time" affairs, frequent and exciting until one early evening after the day's shooting, the looking at the rushes, and the preparatory work for the next day was finished. Nobody was around. The whole studio deserted save for the watchmen who had not yet started their nightly rounds. She was in my office in my arms, and the door opened. It was Bernie, and I was caught. It was terribly embarrassing, and the only thing the poor little girl could do was to grab all her things and flee the office like a moulting chicken.

All through this accelerated sixty seconds of confusion and utter chaos, Bernie stood like a statue and never said a word until she darted past him; then I heard him say very softly, "I'm terribly sorry," which by God he was.

Bernie closed the door, took his coat off, and started for me. I knew what was coming. When he got right in front of me, he told me to get myself ready, that he was going to kick the shit out of me.

I only weighed 150 pounds, but I knew how to handle myself and I did a pretty good job for a few minutes, but each time he hit me it felt as if the ceiling had fallen in. Suddenly

58

I wasn't there anymore, and the last thing I remembered was the floor raising up and belting me, and I went peacefully to sleep.

I woke up sitting in a chair. My head was soaking wet from the cold water he used to bring me to. One eye was closing fast, and my jaw wouldn't work. It seemed paralyzed. He was leaning over me mad as hell.

The blood was dripping from his nose, so I knew I had gotten a couple of good shots in. When he realized I was coming to, he grabbed me by the collar and shook me. That brought me around, and still breathing heavily, he told me to get myself cleaned up, put some raw meat on my eye, and be on the set bright and early. I had this coming to me, and he gave it to me good because there might come a time when he would need me. Then very quietly he added this little bit of startling information.

He told me quite simply that he had a problem. Had this problem for years. He was a periodic drunk. A once-in-a-while bastard. Every so often, he had to let go, and when those times came, he was the worst drunk you ever saw, and the most helpless. Then is when he would need me, goddamned badly. That was all. He put on his coat, said he'd see me in the morning, and was gone. I sat there trying to pull myself together. I had been his assistant on five pictures and up to now had kept my apron clean. It took over a year to make these five pictures, and to my knowledge, this periodic business hadn't reared its ugly head, yet I did remember he was sick a couple of times and wasn't at home. Had gone away to get some rest. Maybe then was it—maybe they hid him away. It's been done.

I had all kinds of experiences with him. In those days an assistant doubled for everything. I did stunts, walked wings for him, airplane wings. Everything you can imagine, and quite frankly he was my God.

Dempsey was a great friend of his, and he used to come over and work out with Bernie in Tom Mix's handball court. Mix had a ring, but the handball court was better. They had more room to kick the hell out of each other. Durning stood up to Dempsey, and this was when he was a young champion.

Everything that flashed through my mind made me realize what a helluva guy he was.

We went on location once in Eureka, California. It was a lumberman's story with Dustin Farnum. Bernie had just finished a long siege at the dentist and came out with a very small, beautifully tailored bridge. He showed it to the cameraman and me. He was very proud of it. It was like a precious piece of jewelry, and he loved sharing its beauty with anyone who would look at it.

The company lived in a lumberman's hotel—rough. There was a comparatively small cast—Dustin Farnum the star, Frank Campeau and Bill Conklin, and a big jerk that played a heavy —George something or other, and the leading lady. It was a melodrama. The simple plot was big lumberman on trip to big city falls in love with New York actress who gives up career to become big lumberman's wife. Comes to live in God's country with him and can't take it. She leaves—he is heartbroken but carries on nobly—he still has his trees.

In those days, the days of the silent movies, a company had with them a three-piece orchestra—a fiddle, a cello, and a portable organ. Their job was to keep people happy and, if necessary, to evoke tears. On this particular day the leading lady was to have her big scene. She stood at the trunk of a huge pine tree and gazed off at the unending God's country—full of trees, big ones. With trick photography the New York skyline was superimposed over the landscape, and her highness was supposed to trump this effective bit of hoi polloi by giving vent to her feelings with rivulets of tears streaming from a breaking heart. Everything was all set. The cameraman had the counts all figured out; the fiddle, the cello, and the portable organ started to play a sad, mournful tune. Bernie had finished his directions, describing her supposed feelings, her fight to do right, her unbearable loneliness, and then he screamed for quiet. The world stopped, all except the fiddle, the cello, and the portable organ. The script girl sniffed, the wardrobe mistress started to cry softly, Frank Campeau, with a horrible hangover, looked as if he might break into a crying jag, and Bernie looked at his leading lady with hope in his eyes. Nothing happened; she was as dry as a parched throat. Bernie yelled cut, and the world came to life and the fiddle, the cello, and the portable organ muted.

Bernie started to work again. He talked quietly to her, pleading, begging, beseeching. Then, thinking he had her, screamed for quiet, the world stopped a second time except the fiddle, the cello, and the portable organ. The script girl again sniffed, the wardrobe mistress again started to cry softly, Frank Campeau again looked as if he might break into a crying jag, and Bernie again looked at his leading lady beseechingly.

Bernie again yelled cut, and the world again came to life and the fiddle, the cello, and the portable organ again muted.

This was repeated, over and over, and each time Bernie tried a different approach, from the pleading, begging one to the angry one—and his anger was most profound. Everybody watched Miss Parched Throat as if she were about to be swallowed up by the blue haze caused by the fury of the past master of the temper. The music went off key. Once again he screamed quiet, camera—and once again, nothing happened. He whispered cut, and as he started to walk away, she called to him in a very sweet unaffected voice—"Mr. Durning, may I speak to you"—and he turned back and walked over to her, and they indulged in a whispered conversation. She apparently was asking him to do something that he did not want to do. She talked on and on, getting more persistent, and all he did was keep shaking his head no. Eventually she gave up, and Bernie walked behind the cameras and motioned for me. I joined him. The big man was flabbergasted. "You know what she said? She said call me dirty names and then hit me. How the hell am I going to hit her?" Then came a gleam in his eye, and he looked at me and said, "Look Bill, you do it."

"Now, wait a minute, Bernie, I'm just the assistant director."

"No, no, Bill, do it for me, will ya please, just this once."

"No, Bernie."

"*You* don't have to get along with her—you don't like her

anyway," and he started to walk off the set, with a last comforting three words, "It's all yours." He kept going, and I was on my own.

I walked over to our dehydrated heroine and asked her what she wanted me to call her, and she said anything. I hadn't even thought of how to start, and then I realized how little I cared for the dame, what a lot of trouble she had caused me, late on the set, late to makeup, forgetting what she had on yesterday, the works, so suddenly this became a great opportunity to let her know how much in love with her I wasn't and to release a lot of pent-up anger, so I let go right at the top. There was no build to my cursing. I threw her the roughest, dirtiest language that any dame ever heard anywhere. I started at the peak and I stayed there—and my voice is very resonant and very loud. I was so convincing that Frank Campeau blushed, and suddenly there appeared a faint mistiness in her eyes. I was about to run out of breath, and I knew that if I quit now, all would be lost, so I did the one thing I had wanted to do ever since I started working with her—I kicked her right in the ass. That pulled the finger out of the dike, and she cried and cried and cried, and the mascara got in her eyes and she cried some more, and the camera got it all. And when Bernie yelled cut, the troop applauded; the dumb dame thought it was for her and with bowed head took her curtain call.

This was the wrap-up scene, so we all retired to Dusty's room in the hotel. He had finished work earlier, so we all barged in. Bernie, with his arm around my neck, gave Dusty a complete and picturesque description of the whole blasphemous adventure, including my kick, which he said was like a kickoff of a football game at the Rose Bowl. I was the big hero, and we celebrated—and the fiddle and the cello and the portable organ played on and on, and the drinks were unending. It was a party.

All good things come to an end. At the height of the festivities, an out-of-breath property man flew into the room. With some difficulty, he told us that George what's-his-name, the disliked heavy, was getting a good going-over at the only bar in the town. Disliked as he was, he was still a member of a motion picture company (and believe me, in those days, they all stuck together through thick and thin). So, to the rescue, led by Bernie, followed by me, the camera crew, Frank Campeau, Bill Conklin, the violin, the cello, and the portable organ. En route we were joined by a couple of grips, three electricians, Scotty the property man, and the two stunt men. Don't let anyone tell you that a picture company isn't rugged.

In this group were a couple of ex-plugs, two old ballplayers, an ex-pro tackle, an ex-jockey, and a few G.I.'s thrown in for good measure. I represented the Foreign Legion and two air corps, the French and the American. Somewhere along the line, we had all learned the hard, dirty way; when we barged into the bar, it sounded like the arrival of Jack Ford's cavalry in the nick of time.

George what's-his-name was down in a corner, covered with blood and screaming like a stuck pig. He was surrounded by the enemy, perhaps a dozen lumberjacks, all loaded and mean. George must have gone all out to become this popular. They were teeing off on him individually at this stage of the ritual; then the donnybrook started. There were more wild round-house rights thrown by the lumberjacks that night than you could count, and most of them fanned the air, but the low illegal blows that were delivered by the movie gang hit the mark (to put it politely) and the headhunters were losing the battle royal to the lower-gut shooters. Bernie was swinging with his right, his left covered his mouth, protecting his precious bridge. It was enchanting, and suddenly the sheriff and his men appeared. They had a different kind of convincer in their hands, and the melee was over. All the victorious were escorted to the clink, all save George what's-his-name, who took a powder when things got hot.

We had with us a business manager, a gentleman from New York. He represented the money side of the business, and this was to be his baptism in the intricate undertaking of the making

63

of a motion picture. Only yesterday, he had complimented Bernie on being ahead of schedule and under the budget. That was yesterday!

Tonight he was called from his warm bed to bail out Bernie and his devoted followers. But that was not all. In the morning the fixing must start, and fixing costs money, and a busted-up bar had to be restored, and a few hospital and doctors' bills made good. He thought for a day or two that he was in politics and thanked the good Lord that at one period in his younger days he had aspired to be a lawyer, and in fact had finished law school and was about to start practice when the golden cornucopia filled to the brim by moneys from movies changed his whole life and brought him to Eureka, California, to handle dough for a bunch of insane, daffy idiots who were making the product that bamboozled the public and that filled the cornucopia that he hoped to eventually dip into. Mr. Business Manager was sadly disillusioned, and Bernie was behind schedule, and the budget was shot to hell.

The morning dawned gray and gloomy, and the movie gladiators awoke much the worse for wear and tear and prepared for the day's shooting. There were some fully sealed eyes and many half-sealed ones, a few broken hands and a couple of lost teeth, one lost uppers, and one broken lowers. (The town's lone dentist had started business very early that morning. The drill started its frightening whine even before the burping of the morning coffeepot.)

My alarm sounded its unwelcome good morning, I knew I had to get up and get the show on the road, but I was having trouble. One big head is tough enough, but two big heads was too much for me to handle. One was legitimate, the alcoholic baby, but the second, gathered in the barroom fracas, was a dilly. I remembered how it happened. I was having a personal vendetta with a short, chunky tree-spoiler who fought in a crouch, and exposed nothing but a granitelike skull. I tried every trick in the book to get him to unmask, just once, his flabby beer-developed paunch. Nothing worked, not even a well-executed savate kick, when from out of the blue I was nailed by a wild swing from a guy who had aimed it at our cameraman, who ducked just as I took a step in reverse. It scored, right behind my left ear, and brought strange music.

The goddamned alarm clock was the longest-winded bastard that ever awoke sweet slumbering little children. Finally it ran down, but the jingle was still in my head much louder, and it wouldn't stop. It was an eternal echo, and my skull was a hollow sounding board.

I managed to sneak one leg out of bed. Then I got stuck. I couldn't get it any farther, and I couldn't get it back without moving my head, so I just lay there like a frozen motion picture of a hook slide into second base.

This was getting me nowhere, so I finally decided to trick myself into getting in a sitting position. I was to lie there completely relaxed and, on the count of three, throw caution to the winds and snap myself, head and all, into a new anchorage.

One—two—a scream of agony propelled me past the sitting position to one with my feet planted, not too firmly, on the floor. But I was up and listening and alive and then the flood of four-letter words, and I knew the big man was having trouble, Bernie was always having trouble, but I didn't mind, because it was always interesting.

I flew down the hallway, following the ribald trail, until I arrived at the collective can, and there he was, bending over the washbasin as if disgorging, but it couldn't be that because he was still cursing. I waited until he got out of breath and then asked him what the hell was wrong. He said everything was wrong, life was wrong, the whole world was wrong, that all he was doing was tenderly cleaning his precious bridge when it jumped out of his hand and disappeared down the drain. This was a calamity of major significance, and he told me to hold up the company, get a plumber, get the grips, get the electricians, get going! I got going, and in no time at all, the grips, the electricians, the whole damned company including the fiddle, the cello, and the portable organ were all crowded in the hallway or in the bathroom, all save the town plumber. He had taken a few days off to go fishing.

The board of directors, headed by the chairman of the board (Bernie), held an emergency meeting, and a course of action was quickly decided upon. We would tear up the plumbing until the priceless bridge was found. Stillson wrenches, big and small, hammers, axes, an assortment of tools fit to dismantle a tractor were gathered, and the job was about to commence when in stepped Mr. Assistant Hotel Manager and demanded to know what was going on. Mr. Manager had gone fishing.

Bernie drew Frank Campeau aside, whispered in his willing ear, and Frank moseyed up to the belligerent Mr. Assistant, uttered a few magical words, and they disappeared arm in arm in the direction of Frank's room. Bernie gave me the sign, and I followed them, saw them enter Campeau's room. With my ear to the door, I heard the popping of a cork, the tinkling of glasses—a toast by Frank—"Cold water is the best of drinks. Let temperance poets sing. But who am I that I should have the best of everything? Let poets revel at the pump, and peers debauch on tea. But whiskey, beer, or even wine is good enough for me." A big gale of laughter, and I knew that Mr. Assistant was well on his way. (And incidentally so was Mr. Campeau.)

The dismembering of the sink plumbing started in a very businesslike, methodical manner. It didn't take very long to find out that the missing bridge was not on the second floor. We left the second floor in shambles and made our way down to the first floor.

By this time, we had become toilet conscious, and we wrecked this one much quicker. Bernie started complaining about a slight ache that had developed in one of the teeth that once embraced the lost bridge. Old Cap, the head electrician and chief wrecker, thought it might be from loneliness.

From some mysterious source, a bottle appeared. It became a community bottle and eventually found its way to Old Cap, who took a good slug and then told Bernie that the surest way of stopping the ache was to sluff some whiskey around in his mouth, concentrating on the aching tooth. This Bernie did, and I held my breath. This might be it.

Bernie took the mouthful, and he had a big mouth, started sluffing, choked and swallowed—the fakest choke I ever heard. Then Bernie took another crack at sluffing. Another sluff and another choke, and this *was* it. Bernie was off to the races. Bottles appeared in the hallway, another in the can, and Old Cap tore the place to pieces. The fiddle, the cello, and the portable organ came to life, and the party was on—this time very early in the morning. We had a great day ahead of us, and I did my duty. I snaked downstairs to the telephone and canceled the day's work. We had a job to do, and everybody hoped that it would take a long time. It did.

The work slowed down, and the coffee breaks became more frequent; that is, we called them coffee breaks. Bernie's aching tooth had subsided completely. There was no more sluffing, no more choking. Just good old-fashioned drinking. It was full of wild noise, only subsiding when all the plumbing was ripped up and the careful search for the missing bauble started. The violin, the cello, and the portable organ stopped playing. You could hear a pin drop, and when it was not found, the all-embracing sigh of relief sounded like the soft murmurs of a dozen bedded contented young brides.

The next and last stop was the cellar, the very heart of the plumbing system.

The whole company, now feeling no pain, started down the stairs. For each step there was a chuckle, a guffaw, or a horse-laugh; shrieks of belly laughs drifted up into the now-deserted lobby as Mr. Business Manager came tearing in from the street. He had just finished squaring the beefs of last night's spirited event, and from the raucous nature of the sounds that drifted up from below, he knew that he faced another grim crisis.

I was the last one to go down to the cellar, having been delayed checking on the job Frank Campeau was doing, or should I say had done, on Mr. Assistant Manager. It was superb. They both had passed out and were slumbering peacefully on Frank's bed.

Mr. B. M. grabbed me and with a shaking voice and trembling hands, asked me what was happening. It was really pathetic, because I knew the poor man didn't want me to answer. So I didn't. Instead I sat him down, told him to relax, and proceeded to tell him a few facts of life.

I explained very carefully that he was dealing with a strange but talented group of men, that this company was without a doubt one of the crack units of the entire motion picture industry. From its leader, Bernie Durning, right down to and including the drivers of the cars, trucks, and dollies. That this little outburst of childish play was nothing more than a certain type of escapism that one was bound to run into when working with genuis. I impressed upon him the type of man Bernie was. Intelligent, imaginative, a born leader, a superb director, very sensitive, with a beastly ungoverned temper, and that everybody in his company, including most emphatically me, would gladly die for him.

Then I told him what a helluvan assistant director I was. That this little fling was a worrisome thing but that it would all work out; and, in the end, by hook or crook, the schedule would be met and the budget conformed to.

He seemed impressed and then very sheepishly asked me what we were doing. I told him we were looking for Bernie's teeth. He went into a state of shock, and I left him to join the treasure hunt. As I started down the cellar stairs, they were singing "I left my love in Avalon beside the sea," and some loud-voiced baritone was singing his own lyrics, "I left my teeth in Eureka beside the big trees." The laughter drowned out the rest of his ad libs, and I arrived just as Cap was disjointing an L-shaped piece of plumbing. This important piece was apparently the last pipe in the hotel. From here on, we would have to start excavating in the street. This was the big moment, and Bernie called me over to try my luck at finding the bridge in this our last hunting grounds of filth. The pipe was big enough to admit my hand, and I stuck it in and started pulling out leavings from the years of washing and tooth brushings and shavings of hundreds of men, women, and children. Suddenly I felt it. I knew I had a tooth in my fingers. I looked up at Bernie, and the expression on my face stopped every noise in the cellar but the breathing. All eyes were riveted on my hand as I pulled out the lost bridge. Filthy but intact. The first bridge in history that had a beard.

The cheer that filled that cellar sounded as loud as the ovation that Morey Drury received in his last game before a jam-packed coliseum. Cap passed me a full glass of straight scotch, and I carefully dropped the bridge in it and presented it to Bernie, who was crying.

We decided to do the rest of the mopping up upstairs, so the whole company stumbled up to the lobby, where fresh glasses of scotch took on the job of disinfecting, fumigating, and sterilizing two naked-looking teeth joined together by a couple of unpretentious little gold bands, sort of like a dental bra.

With the help of a borrowed, slightly used toothbrush, the bridge was ready for launching. Someone suggested we break a bottle of scotch over Bernie's head. As Bernie inserted the homesick teeth, Frank Campeau staggered forth looking as if he was walking in his sleep, raised a bottle, and quoted, "There, fiercer from the keeper's lashes, His teeth the fell hyena gnashes," and everybody drank a bottled toast to a quotation that nobody understood, including Campeau.

Bernie's alcoholic gaze fixed on Mr. B. M., who was still in a state of shock. I watched his eyes as an amazing transformation took place. He seemed to squint, to bring the moneyman into focus, and suddenly his eyelids relaxed. This was a new man— or rather the old Bernie. His eyes became clear as a bell, eagle-eyed, and I knew he was doing some quick thinking.

He held his hand up (it reached almost to the ceiling), and everybody became quiet. I think that they all expected some word of thanks. They got it. Bernie's way. He told them that tomorrow was Saturday and the next day Sunday, that today was

Friday and yesterday was Thursday, and that they got their Saturday and Sunday on Thursday and Friday. Tomorrow and the day after, we work from early in the morning, until it's so dark we'll have to feel our way home. I'm going to bed, and if you will take a little tip from me, do the same. He went upstairs, and there was just a moment's still tableau, not a word was spoken, then everybody went very quietly to their rooms. Mr. Business Manager's mouth remained wide open.

This was the saga of the *The Trail of the Lonesome Pine.*

I will never forget the look on Adolphe's face when I charged into the reception room and told him Mr. Durning wanted to see him.

He asked me how I did it. I said I just told him you were a well-educated nut. He likes nuts.

So the debonair Frenchman from Pittsburgh met the Irishman from New York, and a deal was made.

On the way over to Bernie's office Adolphe pointed out that there were all kinds of big Western stars, men of action, that there were an equal number of sex stars, also men of action, but no drawing-room stars, so he was going to be the epitome of such a strange fellow. He explained that he spoke six languages, and although he had never been out of the country, he had trained himself to speak English with the distinct accent of all six English speaking countries, whose mother tongue he spoke fluently. He would some day be the cosmopolitan star, the man in the high hat, the man of experience, the man of the world, and that he became. A guy from Pittsburgh, Pennsylvania.

When we entered Bernie's office, he was working on the script in his shirt sleeves. He looked up, saw Adolphe, and got up, put on his coat, and shook hands. That was the tip-off—the cosmopolitan veneer was contagious.

Adolphe rose to the occasion. The great gentleman with a gift for gab; and it was not long before he had Bernie laughing so hard that tears were in his eyes. Story after story. Some a little risqué, but none were dirty, and all were hilariously funny.

Finally he stopped, and Bernie dived into the script, read for a minute, and then told Adolphe that there was a part, a good part, of an English gentleman of fine breeding, in the story. Would he mind reading this particular scene? And he handed him the script. Remember, we were still making silent pictures.

Adolphe took his time, carefully read the scene, thumbed back a few pages to get a little better idea of the characterization and then looked up at Bernie and asked him how much of an accent he wanted. Bernie said just enough, not to overdo it, so Adolphe did it, just enough, and beautifully. When he finished, he asked Bernie if he would like it as a Frenchman or an Italian or perhaps as a Russian or a German, or he could do it as a Spaniard. Bernie played it straight and said try them all. So Adolphe did them all, in just the right key. Each one a masterpiece. He topped it off as a Filipino houseboy, changing some of the lines, making the scene slightly off-color and excruciatingly funny. Adolphe got the role and a very dear friend and an engagement that lasted for a year. It witnessed the birth of a great star, and Bernie was the father.

To mention all the successful pictures that Menjou made or all the great roles he played would be like a recapitulation of some major studios' entire product. His versatility was unbounded. For me alone, he played the worried yet understanding producer in *A Star Is Born,* the crazy, crooked lawyer in *Roxie Hart* with Ginger Rogers, the French-Canadian guide in *Across the Wide Missouri* with Clark Gable. Three very demanding but completely different characterizations, and all beautifully done.

On *Across the Wide Missouri,* we were on location at Durango, Colorado, and I had a certain tribe of Indians working for me. I think they were the Blackfoot or the Black Hawks or something or other Black, but they were the real thing and had a wonderful old chief. He looked exactly like the Indian on the nickel, only much older. He and Adolphe became great friends, and whenever Adolphe was not working, you could always find him sitting and talking to the old chief. We were at Durango for about eight weeks, and that was all the time he needed to learn the language of the Blackfoot, fluently.

Adolphe Menjou died today. There has never been anyone like Menjou in the motion picture business, nobody you can mention, that even closely resembles him. Brilliant, opinionated, smart as a whip, lovable, and a character. Adolphe was unique!

THREE

I was still bedridden, except for the few long, painful trips to the bathroom, and still on the lousy medication—and for good reason; I was still full of pain, so I took my relievers, the green hornets, and I became painless.

The doctor and I had a long, serious discussion on the problem of my gradually breaking myself of *the habit*. He told me that he could trick me into this, by cutting down on the contents of the hornets, but that he didn't believe in such measures, so he laid it right in my lap. Simple: First, don't take them every four hours. Start with four hours and twenty-one minutes. Then gradually increase the time between until your system is rid of the goddamned stuff and you are once again a man with natural cravings, such as ice-cream sodas or a steak or a shot of bourbon, or maybe even a little sex. Sex—how the hell are you going to indulge in that, when even the slightest noncarefully executed movement makes you cry out in agony? Frustrating. Frustrating? Hell, deadly.

I told the doctor I understood the problem and that I appreciated his confidence in me and that I would not let us down. After all if I could look at it as some sort of a game and it, the habit, as some sort of poisonous venom, I would have something to strive for, a big something to help me make the hours less boring. We shook hands, and for the first time in weeks, I had a semblance of a grip. It was a good start.

After the doctor left, I lay there thinking of some way to make this a more even fight. For weeks I had just waited for the passing of four hours, and some few times I could have kept going without the pain-killing relief of the green hornets. It seemed nice to call them green hornets instead of using that constipating word "codeine" or the name of that other killer-diller they mix in with it, the dream-maker. I could have kept going, but I didn't; I wanted it badly. So now I'll find out what kind of a man I am. This one I've got to do all alone. No AA to help. Just me, and as I lay there recalling some of the horrible mistakes, repetitive horrible mistakes, that I had made during my should-have-known-better years, I was a little worried

What gadget could I think of to make this a game? Whom do I hate enough to make him Mr. Codeine, and who is so revolting to me that he or she could replace Mr. Dream-maker?

I got it. Golf, or rather the way—the hard way—I learned to play good golf.

Years ago, when I was under contract to Warner Brothers and making my pictures for Zanuck, Bobby Jones was the— the—of golf. He was making a series of golf shorts at Warners, with George Marshall directing.

I had just finished *Public Enemy with a fresh, new, talented* young man named James Cagney. I received a letter from my brother, who by now was one of the biggies in the wool business in Boston.

He was coming to California on a business trip and would like to play golf with me for a hundred-dollar Nassau. He had a very wealthy millowner from the South with him, and they looked forward to seeing me, playing golf with me, and taking my money.

Since I had never played golf in my life, I didn't know what a Nassau was. I showed the letter to Bobby. He explained what the Nassau meant and asked me my handicap. I told him a misspent youth. He said not that one, your golf handicap, and I told him I had never played the game but was going to learn how before my brother got here, which would be in about three months. I had just finished my year's contractual pictures and could concentrate on golf for three months. Could I learn in that time? He said you might learn how to hit a ball, but God knows where it will go. Then I realized there must be something to this game. He asked me how serious I was about learning. I told him dead serious, that my brother hated to be beaten by me in anything, and I felt the same about him. I gave him a brief résumé of my athletic powers, mainly baseball and ice hockey, and he saw that I meant business and offered to help me.

He explained most carefully his reasons for not teaching his own wife the game—wanted to keep the sport out of the home. Instead he had her under the instruction of a professional he considered one of the finest teachers of golf in the country. Mr. Harry Bassler, the pro at Lakeside, practically across the street from Warner Brothers.

Bobby made an appointment for me; and the next morning, bright and early, I met Mr. Bassler, explained my problem and my profound desire to beat my brother. Before I knew it, I had a full set of matched woods and irons, and a golf bag, glove and shoes and membership in the Lakeside Golf Club. This was the most expensive first lesson that any would-be golfer ever had.

We went out to the practice tee, and Mr. Bassler told me to take the five iron. I said how the hell do you know it's a five iron, and he said it has a five on it. I pulled out the club with a five on it and took a couple of baseball swings to warm up. He put a ball down and gave the greatest instruction a teacher of golf ever gave. He said *hit the ball,* and by God I did. I had been shooting a puck all my boyhood days or batting a baseball, and at least I knew you had to keep your eye on the damn thing or you might fan it.

I kept on hitting it, not too straight, but they were hit. He showed me the proper grip, which felt very uncomfortable, but outside of that said nothing. I hit a pail of balls, and all he did was place the balls in front of me, stand back, and watch me hit them. When the pail was empty, he said he thought that was enough for the first day, made an appointment for my lesson the next day, and went about his business. I learned a helluva lot about golf, but if Bobby said this guy was a good teacher, I guess he must be, but I sure couldn't write home about what I'd mastered my first day.

The second day was almost like the first. The only difference being that Mr. Bassler told me not to lug the bag out to the practice tee, it was too heavy. All I would need was the five iron. As a matter of fact, that's the only club you will need for quite some time, and he wasn't exaggerating one bit.

He kept me on that five iron for one month—four whole weeks of great instruction, sore hands, blisters, patience, on his part, not mine—and whenever I beefed, he just looked at me with a funny little smile on his face and said, "You want to beat your brother, don't you?" Then I'd go back to the goddamned five iron and belt my brains out. If you say "five iron" to me today, it's as self-destructive as saying "in-laws."

As time went by, I graduated from one club to another, first down as low as the wedge and then up to the two iron. Finally the woods; and then, on the last week, he asked me if I liked the beach. I said I did, and he took me into the sand trap. After a few days of playing in the sand, he began placing the pail on the green in different positions, far away and very close to me. He told me to put the ball in the pail or at least hit it. Try this sometime; it is very invigorating.

I had now finished three months of nothing but lessons and practice, practice and lessons, never getting closer to the real links than the practice tee, when Harry very nonchalantly informed me that we were now going to play my first round of golf—and with the great Bobby Jones. I said when, and he said right now, and I broke into a cold sweat. But Harry, I don't know how to putt. I'll show you on the way to the first tee. He showed me. It took him five minutes and I was off to play my first game of golf, and with the champ. For the record, and because of Harry, I shot an 88, and I never shot higher than that for thirty years.

My brother's trip was postponed until the spring, giving me another four months to get ready, and I had fallen for the game hook, line, and sinker. When he did arrive with his millowner friend, my handicap was down to four.

The day of the match arrived sunny and warm. An ideal no-wind day, and the course was in perfect shape. My brother, his friend, and I started practicing putting at nine sharp. I saw that my brother paid more attention to my putting than he did to his own, so I came up short on putt after putt. Then to the first tee. No one would take a practice swing, and nobody asked anybody what their handicap was. Finally I suggested that we toss for choice of positions on the drive. I won, so I chose last. My brother was first. He hit a good ball for him, and then, before his friend drove, I told them I would play their best ball for another hundred-dollar Nassau. This they gladly accepted, and then his pal drove, a good ball for him. It was my turn; I split the middle and was a good sixty to seventy yards out ahead of them. They both had handicaps of twelve.

To end quickly, I won both matches on the thirteen green and for the first time broke 70. The three months of agonizing practice and lessons and great teaching paid off, but even with the six hundred bucks I collected, I was still far behind. It's a great game, because you're only fighting one guy, yourself, and as long as you can control *him,* keep him simple, make him stick to his swing, don't let him read any books, and make him keep earmuffs on in the locker room, and as long as he chooses a great teacher like Harry Bassler and *sticks with him,* then you have a chance to play good golf.

I did not stick to these above suggestions. I was so close to being pretty good that I began reading all the books that all the leading pros were putting out. I went to different pros and took lessons, and finally one told me that all I needed to do to become a great golfer was learn the forward press. That did it, and I forward-pressed myself right off the golf course and onto the back of a horse. I gave up golf and took up horseback riding. This lasted for two years; and then the call came again, and I started to play golf once more. I was lousy. I averaged 84, and one day I thought of a device to get me back on my game, and perhaps it might help me in my present predicament. What if I considered the ball as, say for instance, a guy I despised, named Jack. You don't have to limit yourself to Jacks; it might be a Nell or a mother-in-law or a director or an actor or a producer or just your boss in whatever business you're in.

Now, this can't be just an ordinary hate, it's got to be an all-consuming loathing, an abomination, a rancor, and that little dimpled son of a bitch becomes your Jack. Now, you never kill him; you just hit him where *you* want him to go. Now, where you want him to go is as important as he is. With a driver, you want to belt him right in the kisser and propel him to a spot way out in the middle of the fairway; and there he rests, getting over the blow, in the nice soft green grass. Don't let him be comfortable too long; hit him where you want him next, but be sure the hit is always right in the kisser. Now, this kind of a guy likes holes, so you will have no trouble in your putting; you *gently* tap him in the kisser, and he'll help find the cup. But don't let him stay in there any longer than possible, because remember he likes holes. Keep washing his face, because he doesn't like that too much either. Just remember that from now on you're not playing golf with a ball, you're playing with a face, it's a little round, but still very discernible, and it hates you. If Jack smokes cigars, he's blowing foul-smelling smoke up at you. If it's a dame that's done you wrong, she's laughing up at you. Whatever you hate about your Jack must be pictured in that miniature puss that is constantly *glaring up at you.*

This Jack kind of hatred will do one great thing for you. It completely eliminates the are-my-wrists-cocked, is-my-chin-pointed, is-my-left-knee-flexed, has-my-shoulder-turned, is-my-left-arm-straight, is-my-heel-raised type of thinking. You just concentrate on one thing, belting your Jack right in the kisser. So Mr. Codeine has now become my Jack, and the dream-maker my Nell; and each time I take a green hornet, I am playing right into the hands of the two people I despise most and who share the same opinion of me. (By the way, Jack was

78

a well-known producer, and Nell was an ex-mother-in-law who I always saved for the sand traps.)

The "nurse's record" is a very dry, very technical report on the daily activities, stoolwise, urinewise, medicationwise, and conditionwise of the suffering patient. It gets a very light going-over by the attending philanthropist, your doctor, each morning.

The last column is reserved for remarks, your nurses' bits of wisdom, usually pertaining to the eccentricities of the idiot lying there, who apparently thinks he is the only one in the world suffering.

What great reading they would make if a Gene Fowler or a Ben Hecht were writing the remarks, or a Dorothy Parker.

When I arrived home from the hospital, my doctor gave me this job to do. It was boring at first, a chore to be done, like being my own nurse, but eventually I got the swing of it and started to add a few remarks about this mad suffering moron who squawked all day long and part of the night and had the goofiest thoughts.

NURSE'S RECORD

Care No.———

Patient's Name Wm. A. Wellman   Physician C.H.B.   Room No. ——

Date	Hour Given	Medications, etc.	Urine	Stool	Remarks
7/9	10:00 A.M.	2 green, 1/2 yellow			She had a great gift,
7/9	1:00 P.M.	1 Aristacort			she could always look
7/9	1:45	2 green, 1/2 yellow			intelligent even though
7/9	5:40	2 green, 1/2 yellow			she didn't even know
7/9	7:00	2 green, 1/2 yellow			what the hell you were
7/9	8:20	1 co 1 Aristacort			talking about—a
7/9	9:20	Spud T 1 Aristacort			mother will talk about
7/10	4:00 A.M.	2 green, 1/2 yellow 1 co			her son over and over
7/10	8:40	2 green, 1/2 yellow 1 co, 1 Spud cap			and over, then suddenly you realize he is dead.

7/10 9:40	1 Aristacort	
7/10 11:30	B.M. goodie—minus enema	

Thus it went, on and on, day after day. A few samples at random.

7/11 9:30 A.M.	The works	
7/11 9:30 P.M.	The works + sleeping pill	Guard your dreams jealously, that is all you
7/12 10:20 A.M.	2 green, 1/2 yellow 1 co	have that's all your own. Enema successful but rugged—an angry experience.
7/14 1:30 P.M.	Bowel movement *sans* enema	Great day. We don't
7/15 6:45 P.M.	The works + 2 modane	look far enough into the forest. Boring—she talked and talked—it was like the smoke that comes from the chimney. Suddenly a puff of wind and it's gone forever. My life has the promise of an old shoelace.
7/15 12 midnight	Gas—stomach	Ouch.
7/16 4:00 A.M.	Took shower	Chee-rist! Had bad
7/16 1:30 P.M.	2 green, 1/2 yellow	time getting out or in! Pain from 1:45 to 3:45 terrific—stopped by 1 co then the gas—a shiver of cold wind.
7/16 4:15	Went to sleep	If in making love to my wife, I had to say some of the things they say in the movies, I'd laugh in her face.
7/17 6:10 A.M.	Dopey	I have often wondered how some housebroken married actress feels when being made love to by an attractive,

young, virile leading
man who kisses her
neck, her shoulders,
her lips, and whose
inquisitive strong
hands meander through
forbidden grounds and
who speaks wonderful
words beautifully. How
disappointing it must
be to take that pro-
tective suit of armor
off at home.

These reports all had a very boring sameness about them—did you or didn't you, and how was it? But there was something else: I have a plate in my head because once in a crack-up I forgot to keep the control stick out of my mouth—hence the plate, and sometimes if you feel lousy or you get overexcited or lose your temper, it plays its own music—but I don't care for it, I don't like its funeral beat.

Skipping ahead to July 28 at 2:30 A.M., as usual the works, then to 8:15 A.M., again the works—but I had gained one hour and forty-five minutes on Jack and Nell and in the last twenty-four-hour period, five hours and five minutes. My golf gadget was working.

Another fitful night, and who should step forward but a guy named Lester Cowan. He rang my doorbell; I answered the ring, and he introduced himself as a producer of motion pictures. I had never even heard about him, but he came in without being invited and took over. Said he was preparing a picture to be called *G.I. Joe*, written by Ernie Pyle. This stopped my throwing the bum out, so I sat and listened; in fact, that's about all you can do with Cowan, just sit and listen. He told me how much he had admired my work and that he and Ernie had decided I was the man to direct this story of the doughfoot.

Finally he ran out of breath, and I politely declined the great honor that they would bestow on me. It was like water off a duck's back to Mr. Cowan. He wouldn't take no and kept arguing until finally I shut him up and told him the truth. I was not interested in working my ass off for the infantry. I was a pursuit pilot in the first war and for a long stretch was assigned to nothing but close-to-the-ground work. Tommy Hitchcock and I. We two shot up more airdromes, made passes at advancing infantry, dropped President Wilson's message to Congress in the front-line trenches, did every dirty job that came along. Naturally the German ground troops resented it and did everything but throw their helmets at us, but unfortunately the Frenchmen did the same thing. We fliers were not too popular, we led such an easy, clean life—my ass. In short, you know where you can stick the infantry, and in slow motion. There was such a fury behind this that I frightened him into getting the hell out of my house. That was that, I thought.

A few days later, my doorbell rang, and I answered it. There he was again, this time with a letter in his hand, which he asked me to read. I wanted to know why I should read the goddamned letter, and he said because Ernie Pyle wrote it. Now, I didn't know Ernie then; naturally I had heard about him but had not bothered to read any of his writings because they touched on but one subject—the infantry—and to me, that was like waving a red flag in front of a bull, so I slammed the door in his face.

It's a heavy door. The whole house shook, and I thought that was the end of Mr. Cowan.

Three or four days later, my doorbell rang again. I answered it, and there was that man again. This time he was playing Santa Claus. He had so many packages in his arms, I asked him who the hell he was delivering for, and he had an answer. For your kids, all of them, Pat, Bill, Kitty, Tim, Cissy, Mike, and Maggie. The son of a bitch even knew their names. Wait a minute, I am a little ahead of myself. Scratch Mike and Maggie; we only had five then. Funny, but all the kids are so wonderful that it seems as if they had always been with us. So he had a few less packages.

This time I really let him have it. I told him, in well-chosen four-letter words, to get out and this time stay away, or so help me I'd put him in the hospital. It was tough enough not to spoil kids, especially when they could have whatever they wanted, within reason, so long as you stuck to that "within reason." I told him that Santa Claus didn't come for another three months and that he looked about as much like Santa Claus as Sam Jaffe does. I slammed the door in his face again, so hard that I heard him drop a couple of the kids' gifts. I suppose I played a dirty trick on my kids, but no, I was just being a good, stern father. Taking presents from strangers. I wouldn't have done that when I was a kid. (You're damn right you wouldn't have, you were such a snotty little bastard no one would have offered you a present.)

That night, a long-distance call from Albuquerque. It was Ernie Pyle. That Cowan was a persistent bastard.

I got on the phone, and Ernie said you won't remember me but we met a couple of years ago. I didn't remember. He said that Lester had called and told him about his interesting experiences with me, that I had refused point-blank to even discuss the story. I told him that was true, and then he invited me to come to his home and spend a few days. He was sure that I would change my mind after I had given *him* a chance to tell the story and to make me realize the great need for such a picture and what it would mean to the thousands of kids that were fighting for his and my country. He damn near had me crying on the phone.

Two days later I landed in Albuquerque, and there he was, all alone, waiting for me. He wasn't very big, maybe 125 pounds. Not the kind of guy you would imagine fooling around the front lines, living the hard, brutal reality of personal participation in a war.

We shook hands. He told me he was glad that I came to see him, that I would give him the opportunity to convince me that I should make *G.I. Joe* the important and successful picture he knew it could be. I told him that I didn't convince very easily and that some of my strongest convictions had resulted in very weak pictures. Weak is hardly the word; lousy would be more fitting.

We climbed into his old Chevy, and on the way to his home, he reminded me of the time, place, and reason for our meeting some few years ago. He had been writing a column of everyday happenings for a small chain of equally small newspapers. He said it didn't amount to much, that it was all he could get, yet he had a great pride in his work, and occasionally managed to write something that had a meaning, a purpose, an idea.

Some screwy flier that had flown with me, when I made *Wings* in 1926 in San Antonio, told Ernie about some of his experiences, good and bad, with the so-called Wild Bill Wellman. For some daffy reason, Ernie's curiosity was aroused, and he did a little research on me and found that I was shooting *A Star Is Born*. What appealed to him was the why and the wherefore that made a director out of a crazy ex-flier. He arranged an interview and arrived on one of the sets at the David Selznick Studios in Culver City, had a short few minutes, between takes, to ask Wellman some questions, got a lot of not-too-brilliant replies and a distinct feeling that Wellman was not particularly fond of newspaper people. He did not get the slightest clue of the why and the wherefore, and as a result, he wrote a not-too-brilliant story for his column. He did remember, however, that when it came time to go, Wellman was most polite, very thankful, and extremely relieved.

He asked me if I remembered him now; I said vaguely. And if I had happened to read the article; I said yes. And what what did you think of it; I said I thought his writing had improved. Silence!

We rode on for a few minutes, then he turned to me and said, "You know, most guys would have taken the easy way out and told me that they liked my article very much. I appreciate what you said, and I am most flattered."

We turned into the driveway of one of the many houses on the street, all almost identical. Same size lots, same style

84

houses, all FHA projects. As Ernie said, the only difference was that his house had just been painted, by himself, and he had no garage, or rather he had made his garage into a guest room. His car stayed out; it had been doing this for five years and had become acclimated.

We went inside; I sat down, and we had a drink, and then I met Mrs. Pyle. It was very strange. She seemed ill at ease, almost frightened, and stayed for just a moment, excused herself, and left the room. I thought I saw a slight stagger. Ernie had acted in an odd sort of a way, and for some unknown reason, I felt embarrassed. I stayed there for two nights and two days, but I saw her only once more, and then not even to speak to.

Ernie and I ate dinner at a comfy little home-cooked dinner-style café. Apparently he dined there frequently, for they treated him like one of the family. We talked of flying, of moviemaking, of my wife and five kids, as a group and individually, but not one word about Ernie, his experiences, or *G.I. Joe.*

During the meal, I saw two G.I.'s who had recognized Ernie, though his back was to them. I could tell they were talking about him by their frequent glances in his direction. Unknowingly, this was to be my first baptism of the greatness of this little giant of the G.I.'s.

When we were halfway through our dinner, the two G.I.'s got up and left. Just before they passed through the door, they took a last look at Ernie, said a few words to each other. I felt that they wanted to come over and talk to him but thought that perhaps this wasn't the time or the place. Not right in the middle of a man's dinner. I'll never forget the expression on their faces when they looked at Ernie.

We finished our dinner, and I finished most of the talking. Then we went outside, and there they were, not only the two G.I.'s that had spotted Ernie in the café, but nine or ten more, a few with books under their arms, in their hands, or stuck in their belts.

There was not the movie-type charge of squealing autograph hunters. They didn't even move, just stood there—eyes riveted on Ernie, waiting and hoping that he would notice them. He did and went over. I decided to remain where I was, feeling that a stranger in their midst might become a little embarrassing to them, so I witnessed a pantomimic ritual that I will never forget. Ernie shook hands with them all. You could tell that they asked him to autograph the books, and I suddenly realized that they were probably copies of Ernie's *Here Is Your War* or maybe his latest, *Brave Men*. He asked each of the boys their names, made a few more inquiries, held a brief little talk with each one, and then wrote a something in each book. It was not the usual "Best Regards—Ernie Pyle" stuff; he took time and wrote each a little note. When he had finished, he said good-bye to them with a funny half-wave, half-salutelike toss of his hand, joined me, and we went for the car.

As we drove away, I looked back. One of them was reading what Ernie had written in his book. As he finished, there was a roar of laughter. You couldn't hear it, but you knew it was there, and some passing moron probably thought they were looking at pornographic pictures.

Home, a couple of short ones, a little light talk, and then to bed.

Ernie showed me to my room—his room. I thought I should take the guest room in the garage. I told Ernie I didn't want to take his room. He said that it was just a mock-up of a room to him, that he slept out in the garage. It was his sanctum.

I put out the lights and crawled into bed, but couldn't sleep. I kept thinking of that verbal portrait of Ernie's "mock-up of a room," his "sanctum." To me a mock-up was a model of an airplane, built to scale, that couldn't fly. A sanctum: a retreat, or a place of refuge.

To Ernie, it must once have been a beautiful, graceful airplane, then suddenly something horrible happened, and it became too big to get out of the house, but you could get away from it, in the garage. A sanctum for a poor lost guy.

A door opened. The door across the hall. Soft bed-slippered

footsteps padded toward the kitchen. A door opened and softly closed.

I turned on the light and looked around for something to read. I picked up a book on a table across the room, crawled back to bed with it, and I heard the kitchen door open, the footsteps getting closer and just as they were passing into the room across the hall, the faint tinkle of a glass. Then the door closed softly, and I remembered that slight stagger as she left the room when we first met.

I opened the book. It was Ernie's *Brave Men,* and I read the prelude:

> In solemn salute to those thousands of our comrades—great, brave men that they were—for whom there will be no homecoming, ever.

I started to read and became fascinated. I read on and on until early in the morning, with but two interruptions. The door quietly opening, the bed-slippered footsteps, the tinkle of a glass, the door softly closing, and silence. Sometimes you can hear silence.

Early in the morning, I awoke. I never was a day sleeper. I washed and dressed and stole out of my bedroom. The door across the hall was very quiet. Ernie was sound asleep in his sanctum. I went into the kitchen, and the coffeepot was on the stove already prepared. I lit the gas and went outside for the morning paper. There it was, all screwed up with the hedge, just as they were all over the country, never in the middle of the walk.

On my second cup and just getting into the sports section, the doorbell rang. I answered it, and there was that man again—Mr. Cowan. He shook my hand, acted as if I were a long-lost brother, and breezed right by me, on his way to the garage. I stood there like a goof with my mouth open as I heard him awaken Ernie, "How ya, Ernie old boy? Yah missed me?" Well, I'll be a dirty so and so. This guy is incredible.

They both came out in a few minutes, Ernie half asleep

and in an old bathrobe and Cowan talking like a magpie. The strange thing about it was that Ernie wasn't annoyed or bored by his chatter, but seemed very amused. He acted as if he liked him, so I guess it must be me. There must be something down deep, *way* down deep, that I haven't recognized.

Ernie cooked us a man's breakfast, but I noticed he started off with a Bloody Mary, in fact two Bloody Marys. Cowan and I stuck with the orange juice, unadulerated.

After breakfast, Ernie started to unwind. He told of men, and kids that were men, that had been killed fighting our war, and a lot about a lot that were alive, and *still* fighting. He talked about D Day, the medics, the engineers, artillery men, dive bombers, and of course the infantry. He took us into England, to Italy, Africa, France, and a city I knew a little about, Paris. It was a hell of a tour. Funny, always exciting, sometimes heart-breaking; and, through it all, Lester never said a word. I was beginning to locate that something.

Ernie talked all morning, during luncheon, and well into the afternoon despite the annoyance of a jalopy that kept clanking by every half hour on the dot. It had passed, the trying-to-sell-me period, and it was now a man emptying his heart. My reaction was a strange one, for me. I began to wonder if I was good enough. Ernie sensed that something was wrong and asked me point-blank if I was becoming interested in the story. I said Christ yes, but I was trying to make up my mind if I was the best man for the job. I had always felt that to make a really fine picture, one must know all about the people. Fliers I know, I was one of them, from the beginning, right through to the end, with all the joys and sorrows and crazy living that went with it, but I didn't know one single foot soldier intimately. I was not in love with the infantry, and I didn't agree at all with their attitude toward the flier. I think they call them the fly boys. God-dammit, it's easy to fight if you have a couple of guys right along with you, but try this sometime when you're all alone up there and there's a way out. Which route will you take? Nobody is going to know except yourself. There's a horrible after-birth when you've taken the easy one. I happen to know.

This kinda stopped things for a while. It was very quiet in the living room. The jalopy that had been circling Ernie's block for the last hour now sounded like a big Mack truck. Ernie couldn't stand it any longer and with an "I'll chase that bastard out of here" stormed out the front door. Lester had to go to places, and I was alone, trying to figure out what to do, and I wasn't sure of myself. I didn't want to bollix this one up.

I started to walk over to the window to see how Ernie was making out, and I heard the bed-slippered footsteps again. I turned around and got a flash of her as she passed by on her way to her room. I'm sure she didn't even see me. She looked as if she was walking in her sleep.

A few minutes passed by, and Lester came back into the room. He asked me what I thought of Ernie. Before I could answer, Ernie came in from the street. He was no longer angry. There was a sadness on his face. He looked at me and said, "Do you know what that was? An old man and his wife. They had driven through three states just to thank me for a lousy little paragraph I had written about the death of their son. I asked them to come in, but they refused. They said they just wanted to thank me and drove away."

Poor Ernie—a pathetic little guy with fifty thousand obligations and one great personal tragedy. I knew I was going to make that picture.

Three weeks later, Ernie came to Hollywood. The script of *G.I. Joe* had been completed and now the polishing job, and Ernie was to be the shine boy. We worked together day after day, and it gradually became a great shooting script. Cruel, factual, unaffected, genuine, and with a heart as big as Ernie's. This was *the* story of G.I. Joe.

Midway in our work, we became stale, as so often happens when two guys are driving day and night. We hit an impasse and found ourselves just staring at the ceiling and seeing nothing but ceiling. It was time to quit, to do something that could get us away completely for a day or two. Ernie knew that I loved golf and suggested that I get out and take a few belts at my old pal Jack. It sounded like a helluvan idea for me, but what about him. Did he have a hidden Jack? A golf ball or a tennis ball or just a hiking Jack. He said no, he didn't go much for athletics, too much effort—and then he sort of hesitated. He realized this was a stock request in Hollywood—could I introduce him to two personalities he had always wanted to meet? In the few weeks that I had known Ernie, I had never heard him mention any dames, and I wondered who the lucky two could be. I said of course. Who are they? They were Bill Fields and Gene Fowler. I should have known. I apologized to Ernie silently.

I told him Gene was a cinch; he lives two blocks up the street from me. But Bill was a problem, that is, as far as I was concerned. Ernie's face fell, and he said you mean that you don't like Bill Fields? I said, "Hell, I love him, but I went on the wagon six months ago and Bill never forgave me. Said I was an imbecile, a half-wit, caught in two rat traps, fear and self-interest; and that although he considered me, some few times, a very brilliant young director, I should remember that a brilliant man can well be a madman. These Fieldisms he yelled down at me from his window on the second floor of his home. I had rung his bell but he wouldn't let me in. He punctuated each vitriolic brickbat by throwing at me whatever he could lay his right hand on, including an occupied chamber pot, but never the bottle he held in his left. As I made a fast exit, I heard his last *bon mot,* something to the effect that if I died, he wouldn't go to my funeral, even if he suddenly got well enough to navigate, because he knew I would look like a beheaded rooster's head, sticking out of an expensive container. For a man who was supposed to be getting ready to meet his maker, he was the wildest sick man I had ever seen or heard. Ernie asked me if he was really that bad, and I told him he was . . . that he knew it, didn't give a damn, and, as he once told me, was keeping himself warm for a long, cold journey.

I called Gene, told him there was a fan of his, in my house, that wanted to meet him, Ernie Pyle. He'd be there in five minutes, and the phone slammed down.

They met, these two keen, wonderful guys, and Gene immediately got Bill on the phone, told him about Ernie, and they left my house without even saying good-bye. Happy as a couple of kids going for a chocolate ice-cream soda with an extra scoop.

Ernie was missing for three days, three days dedicated to the magic of three brilliant men getting to know one another. How I would have loved to have a recording of that fiesta of conversation. Ernie Pyle, Gene Fowler, Bill Fields—the rendezvous of three marked men.

When Ernie came to work again, he was a little hung over, rather pale; and when I asked him if he had a good time, he didn't answer in words, just with a profound little smile. He looked as if he was just coming out of shock. This apparently was a milestone for his memoirs. I never mentioned it again. Nor did he.

"For Bill and Dottie and all the multitudinous little Wellmans—from Ernie Pyle." This was what Ernie wrote on the copy of *Brave Men* that he presented to us; however, the story of *G.I. Joe* was culled from *Here Is Your War,* my copy of which is dog-eared and full of notes. Characters that I loved. Dialogue and adventure, battles and heroics, letters and heartbreaks, boredom and, above all, exhaustion. To this wealth of material was added a fountain of new incidents that Ernie had not novelized.

The multitudinous little Wellmans were then represented by five: Patricia, Bill, Kitty, Tim, and Cissy, who was a little bitty baby, so naturally to her, Ernie was but a hazy motion. The other four worshiped him. They were the Western type of play kids. The guns, the belts, the hats, and a real live horse, named Blue.

Blue was a present to them from a wonderful ex-cowboy named Fat Jones. Fat furnished a great number of the Westerns that were being made at that time, not only with horses, but everything that was needed, stagecoaches, wagons, trick riders, wranglers, the works.

I was particularly fond of Fat and insisted, at whatever studio I was directing a Western, that he furnish what was needed. He never let me down, and some of them were big jobs—hundreds of horses, good horses, for *Beau Geste,* and everything that went with them including feed, down to a carefully chosen few, for the posse in *The Ox-Bow Incident.*

Blue was a little on the old side, still hale and hearty and gentle, and loved kids. Fat told the kids he thought that old Blue had his share of deserts and mountains and movies, and that he was retiring him to them because he knew they would take good care of him.

How the hell did Ernie get mixed up with a horse? Well, that's the way this codeinic ball bounces.

I remember now. The kids were all fast as chain lightning on the draw. Rode like Indians, no saddle, no nothing. They slaughtered all the bad Indians in the old West, right at their home, and learned to fall dead from rocks, trees, hillsides, and Blue's back. After a particularly devastating attack of the Shawnees I witnessed, all four were shot dead from the springboard of Blue's back. It was so fast that old Blue pulled his empty self up and looked back at the scene of carnage with complete bewilderment. They were pros, and they had an inexhaustible supply of ways to fall dead. Each one a masterpiece of extinction.

On Ernie's last Saturday in Los Angeles, I had invited him to a little farewell dinner with the multitudinous Wellmans, after which a few of his most intimate friends were to drop in to wish him well on his trip to the South Pacific.

We had finished polishing the script, and it was now a hooting script, which is the greatest and most unusual compliment that can be paid a writer.

I was a little late from golf, and Ernie was a little early for dinner. As I came through the house, Ernie was in the living room with the four young Injun fighters. I could just see them from the door into the living room, not the door from the hallway into the living room, the door that passes by the little bar into the living room. The door I preferred. They didn't see me, and I made sure that they wouldn't. Ernie with belt and holster and gun was drawing and shooting, first Pat, then Bill, next Kitty, and finally little Tim. They died four completely different deaths, and each one frightened the hell out of Ernie.

Now it was Ernie's turn. They had fallen dead for him, now he must fall dead for each one of them. Ernie tried to get out of it, but it was useless, so he finally made a deal.

They all must shoot together. He didn't care if they riddled him with bullets, he was only going to fall dead once because after all that's all a man is allowed, *to fall dead once.*

They riddled him. You have never heard so many uh-uh-uh-uh-uh-uh-uh-uhs in all your life. Ernie fell. It wasn't an agonizing fall of death, just a very tired, relaxed, amost welcome crumble. I will never forget it as long as I live.

The dinner was finished, the kids were in bed, the guests had arrived.

It was an unforgettable evening. There was a deadline to it, for Gene and I were to drive into Los Angeles in time for him to catch his train to San Francisco—his port of embarkation.

The few hours were filled with vivid bits from the lives of two great reporter-writers. Gene Fowler and Ernie Pyle discussing days of the past, days and characters that they knew so well. We all sat in awe. It was an experience given to but a chosen few. It was history that laughed and cried, and it ended too soon.

Time to go, the good-byes and the wish-you-lucks, and through it all, Ernie remained seated.

Dottie, Gene, and I started for the hallway. I realized that Ernie was not with us. He was still seated. I went back to him and said, "Come on, Ernie boy, we gotta get crackin'." He looked up at me and said, "Bill, I can't move, I took that one too many."

Looking back at it, I often wondered if that was the real reason. Maybe Ernie had found another sanctum; Dottie, my kids, a happy home, and he wanted to hang on as long as he could; even though they weren't his, they represented what he had always longed for.

"Okay, Ernie, let's go," and I helped him up, and we started out to the car. Mommy and Gene were waiting at the open door. As we passed by Mommy, Ernie reached for her hand, held it for a silent moment, then, his voice as clear as a bell but strangely quiet, he said, "Dottie—you will never see me again." They were like the last words of a condemned man. Dottie was speechless; so was Gene, and so was I. It was liable to spill over, so I hurried him to the car. Gene and I tucked him in nice and comfy, and before we could get the car started, Ernie had fallen fast asleep.

As we drove out the driveway, Dottie stood there all alone, watching us go. She waved good-bye to the slumbering Ernie.

Ernie Pyle—San Francisco—South Pacific—destination unknown.

Carole Lombard and Patricia Wellman during the filming of *Nothing Sacred*

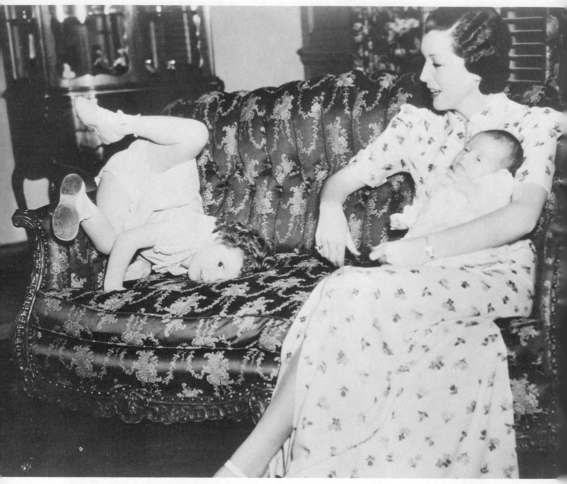

Mrs. Wellman, with Patricia on her noggin and Bill, Jr., in his mother's arms

Carole Lombard and Wellman during the filming of *Nothing Sacred:* Teaching Fredric March how to kick a dame in the exterior while John R. Coonan looks on.

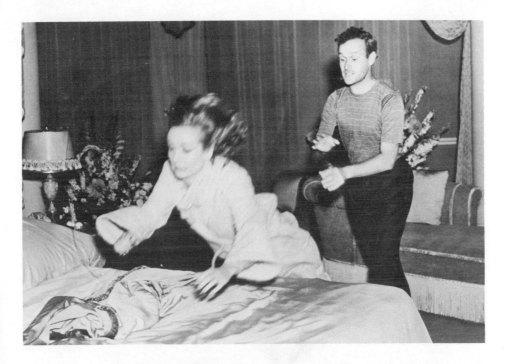

Wings

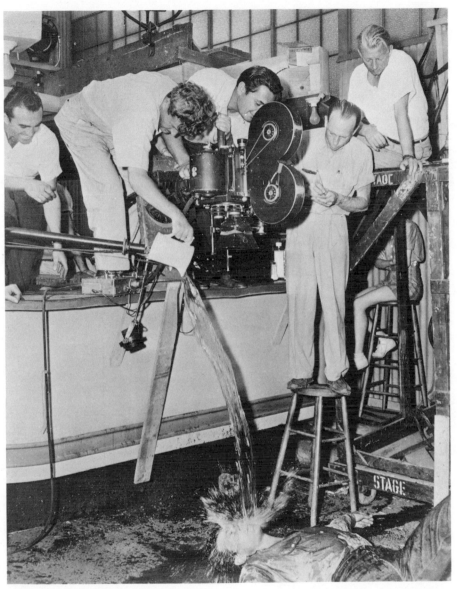

Joel McCrea getting superb direction from Wellman in *Reaching for the Sun*

Wild Boys of the Road—Sidney Miller, Edwin Phillips, Frankie Darro, and Dorothy Coonan (Mrs. Wellman)

Wellman as an assistant director to Harry Beaumont. In front row, third from the left, is Walter Hiers. Behind him (in white shirt) is "Lefty" Flynn. On Flynn's right is William A. Wellman.

Gregory Peck in Death Valley (filming *Yellow Sky*)

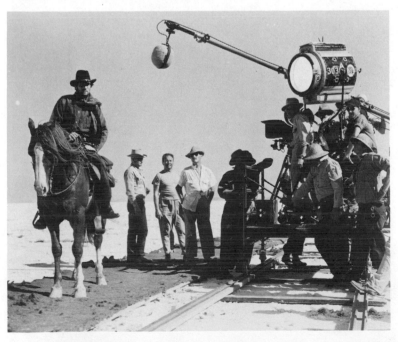

"Looking for the sun to shine"

Barbara Stanwyck and Wellman, during filming of *Lady of Burlesque*

Taking a break during filming of *Magic Town*, with Jane Wyman and James Stewart (*photo by Gaston Longet*)

"This was how tough it was to make *Wings*"

Directing Burgess Meredith in *The Story of G.I. Joe*

Reginald Owen taking a bath during the filming of *Call of the Wild*

Director Wellman filming *The Boob* in 1926, with cast members, including Gertrude Olmstead, Tony D'Algy, George K. Arthur, and Lucille le Sueur. "The picture was so bad they changed Lucille le Sueur to Joan Crawford, fired me, and I enjoy the reputation of making the worst picture Miss Crawford ever made—a great distinction."

During the filming of *Across the Wide Missouri,* Clark Gable and Ricardo Montalban, in costume, get instructions from Director Wellman, who doesn't seem to mind the rain.

A Buck Jones Western (Wellman is "the guy in the golf pants")

Eight Wellmans—with one still to come (Cissy, Tim, Kitty, Billy, Pat, Mommy, William A., and Mike.)

William A. Wellman, Lafayette Escadrille N. 87, Luneville, Alsace-Lorraine

The Wellman clan

Ernie Pyle, en route to the South Pacific, stopped to watch shooting on Lester Cowan's *The Story of G.I. Joe*. (Photo by Ned Scott.) First person he talked to was William A. Wellman, director of Lester Cowan's picturization of Pyle's best seller, *Here is Your War*.

But Ernie never got to see the picture.

David Selznik, President Dwight D. Eisenhower, and William A. Wellman, during filming of TV Special

"Pershing has almost recognized me"

The High and the Mighty (Wellman with John Wayne)

Wellman directing *Battleground*

Filming *Beau Geste*—Gary Cooper, Ray Milland, Robert Preston, and Wellman

Legion of the Condemned, Gary Cooper's first starring picture, with Fay Wray

"How big is a short time?"

FOUR

Doctor has ordered another period of traction. The apparatus all in place and here I go again. They X-rayed me in my own room, looked like homemade movies. The guy that did it was wonderful. No chiropractic pulls or jerks, just gentleness. I told him about the antisocial bastard that had outraged me at the hospital and asked him why he was so gentle. He told me that he broke his back once years ago; and perhaps because of that, he had a little more compassion for his fellow sufferers.

He asked me how I broke my back, and I told him in a crack-up in World War I. He said you were a flier huh, and I said yes a fighter pilot. With the Americans? No, with the French. I was in the Lafayette Flying Corps. He asked me what sector I was flying in, and I told him the Alsace-Lorraine. He said out of Lunéville, and I said yes, how the hell did you know. With a little shrug of his shoulders he said, who can tell, maybe we met before. He had packed up everything and was ready to go. As he reached the door, he turned and said very sincerely, good luck to you and saluted me. It was the German salute.

I had a visitor today. Paul Fix the actor, or rather Paul Fix the fine actor. Paul has had, at various times in his life, a slight grog distress. He never let it interfere with his career, but between pictures it gave him a little trouble, a touchy tummy, and a slight change in the contour of his profile. Perhaps that is what made him such a good actor.

Sometime before my illness (God, that sounds awful), I made a deal with Duke Wayne to make a few pictures for him.

95

I started out like a racehorse, with *Island in the Sky* and *The High and the Mighty,* and then fell on my skinny butt with *Blood Alley.* In fact, I didn't gather any directional huzzahs with *Track of the Cat* or *Goodbye My Lady.* I was in a rut, a deep one. I pulled myself out a little by doctoring up a bad one that Duke's company had made, a circus picture called *Ring of Fear.*

Ernie Gann wrote *Island in the Sky* and *The High and the Mighty.* These two I couldn't ruin; and since I own a share of them both, as does Ernie, we both did very well financially, which of course makes one feel very melancholy, taxwise.

I own a small share of *Ring of Fear,* which added to the melancholy.

I also own a goodly share of the other three, and I would gladly sell out for a ten-dollar bill, all three.

Ring of Fear had already been completed. It was not good, so Duke and his then-partner, Bob Fellows, asked me to help them out and do a little doctoring on it. I had made enough for that year, so I consented, provided I didn't get paid and didn't get credit. That was agreeable to all, so I got me a couple of writers and went to work.

Clyde Beatty was in it. He and all his lions. In the original version he performs his usual act. A good one, but for some strange reason it didn't come off on the screen. Good, but not spectacular. I talked him into putting a bad lion in the cage with the others, and the results were very exciting, a masterpiece of understatement. It was rugged for Beatty, to say the least, but he came out of it in one piece, and we had a little bit of lion pandemonium that kept you holding your breath. I don't know if you have ever seen and *heard* a lion gang fight, but that's what we had, and you have to see it to believe it.

Most of my work was done in Phoenix, where Clyde had his winter quarters. We changed the story here and there, added a bit of tiger action, such as breaking out of his cage at night and tracking down the heavy, and I mean tracking him down all the way through the city to the freight yards, and finally getting his quarry in an empty boxcar that was just pulling out. Sounds simple; it wasn't, but we did it.

We cut here, added there, eliminated shot after shot of the Phoenixian debutantes strolling through the scenes, and stuck with the atmosphere and the smell of a circus, and it paid off. Warner consented to release the picture, and it made a lot of money.

After the preview and the good news from Warners, Duke gave a little party at his home to which I was invited. Duke was happy and a little gay, and in an unconscious moment sat down and wrote me a little gift, a small percentage of the profits, if any. There was, and still is, and I have often wondered what his true feelings are when he has to sign those checks to the half-wit that wanted to do it for nothing. Putting myself in his place, I wouldn't be happy; there goes that false rumor again. First in a hospital, then in a shoe factory, and now just thinking about a sometimes very nice guy.

Goodbye My Lady, by James Street, was a financial fiasco. I don't know why. The story was beautiful, the performance superb: Walter Brennan, Brandon De Wilde, Phil Harris, Bill Hopper, Sidney Poitier, and the cutest, gamest little dog you ever saw, a Basenji. How could you miss? But I did.

We went down in the swamps in Albany, Georgia, all through the peanut fields, with the snakes and the heat, and worked like Trojans. For what? For a plaque that reads:

> To William A. Wellman for his outstanding contribution to the technique of Motion Picture Direction and for "Goodbye My Lady" the National Society, Daughters of the American Revolution awards its CERTIFICATE OF HONOR for producing the Best Children's Picture of the Year 1956—Josephine T. Nash—National Chairman—Motion Picture Committee—Allene W. Graves—President General.

Now, don't misunderstand me. I am a father of seven kids and, up to yesterday, seven grandchildren. I am very proud and happy to receive such a certificate of honor and am doubly proud to have made the best children's picture of the year, but why didn't the kids go to see it? Why didn't they drag their mothers and fathers to the theater? I guess you can't make a good clean picture anymore and make any money. What am I talking about? Disney does it all the time. So it's as plain as the nose on your face. *I am just not Disney.*

Most motion picture directors are a little screwy. I know that fliers are, and I have been both, so draw your own conclusions. Now, add to this my illness—there goes that horrible word again—the green hornets, and a hatred for inactivity, and it's a wonder they haven't rolled the wagon up, put me in a straitjacket, and deposited me in a padded cell. I guess I'm still all right though; I haven't screamed. I've given vent to every other sound you can imagine, but that one I'm holding back until I become a vegetable. What kind of a vegetable? Not a potato or a lettuce or a carrot. An onion, that's it. That seems to suit me better. Strong to stomach, has a pungent odor, and makes you cry bogus tears.

For years, I have wanted to make a black and white picture in color. Reread that sentence again. Now reread the above paragraph. Now we understand each other.

The secret was to get a story that had little color. I am speaking now of color from a visual standpoint. I found that story in *Track of the Cat,* written by Walter Van Tilburg Clark. The same man that wrote *The Ox-Bow Incident* that I made for Zanuck.

It was a very intimate story with but a handful of characters. Practically the whole story took place in or around a ranch house, in the winter with snow on the ground.

This was it. The ranch house was painted off-white, the snow was white, the cattle and horses black and white or a combination of the two. The big pine trees I shot from the shady side so they photographed black. The characters were all clothed in black and white. The only splash of color was the red mackinaw that Mitchum wore and a little flimsy yellow silk scarf that Diana Lynn wore. Bill Clothier, than whom there is no better, was my cameraman. He shared my enthusiasm, and the result photographically was fantastic. Never have I seen such beauty, a naked kind of beauty. Bill and I saw the first print back from the lab. We sat there together, drooling. We had it at last. It was a flower, a portrait, a vision, a dream come true—it was a flop artistically, financially, and Wellmanly. Neither the critics nor the audiences paid any attention to the unusual color, or rather the lack of color, the non-Easter card type of color we had striven for and succeeded in getting. Most color pictures remind me of scrambled eggs, only they don't use eggs—just paints. All the colors of the rainbow, scrambled. *Track of the Cat* had but four colors: black, white, a red mackinaw, and a yellow silk scarf.

The black panther was the symbol of the picture. It was the black panther that represented all that was bad in Mitchum and that finally kills him. In a fit of sophomoric thinking, I decided that we should never see said panther killing our hero. We would just hear it, and the audience could use their imagination, and the effect would be much more powerful. Once more I was wrong. The audiences' imagination failed to imagine, and my arthritis became my black panther and the son of a bitch has been prowling through my system ever since.

The great motionpicture-going public have never known what a helluva job the making of a picture is. I am not speaking of the physical or mental aspects. They can be rugged in any kind of a job. I am speaking of it purely from the standpoint of the nerves. You know, nervous tension, strain, stress, the jitters, the willies, the heebie-jeebies, all wrapped up in that thing called "a director's stomach," and I have a pip. You get it from actors and actresses, writers, producers, the *Hollywood Reporter* and Louella and Hedda and Harrison and a lot of black panthers, and you, The Public. Most of all you get it from you. You don't know what you want, and when you do get it, you don't want it. Sex of course, the old standby, will always bring you in, provided it's nasty sex. Killings are good too, provided you do it in a different, more terrifying way. We, the motion picture makers, have killed thousands. I trussed the dead Cagney up and leaned him against the front door so that when his brother Donald Cook opened it he got a package delivered to him in a cozy little way.

Widmark pushed an old dame in a wheelchair down a long flight of stairs. That brought you in. One of my kids just saw a picture where a gentle person pulls arms off people and cooks them and eats them. Where do we go from here?

The sneak preview. This is the big moment. This is what you have been dreading. This is your stomach, your moment of prayer. Weeks and months of preparations and shooting. Clashes of personalities. Arguments with writers, producers, actors, actresses, juvenile performers and their mothers, unions, New York, musicians, and the friends that need a job. A director is a very popular guy before and during the making of a picture. If the picture is a hit, your popularity remains high. If it's a bomb, you're a bum. They can all sneak out of it—that is, all but you. It's your baby then. If it's good, you're just one of the many of the great team that contributed to the whole. Anyone could have made a great picture out of that wonderful script. I know a few actors and producers who have taken a fling at directing; but, for the life of me, I can't recall any one of their efforts having that lasting quality of a great picture, with three exceptions— Erich Von Stroheim, Orson Welles, and Cecil B. DeMille.

One of our greatest producers tried this simple directional stint, and got everything so confused that his jigsaw puzzle is still on the shelf. A million-dollar shelf. His excuse to me was that he couldn't get up early in the morning.

Your *sneak* preview is held in a theater in a nearby town. The theater is part of the massive chain of theaters that your producing company owns. This theater averages a sneak preview a week. Sometimes even more.

It's going to be a sneak, all right. The manager has notified all his best patrons. Who the stars are. What the picture is all about and even in some few instances who the director is. There is a big banner extending the length of the lobby, announcing the preview, and the red carpet is out for the giant of the industry, for whom you have been busting your gut.

The audience you are going to sneak up on see more pictures than you do; and the ones that you have seen, they saw months before you did. They saw the sneak previews.

There are cards in the lobby with simple little questions to be answered. They rate the picture. The audience write their criticisms good or bad; in truth you are sneaking your picture before a couple of hundred frustrated picture-makers, any one of whom could do what they wished they were doing better than it's being done in the picture they are about to criticize.

The only sneak about the whole deal is you. You sneak into the theater, and an usher sneaks you down beside the great man who is sitting with hand on fader. This fader increases or decreases the volume of the sound.

I am deaf in one ear, my right ear. I got it diving too fast years ago. I had a reason, I was being pursued. Mr. Big has excellent ears, a little too big, but very keen. After sitting through a preview with Mr. Big attacking the fader, my good ear was still good but there was chimes in it. Not joyful Christmas chimes, more like gongs, melancholy gongs of misery. Scenes that were quiet and unpretentious, as I had thought they should be, became raucous and inflated. A rather loud angry scene became a bedlam of fader-inspired yelling. The audience of self-esteemed critics laughed at the wrong time. This wasn't a comedy, or maybe it was; maybe I'd made a funny picture when all the time I thought I was making a tragedy. It wasn't hot inside, it was very comfortable, but I was wringing wet. I closed my eyes, but I couldn't close my one good ear. It kept hearing the rise and fall of the fader. It made me think of something funny, and I laughed at the wrong time, of course, for the house was still—the star had finally gotten to them. Mr. Big nudged me with his elbow. I stopped laughing outwardly.

Next—the meeting in the manager's office. You're pooped, but Mr. Big isn't. No sir, he's fresh and full of ideas, of course his day is a little different from yours. He doesn't get up until noon, and your lunch is his breakfast, so it's eleven o'clock at night for him, but it's four o'clock in the morning for you.

I arrived in the yes-den first, all alone. Nobody on my side but me. In came Mr. Big, laughing and saying witty things, at least they were to him and to the little Mr. Bigs that were dogging his footsteps. All were laughing, although you knew damn well that some of them couldn't even hear his stale *bons mots*. The room was full of the enemy, and the slaughter was about to start.

The king's messenger arrived, this one from the publicity department. He had in his hand the questions and answers. The sneak preview audience was about to edit your picture.

Mr. Big began to read aloud the lampoonery.

There was a deathlike silence, save for the monotonous utterances of Mr. Big. It was like a recitation, with no variation in pitch or expression. It was the death sentence delivered to my stomach, and it went on and on with no intermission.

Outstanding	25
Excellent	44
Very good	41
Good	21
Fair	14
Poor	38
COMMENTS (with instant echos)	
Very draggy in spots	(a good beginning)
Too much yelling	(there's that fader)
Don't touch it	(a masterpiece of understatement)
Stinks	(neurotic bastard)
A hell of a good picture	(won't mean a thing)
Time I trust will give this the denunciation it deserves	(oh, balls)
Could be edited some	(and it will be)
Death scenes too realistic	(death always is)
Love scenes beautiful	(God bless you)
Wellman stinks	(this guy must know me)
Too noisy	(there's that fader again)
I thought the picture was excellent, fast-moving and exciting	(and God bless you too)
Picture dragged	(down again)

Near the end, when the two men get together and have their talk, I believe the picture was adequately explained before. It would be better to let the audience derive what they will from it. The purpose was clear.	(A Harvard man)
First time comedy and drama mixed to my satisfaction.	(ecstasy)
Music too loud	(Mr. Big and his goddamned fader)
Hard to form a definite impression. Believe the picture was trying to put across a definite message but that it was not definitely obtainable because it could not be received definitely by everyone.	(by Mr. Definite—sucking his thumb)
Too loud	(wonder if these "too louds" are sinking in)
Corny	(Oh, Christ, not that)
A waste of talent except Wellman, who has none.	(could be)
A loud stink	(this should do it)

Mr. Big had run out of cards. Nobody said anything, including Mr. Big, who seemed lost in deep, momentous thought. Again the silence was overbearing.

Everybody waited breathlessly for the pearls of wisdom to fall. Finally Mr. Big tore himself out of his philosophical cocoon, looked across the room at Mr. Medium Big, and uttered these world-shattering words: "I didn't think it was too loud. Did you?" And the equally brilliant soul-searching reply. "No—I understood every word." Mr. Big nodded. Every other head in the room nodded, in unison, and the big Gordian knot was resolved, and I was going nuts. He then looked at me. He said that he thought the love scene was good but too short. Got to expand it. Get ahold of what's-his-name, you know, the writer, and we'll chew the fat (these were his words), chew the fat, and we'll make that love scene unforgettable.

My quiet, delicate little love scene. Chew the fat. You can imagine what the final results would be. A bawdy, oversexed version of something simple and honest and tender. I didn't know how the hell I could carry it any farther, unless of course they had an affair right in front of your eyes. This might offend the Breen Office and the Legion of Decency and all the other censorship organizations, but I might cut away to an old tomcat on a fence in the moonlight, giving vent to a wail of passion and springing at some unsuspecting little pussycat in a bed of violets just below him and cut with the old boy about to hit the target. Better still, a couple of rattlesnakes in the desert, wound around each other like two pieces of rope, thrashing over the sand and through cacti, with their rattles rattling in that terrifying sound. This we might get away with. We could explain to the Legion of Decency that they were just wrestling.

This was all I could take. I had a bellyful, so I got myself off the floor and started for the door. As I passed by God, he stopped me with one more question. What the hell were you laughing at, at the wrong time, when the audience was being held? Hell, you could have heard a pin drop and then you laughed, loud. Why?

He asked for it. You know, Mr. Big, that I have a lot of itises, arthritis, colitis, radiculitis, and fibrositis, acute fibrositis. This last one is a dilly. You get a pain in your knee, your elbow, your shoulder, your neck; and right now, I have a pain in the ass, but it isn't from fibrositis. It's from a new "itis" called faderitis; and I went out and got loaded.

There's a war going on in my bedroom. It's not noisy, it's very quiet, it's deadly. One combatant is fresh and full of poison, the other is old and tired and full of pain, but he is winning, because he knows if he loses, he loses all. His wife, his kids, his self-respect, himself.

Six hours between the green hornets. A gain of one hundred and twenty minutes. One hundred and twenty minutes of the most fiendish kind of suffering. Nerve suffering, like having them all exposed at once. You just lie there sweating and watching the clock with the slowest ticking second hand that ever tried to reach sixty. Then it goes for another sixty. This time even slower. These goddamned hornets are lying there right beside a glass of water. You can take them anytime you want. Nobody is going to stop you. Just you. Don't overdo it. Remember, you're not the strongest-willed guy in the world. Remember how Mr. Bottle used to handle you? What a clever pal he was. Remember, you cut out all the hard stuff and went on a diet of Dubonnet, then he showed you how to add a little Dubonnet to a lot of gin. It was the same color, and no one knew the difference, and you were getting away with something. You were real smart. Then you had to start all over again, and finally you got another novel idea. Just beer. For a couple of days that's not bad. Then you have an argument and you get mad; so you give the beer a little more zest by adding anything that's lying around—scotch, bourbon, vodka—and you're off again to the races and that old boy's got you once more. You get loud and boisterous and disconnected. You do silly things, ugly things. there is a mutiny in your stomach, and you have to stop, and everybody is proud of you, and you flout your badge of courage, and sooner or later you begin to believe you did it on your own. You fake. So now you don't drink. You don't eat too well either. For your age you look great, outside; so keep on watching that snail-paced second hand and stick with it. This one could make Mr. Bottle look like an amateur.

I stuck with it; and when that hand hit the sixty, I grabbed for the hornets so fast that I tipped over the glass of water. That was wonderful. I gained a few minutes tottering into the bathroom to get some more water and gained a couple more tottering back because I forgot to bring my buddies with me. I finally got 'em down, made my entry in the nurse's report, lay down on my good side, and just waited for the mumbo jumbo of the black magic. Sometimes it's a long, agonizing wait.

There's a trick. Think of something away off. Something from far out in left field, right against the fence. Something with a little problem, not too big, just enough to make you concentrate, just enough to make you forget that ice pick that's sticking in your back.

I don't know where this came from. Christmas is a long way off, but I'll go along with it. On Christmas I always send my mother a check, with the understanding that she spend it on herself, only. I've got a hunch that she cheats a little, but it makes her happy to share it with some less fortunate friend, so after all that's all that matters. I've always had trouble writing the letter that the check is enclosed in. The trouble being that the letter never seemed to say what I really wanted it to. It usually ended up by being one of those "I love you dearly" or "I miss you muchly" things. So I tried to compose a Christmas letter to my mother, five months before Christmas.

> You know, Mother, this is getting to be a habit. It's exactly sixty-seven Christmases that I have been blessed by you, my mother. Sixty-seven boastful Christmases that I have the most wonderful mother that God ever gave a man.
> When I was a boy you taught me to say my prayers each night. Strangely enough I have always done this, and in sixty-odd years that's a lot of praying, and never once, in joy or sorrow, time or place, have I not thought of you and asked God to watch over you.
> He's done a hell of a job—
>
> Your loving son,
> Billy

I fell asleep.

David Selznick was on the phone. I hadn't heard from him for over a year. All I knew was that, for some reason, he had stopped making pictures. An incalculable misfortune to the motion picture business. It would take pages and pages to describe this monumental loss. The easiest way fo fully realize the tragedy of Mr. Selznick sitting up on a hill is to "look at the record." One great hit after another. All done with great feeling, great understanding, great imagination, and great taste. David had courage, and courage can see a long ways. It was my good fortune to have made two pictures with him. I didn't make pictures for him, I made them with him. *A Star Is Born* and *Nothing Sacred* I made *with* David O. Selznick.

He told me that he was going to make a TV spectacular, to commemorate the diamond jubilee of the invention of the incandescent lamp. He was doing it because it appealed to him. The last twenty minutes were to be devoted to President Eisenhower; and of all the directors in the motion picture business, he had chosen me. It was to be a job of love, not money, and as he said, something for my memoirs. I jumped at the chance, and David seemed pleased and told me that it would take three or four days to get me cleared, and that he would then get hold of me and we would fly to Denver, where the president was vacationing. David had taken over the only studio in all of Denver, and the art director and his construction crew were already hard at work on the set, a duplication of one of the rooms in the White House. Knowing David, it would be an exact duplication, and everybody connected with the undertaking would be the best. Cameramen, grips, electricians, property men, assistant, the works, in the Selznick manner.

I had but one reservation: that I would gladly do the job and naturally to the best of my ability, provided there was no codirector or voice instructor or whatever else might be in the Washington setup that would interfere with my direction of the president. He agreed with me wholeheartedly and said that he would so inform the powers that be.

A few days later, David called me. I had passed with flying colors, and they had accepted my reservation. It gave me a funny feeling, both of pride and of humbleness. I was to direct the president of the United States. For my memoirs.

We flew out of Los Angeles, bound for Denver, one Sunday

night. On the flight to Denver, David read me the entire script. He started by reading the ending, my part of the piece, and then started at the beginning. We stopped to discuss various sequences; and through it all, I kept an ear on his reading and part of my thoughts on the ending. I got what we both thought was a very novel and attractive finish to the president's sequence. It involved Mrs. Eisenhower. No arrangements had been made for this, so we figured on trying to see them both sometime early in the morning and selling them on what we considered a very touching finish.

We landed in Denver, got to the Brown Palace Hotel well after midnight. I was dead tired, David was not, so we went to work.

David had hired a double for the president. He was mine for the whole day, to rehearse with. The president was due to arrive at five o'clock. Over and over, time after time, we were to go over every camera move, every move of lights and props, the unloading of the cameras, the replacing of the microphones, the everythings that had to be done to get twenty minutes of film on the president in a given time, not a minute more. This was no easy job.

Finally David became human and got tired. We went to bed for three short hours. We ate breakfast while dressing, and then the meeting with the gentleman who made the president's appointments. He was both charming and efficient. He said no! No Mrs. Eisenhower. Just that. No explanation, no nothing. So we left for the studio and my day-long rehearsal after rehearsal. This was a double that earned his money. He started right out acting like the president, or rather his conception of the president.

It was pretty bad, but he seemed to be enjoying himself; and since I didn't care how he got to a given spot, as long as he got there and stood facing in the proper direction, I let the poor guy have his fun and be the president of the United States for a day.

After the first two or three dry runs, I got another idea for the last scene in the picture. It meant an involved camera move, the laying of a track, and a lightning-fast job from the grips, the electricians, the camera crew, and the sound. The president was to finish his speech seated before the fire.

At a certain word toward the end of his speech, the camera was to pull back and up, slowly disclosing the president all alone in the middle of this large room, and as he finished speaking, the camera was to stop, holding this lonely figure in a still tableau. I had hoped to get Mr. President to bow his head and the audience could read into it whatever they wanted: fatigue, worry, or maybe prayer; but whatever their impression, he would be a very lonesome figure. It looked pretty good, even with that Denver Barrymore in there. The one bad thing about it. It took five precious minutes to make the change, to bring in and lay the track, to mount the camera dolly to do something that had never been done so fast. It was up to David, but not for long. He thought for a minute, then said it's good, do it.

We were all ready. The last rehearsal had gone like clockwork, and there was another hour before the president was to arrive, so we all went outside in the sunshine to relax a little and try to settle down. We had just picked our spots, when three cars came bursting up. They stopped in front of the little studio, and guys came out of them in droves. A few sauntered off into the nearby trees, a handful entered the studio, and one very important-looking individual asked for Mr. Selznick. Someone told him he was in the studio, so in he went, and we all got on our feet and just waited. It wasn't long. David called for me, introduced me to Mr. What's-his-name, who nodded to me and said he wanted to see a rehearsal. I looked at David who gave me a what-the-hell shrug of his shoulders, and I called the company back to work. I told the double to quit being the president, that this time I just wanted him to be himself. He took it as a compliment. Everything was ready in a jiffy. It was so fast that Mr. What's-his-name was speechless. I didn't explain a thing to him, just ran through the action and the five-minute break of clocklike precision and the pulling back of the camera on the lonesome figure of the double seated before the fire. It was a thing of beauty but not to him. He asked me what I was reaching for by getting the camera so far away from the president. I told him I wasn't *reaching* for anything. Then I explained to him my hoped-for reaction to the lonely figure in front of the fire. He didn't give me any reason, just told me the president wouldn't do it.

I asked him how did he know. The president didn't know how I was going to shoot it, The word "shoot" seemed to scare the hell out of him, so I kept repeating it. I told him that the president must have been told who was going to direct him and that he must have been satisfied by whatever they told him about me, and that he didn't object to my insistence on being the *only* director, and that I still felt the same way. This angered him, but before he could answer me, I told him flatly that when the president got here I would explain the whole scene to him, including my reasons for getting the camera so far away from him and what becomes of it is something between the president of the United States, and a lousy motion picture director. I went outside and lay down in the sun. I was safe. There were guys all around me, on the road, in the trees, in the windows, upstairs and downstairs. What a hell of a way to have to live.

Twenty minutes before the great moment. The company went inside the studio for a final check. This was like a countdown; and after each had seen that his equipment, whatever it might be, was ready to go, he sat down beside it, lit a cigarette, and just waited, quietly. This was a no-talk, no-laugh time. They all looked like linemen waiting for the snap of the ball. They seemed to crouch as they sat.

Cars were arriving—not one; cars. The whole company sensed that this was it and went into action. Lights, cameras, sound, the works, and in they came. The others might just as well have not been there. He stood out like a beacon. He was dressed in a very light gray suit, and he walked like a soldier. David was bringing him to the cameras. The company started to applaud; he acknowledged it with a wave of his hand, and I was introduced. We shook hands, and I led him to the leather chair in front of the fireplace.

I explained as quickly and clearly as possible the business at hand including the five-minute delay and consequent camera pull-back and my reasons for so doing. He told me that it all sounded fine to him, that he was in my hands and tickled to death to be there. You can imagine how I felt. I started to walk back to the camera, feeling rather smug. I had put it all over Mr. What's-his-name, but I hadn't told the president of our little disagreement. A fine way to treat this kind of a man, so I went back and explained the entire situation to him. I left out nothing; and when I finished, he just looked at me with a funny little smile and said, "You're the boss." Well, what did you expect? That's the man I voted for.

Everything went so smooth, it was unbelievable, and the president acted like an old-timer who was making his fiftieth picture, completely relaxed, oblivious to the camera, and with a natural gift of timing. This was going to be fun.

Came the rugged five minutes. While everything was being changed, I sat down on the floor in front of the president and asked him if he would do me a great favor. I just sort of threw this at him, and it kinda took his breath away for a second, and then he said not too enthusiastically, "Well, yes, if I can." I said, "Yes, you can, if you would just divorce yourself from the presidency for a few minutes and become a kneeler with me and bow down and worship the great God Golf." He started to laugh and said one word, in fact he almost sang it; it described his relief and his happiness: "Hallelujah."

Before we could get into the "Palmer told me this" or "Boros showed me that" or "Jones used to say" business, I quickly came to the point. I explained to the president why in California we were better golfers than you fellows who live in the seasonal type of country. When it's snowing in Washington, I'm banging the ball around in Los Angeles, Ojai, San Francisco, Palm Springs, or you name it. When nighttime comes, we have to quit, but not me. I've got me a practice net and I put on the lights and get drunk on golf when the rest of you addicts have to go on the wagon. Now, please remember that just for these few runaway minutes you are not the president of the United States, you're just like me, a psychopathic, demented, deranged, unbalanced golf kooky.

Furthermore, what I want to do I can afford. I just want to send you one of those new golf nets, have you put it up somewhere in the White House, and use it all winter long. If you do, I will guarantee that you will cut your handicap by at least three strokes. Don't say anything about it to anybody, it's classified, and imagine what fun it will be the opening day of your next year's golfing season to take those gentlemen that have been taking you this year. To give them strokes and still beat them. To live again.

I had him convinced, so much so that he gave me a special address to send it to. Wanted to be sure that he got it. He got it, he used it, it worked, and I got a letter of thanks for two things: the picture and the golf net. We're even; he's got his net in the White House, and I've got his letter framed in my den.

The president—"You know this golf is not too easy for me to play at times. There's a course here in Denver, it's beautiful, it's tough, it's a challenge, and they won't let me play it. There's a road that runs right through it, and it's hard to control; and, well, you know some idealist might take a potshot at me, so it's off limits. And there are a lot more just like it. I wish I played half the golf people think I do. Someday I will."

"You mean maybe after this term?"

"Exactly. This is no easy job, you'd be surprised."

That's all he said, but it said everything.

Funny, the lightninglike impressions that fly through your mind. The crackpot taking a shot at him didn't mean as much as his not being able to do what normal men leading normal lives can. He'd been shot at before and missed, probably close enough to hear, but with his experience, he knew that if you hear it, it's past you. It's when you *don't* hear it.

Everything was ready. Lights, camera—and quiet. We did it twice. It wasn't necessary. The first take was perfect, but we had to have another for insurance.

The scene was very effective, and the hard-boiled bunch of moviemakers got their little lumps, and the president looked like a very lonesome man.

The president was not acting.

FIVE

Sweat, blood, and tears; I saved another hour on my green hornet fight, saved an hour and spent an hour, sitting on the porch in the sun. It was wonderful, but awfully good to get back to bed again. Nobody as patient as a bed, nor as wise as a pillow. A bed and its pillow. Love, tragedy, inspiration, intrigue, backbiting, and babies. A little fella tucked in a pillow, gurgling his own happy little patter; an old, old weather-beaten couple reminiscing softly; a beautiful young thing whispering to an eager ear; a drunk babbling to nobody. A producer's wife ruining your picture. Thousands of pillows in thousands of beds. All over the world. The universal language—bedpillowtalk.

NURSE'S RECORD
8/15   9:40 A.M.

Got mad and decided to walk downstairs and surprise Mommy—this I did, slowly, carefully, and painfully. Got back, after a short rest, the same way. Now I ache badly, can put my finger on the place in my back; I feel so old and so lousy that if I had any guts, I would blow a hole in my head and let out all the foul air—a magnificent breaking of wind. Took my green hornets, saved two hours, thirty minutes.

Models—all slender and willowy and half starved—they stand as if leaning against a tailwind, or maybe they've just been goosed. Always leaning back, stomach sticking out; on their faces a most constipated expression (maybe they are). Mouths always awash, showing rows of white teeth. They have just said

114

to the camera, how love—ly I am, or if exploiting the sex angle, the pouty, puckering lips behind which lurks the passion of a pelican. And those eyes, dark and looking right through you, soul-searching for that inner substance—money. What about the little bitty ones, with the curves and the things that you can see where they should be seen, long hair and freckles and strong legs? Who stand on their feet naturally, not in the first position, or the fourth position, or about to leap into an entrechat.

Stumbled against the bedpost and wrecked myself—this to add to the rest of the miseries, completely discouraged. Beginning to think I have a frightful allergy—me.

11 hrs., 45 mins. since last hornets

Poor miserable, lonesome, unloved old man: he died this morning; he was so old that he had just been taking up room. Suspicious of everybody, loved nobody, frightened. In his heyday, with a lovely wife and six kids, he fell in love with his partner's wife, she with him. Two families mangled. His with no money, no food, just a big avocado tree in the backyard. Avocados morning, noon, and night.

He lived his life—they theirs—years later, he came back, broken, nowhere to go, no one to turn to, so he came home or as close as he could get. Because he was their father, two of the six—the son and one daughter—watched over him. A little house on a little plot of ground in the country, money to live on, everything but companionship.

Their mother never forgave him, saw him but an embarrassed once or twice. For two long years after he left, she cried herself to sleep each night. Suddenly the sorrow was gone, in its place a loathsomeness, but she never fell in love again. Once was too much.

Five daughters and one son, four daughters ignored him; one daughter and the son tried to untangle a birdcage of attitudes, and took care of him.

Today, they buried an obligation.

115

9/15   11:45 A.M.

Going to keep track of my exercising—got up very slowly and sort of floated all over the top floor like a wounded ghost, came into Maggie's bedroom: it looked as if a hurricane had swept through. Sat down and surveyed the damage—gruesome. Got up and staggered downstairs and into the den, sat down and had a peculiar feeling that I was being stared at—I was, from the mantelpiece. The Oscar, the awards, citations, nominations for best director, the medals, the three wings: French, Lafayette, American, holes-in-one, letter from a president and a picture with a president. Pictures of me with Tom Hitchcock and General Pershing—about to take off in a Nieuport at Lunéville on Christmas Day 1917, with snow on the ground and no brakes, no parachute, no nothing. Not to mention the little goodies in my safety deposit box—just one certificate of marriage, my present, thank God, but several copies of the afterbirths of regrettable wedlocks—the property settlements—all a part of an interesting life, *you bet*. They all stared down from the mantelpiece, just stared, for they were all gone. I pulled myself up and arthriticked out of the den, struggled upstairs into my room, and crawled into bed, a very painful crawl. A hell of a lot of good those goddamned knickknacks are doing me know. If it weren't for them, I wouldn't be pussyfooting around with an ice pick in my spine and a lot of darts sticking in my joints. Just what did you get out of this hodgepodge of confusion? Arthritis and a fortune. I took my window-pain-killers and waited for Mr. Sleep, a very happy man "yuk." And then I saw it ranging on the wall by my bed, and it was big and in color, and they all were smiling at me—Mommy, Patty, Bill, Kitty, Tim, Cissy, Mike, and Maggie—and I smiled back and went sound asleep.

Did you ever come home from something *something* and end up a nothing? In retrospect, it's very amusing; in actuality, it's upside down.

I came home from the war in a neat blue uniform, with two pairs of wings, French and Lafayette, a couple of medals, wounded with a slight limp that I never let myself forget for a moment. One of the very first daring young American fliers to return to his native land. I got attention everywhere, and I got a wife, and I played it to the hilt.

I changed uniforms and became a first lieutenant in the United States Army—Air Service (Aeronautics), stationed at Rockwell Field in San Diego, teaching aerial tactics. I now had three pair of wings.

I had the only Spad in the country, and my pupils were flying Thomas Morse Scouts, monstrosities supposed to resemble the French Nieuport. Thomas Morse Scout against a Spad. It was like a Nieuport fighting a Fokker; of course, in San Diego we were shooting at each other with camera guns. You could get your picture taken, but where I had come from, you could get your brains blown out and splashed right back in your dead face.

Among my pupils were a couple of insignificant second lieutenants by the names of Eaker and Spatz. Camerawise I splattered them all over the San Diego countryside.

Good-looking tailored uniform with decorations, three wings, and a slight limp. If she was a real pretty little thing, the limp became more pronounced. It stepped up their mother instinct. I always remembered to be humble—above everything, be humble. I learned how to be great by inference. Always told of the exploits of Tommy Hitchcock or Duke Sinclair, Dave Putman, or Jules Baylies, or of a little Frenchman by the name of Ruamps, but I always threw me in as the guy who was there. Made certain that I told them of the deal that Tom and I made. One day he would be the leader. The next was my turn; and no matter where we led one another, we stuck together. Then I'd describe a dogfight, but always from Tom's or some Frenchman's point of view. I might throw in a "I didn't see it all because I was a pretty busy guy myself" just to remind them that I wasn't up there on a sight-seeing tour.

All this mythomania came to a sudden stop one night at a dinner given in my honor by a French producer, Louis Gaznier. He was producing the Pearl White serials with Tony Moreno and a beautiful little ingenue, Helene Chadwick. This was my introduction to a new wonder world, the land of the cinema. There were a lot of strange new people there, actors and actresses, and they liked me and the uniform, and the medals; and I was very humble, and my limp was eye-catching.

Then I met her. The ingenue. She was lovely, and her voice was low and much older than she. I forgot to limp, and my humbleness began to leak. I was like an airplane trying to get into a fogged-in airport.

A beautiful girl and a crazy flier and youth and desire. An unbeatable combination. But all good things must come to an end: I met her mother.

She looked me over like a judge inspecting a prize dog, even walked behind me to see the position of my tail. I saw a dollar sign twinkling in the pupil of each of her ferretlike eyes. Her husband had deserted her—deserted her, hell; he fled from her. There wasn't one single thing about her that even suggested that she was the mother of this beautiful, dainty, talented daughter that I had fallen head over heels in love with. She talked— oh how she talked, a never-ending babble of dull words. Her horn was stuck.

Helene signed a new contract with the Goldwyn Studios, and I was within flying distance of her. We spent the weekends together, either in Hollywood or at the Del Coronado Hotel in San Diego; and on one weekend I met her halfway, at Riverside, and we were married in the old Mission Inn. Mission accomplished—all but telling her mother.

This was my job; and all the way from the Mission to my wife's apartment in Hollywood, I tried to figure a way to combat the multitude of objections that this frightful woman would expound. I had to be careful for my wife's sake, although I had a sneaking hunch that the mother had already started to work on her daughter. I can just hear her. Oh, he's a nice boy, but he's a flier, and they are all very unreliable. You have a great future ahead of you. You are going to be a great star, but he can only be an aviator, and what good will they be after the war is over. He is just like Ralph (the late husband), attractive, impulsive, and treacherous, and he has killed men. I don't care if they were our enemy, it's a very unnatural thing to do, and it's bound to leave its mark. There must have been something to make Helene steal off and marry me without her even knowing about it. I asked her what I could expect. She changed it to "you mean what we can expect." Anything; but don't let it bother you. It will quiet down in time. After all, she is not marrying you; I am. I am of age; I am very happy, and I am terribly in love.

That was good enough for me, so we drove up to the apartment and went in to meet the enemy.

It was in the afternoon, but she was still dressed for the morning. Slippers and a robe and a sort of nightcap on her head with ugly little curls sticking out. Life had not been kind to her.

She threw her arms around Helene and started to cry. This was even before she heard the bad news. She kept saying, "Oh, my little girl, my little girl"; and there was nothing wrong with her little girl, she looked ravishing. Then I thought there must be something wrong with me. I felt the same. I hadn't even said hello, but just in case, I looked down to see if maybe my fly was unbuttoned. It wasn't, and then she stopped her crying, looked at me, and snapped one word: *"Well!"*

I said, "I just married your daughter."

"You what?"

"Just married your daughter."

A funny sort of exhaling wheeze came out of her mouth, her eyes rolled over, and she fainted dead away. I didn't catch her.

Six months of weekends together, most of them at Coronado. Those spent in Hollywood were comparatively silent ones, uncomfortable hours of being constantly screened. My mother-in-law never just looked at me, she audited me, over and over, up and down, inside and out, and with never a change of expression. The least I expected was a Mickey Finn. It made Helene very unhappy. I began to get worried.

Then came the two armistices. The first, a false alarm. The second, the real thing. I got a short wire from my wife with but two words, "Thank God."

We—by we I mean the fliers—celebrated the false alarm. We all got loaded, had a fight with the navy, made a shambles of the Coronado bar, and twelve of us goose-stepped off the long pier that used to extend out from the beach of the hotel. It was at night, there was a strong wind, and the waves very very high. We had on our uniforms, complete with the officer's high boots. It was great fun. We did pretty well. We managed to reach the beach, half drowned, that is all but one, and then we found out the armistice was just a rumor. That sobered us up, but it was a little late. *C'est la guerre.*

The real armistice was celebrated with a little quiet drinking. No fights, no laughter, no talk, no goose-stepping, just silent sorrow. I went to bed early. I didn't sleep.

I asked for, and got, a complete divorce from the air corps. During the time I waited for my discharge papers to come through, I became a member of the ever-growing group we called the Ruptured Penguins. There was no more flying. You reported in and then retired to the Coronado Hotel bar. You were forgotten.

You drank a lot and did a lot of thinking, trying to decide what to do now. This was a new kind of war. A war that you had not been trained for. A lonesome war.

I wondered if I had wasted three years; I decided I hadn't. They had been three years in time but a whole lifetime in living, the kind of concentrated living that comes to those who don't quite know whether tomorrow will be theirs or just a memory of them.

I got a letter from my wife. She was on location at Catalina and would be away for another two or three weeks. She said that she was so thankful that I was through with flying, that I could now come home and wait for her and concentrate on choosing a career. Whatever I wanted to become would make her happy.

It sounded so simple. What if I wanted to become a bum? What if I didn't want to, but just became one?

My discharge came through. I bought a couple of suits and became a civilian again. It was an empty feeling, and I was lost. A Joe Doakes with a couple of little narrow, colored ribbons in my buttonhole. You had to get real close to notice them, and even then they didn't mean anything; probably just came with the suit. I threw away my limp and joined another war.

I arrived at my new home in civvies and a dufflebag full of memories. I didn't ring the bell; I just walked in—after all it was my home. How the hell I was going to keep it up I didn't know. She was in the kitchen. I dropped the dufflebag on the floor in the living room and pretended a merry "Hi." She had been rattling some pots and pans. The rattles stopped, and an unwelcome silence took its place. I just stood there, and I have never been more alone, when In she came. She was dressed as she was the last time I saw her, bed slippers, robe, and that uninviting nightcap on her head with the protruding curls that looked as if they had been picked off the floor of a not-too-clean barbershop. They seemed dead and dirty. She stood framed in the doorway like an overstuffed spook, her puzzled gaze riveted on me. She swayed a little as if in a breeze, then her expression changed, like a cloud passing before the sun. Suddenly it grew cold. She turned and went upstairs. A door slammed shut. I should have stayed in the air corps.

My bed that night was very lonesome. I wondered if Helene's was the same and then got mad at myself for thinking that way. Who was her leading man? (What difference did that make? I was.) All kinds of screwy thoughts popped into my mind. I tried to control them but failed miserably. I almost wished for the days of sexual independence that I enjoyed for the years before I met her, but we in our short time together had gone beyond that. I needed her now, more than ever before. I needed her help. What the hell did I want to be? My short experience businesswise had been a washout. There must be a lumberyard in Los Angeles. I still could be a good lumper. That would tickle the old witch to death.

Then I remembered, and I got out of bed and dove into the dufflebag, and I found it, a worn cablegram from Douglas Fairbanks after the news services had proclaimed to the world that I was winning the war single-handed. It read: "Great work boy we are proud of you when you get home there is a job waiting for you—Douglas Fairbanks." I had just struck gold. I felt like breaking into the old bag's room, sitting on her bed, and reading it to her. I almost did. The thought of Helene was the only thing that stopped me; after all, I was their guest. I would call on Mr. Fairbanks in the morning in full dress uniform, shined boots, decorations, the works. I will reenlist for a day.

There were a few things I did fairly well. Getting loaded, getting involved with the opposite sex, getting in all kinds of trouble, this I did very well, flying, and playing ice hockey. I was born with skates on, double runners. Where I came from, mothers never said, "My boy walked today"; it was "My boy skated today."

Way back in 1914 or '15, I was playing a game of hockey in the Boston Arena on a Sunday. I played rover and was captain of a very fine high-school team, good enough to be invited to all the big eastern colleges. I didn't play as much during the games as I should because of my devotion to the penalty box, but at least I made things interesting.

On this Sunday, Douglas Fairbanks was in the audience, seated in a box just across the way from our bench. He was starring in a play called *The Red Mill,* with Fred Stone and Phoebe Foster, at the Colonial Theater—or was it *Hawthorne of the U.S.A.?*

I had a good day that Sunday, and between periods, Mr. Fairbanks asked to meet me. I skated over and met him and his party, and was invited backstage the following week. This was something new for a kid and very intriguing. I made several visits and became very fond of Mr. Fairbanks. Hence the cablegram.

The next morning, I got my own breakfast, put on the uniform, and was on my way to conquer a new world. As I walked down the front pathway. I was conscious of being watched. I turned; and, sure enough, there she was, peeking from behind the curtain of her bedroom window. She was caught, but she didn't pull back, no sir, not that gal. She just froze. I threw a salute at her. It bounced off the windowpane, but she never changed her expression. It was like throwing a kiss at the Sphinx.

Meeting Douglas was like old times. I called him Mr. Fairbanks, and he immediately changed that to Doug. You would have thought we had known each other for years. He didn't ask me what I wanted to do, just cast me as the young brother of Marjorie Daw in the Western he was about to start in a week. He introduced me to Albert Parker his director, Ted Reed the production manager, Bernie Ziedman the publicity director, and to the assistant director; and, presto, 1 was an actor, playing the juvenile lead with Douglas Fairbanks in *The Knickerbocker Buckaroo* at $250 a week. Hell, I would have committed murder for that kind of money. He asked me if I could ride a horse. I told him I hadn't but I could, that I had ridden everything else, so he sent me to the wardrobe. The uniform once more had served me well. It came off, and like magic I became a cowboy, boots and all.

The assistant director then took me out to the back lot, and an old cowhand took over. He introduced me to my horse and saddle, and I got my first riding lesson and a very sore backside. My life had not slowed down.

I lounged around with the cowboys, listened to the way they talked. Watched them ride and walk; and when it became time to go home, Doug called to me and told me to wear the outfit as much as possible. He wanted me to look as if I had never worn anything else. I slept in it, hat and all.

I didn't ring the bell, I just walked in; after all it was really my home—now. She was in the kitchen getting dinner ready. I hoped, for me. She hadn't heard the front door close, so I Hi'ed my presence, but the Hi had a western twang to it. In she came. She had a dress on, and all her hair was showing. She looked very presentable. On her face, a struggling smile, which quickly changed to a look of puzzlement. I told her I had flown out of the air corps and onto the back of a horse, that I had landed a very important role with Douglas Fairbanks, who, thank God, was her idol. I was in. Within the short span of twenty-four hours, I had risen from a bum to a western Sir Galahad. Dinner that night was in my honor.

I sneaked out of the house and brought back a couple of bottles of wine. It was a good thing that I got two. She finished one without batting an eye or losing a syllable. On the second, it began to hit bottom, and my mother-in-law pinned one on. Her horn again became stuck; and when at last she retired and weaved herself upstairs, I knew the whole history of her life from childbirth. You can't go back further than that.

I was alone and exhausted. Have you ever been bored to death for three hours of listening and striving to pay attention? During that interminable monologue, my vocabulary had consisted of but three words: "yes," "no," and "really," with all the inflections, modulations, and pitch of tone. When I heard her door close, I summed it up with one word: balls!

I started to read the script. Upstairs, a discord of strange sounds. I stopped reading and played a game with myself: On each odd sound, I would guess what she was doing. The shoes being tossed on the floor was easy, hanging something up and missing the hangers, throwing an empty bottle into the waste-paper basket that wasn't there, a dull thud. I hope she fell. Four-letter words. She did.

The door opening, her door, unsure steps to the bathroom,

that door opening but not closing, a moment of quiet, then—the game was over. There was no more guessing.

This was a horrible woman. After all I had been through fecalwise in the Foreign Legion, using latrines that had to be whitewashed weekly because of the lack of paper, those finger-drawn feces paintings, being lousy for months, boils and dysentery from lack of wholesome food, greybacks that hid in your navel. None seemed as disgusting as she.

I couldn't read anymore, so I went up to bed quietly. I didn't want that horn to get stuck again. As I passed by her boudoir, the door was slightly ajar. She was sitting in front of her dressing table fiddling with her hair. No, by God, she was taking it off. It was a wig, and when she got through peeling, she was as bald as an eagle. She looked like somebody from somewhere else, as grotesque and eerie as a horror picture.

I stole into my room, undressed quietly, and slipped into bed. I hadn't locked the door. I slipped out of bed, tiptoed to the door, locked it, crawled back to bed, and breathed a sigh of relief. So help me, I was scared. How would you like to wake up in the early morning with your hand on a naked head?

I couldn't go to sleep. I couldn't erase that bizarre picture from my mind. I tried everything. I tried to think of Helene, of Doug, and the picture and the horse. It wouldn't work. I tried to remember back, of things I had done or that had been done to me. Tried to remember sex of bygone days, but that was impossible because there was so much of it. But a woman taking off her wig and disclosing a head like a billiard ball will never be forgotten.

I awakened with a bad taste in my mouth, put on my western outfit, and started downstairs to get my breakfast. On my way past her room, I stopped and listened. She was snoring, not an orderly snore, a convulsive snorting, like a pig rooting in a pile of wet mud. I ate a hurried breakfast and got out of there as fast as I could.

The next few days were full of a new excitement. Learning how to ride, interviews, rehearsals, photographic tests, meeting friends of Doug's. Charlie Chaplin, Mary Pickford, D. W. Griffith, Allan Dwan, Harold Lloyd, Buster Keaton, Will Rogers, Thomas Meighan, Rudolph Valentino, Norma Talmadge, William S. Hart, Mack Sennett, and Doug's cameraman, Victor Fleming. I was living.

The only dull part of it was that I had to keep changing clothes to be photographed with them. Some wanted me in the American uniform, others preferred the French. None wanted me as a civilian. I finally got sore and told Bernie Ziedman that as far as I was concerned they could stick their pictures you know where and in slow motion, that if they wanted me they could take me as I am now or not at all. I was not going to use my flying as a crutch to get somewhere as an actor, and besides there was a rip in the seat of the pants of my blue uniform and a tear in the state of my ego. He didn't like my attitude and told Doug that I was not cooperating. When Doug heard my reason, he agreed with me wholeheartedly, so I filled up the dufflebag again, this time I hoped forever.

We were not going to work during the weekend, so I made arrangements, with the help of Doug's business manager, to get passage on a water taxi to Catalina Island Friday night. It wouldn't get in till rather late, but I knew Helene wouldn't mind what hour it was, and it would be a wonderful surprise. She was staying at the Saint Catherine Hotel.

I had three nights that I must spend with my personable mother-in-law, but fortunately Doug asked me to dinner one night and Vic Fleming another, and I took a couple of the cowboys out the third, so I missed her as much as she missed me.

Friday night came at last. We had late tests to take, and I just did make the water taxi at San Pedro dressed as a cowboy. A seagoing cowhand. I wondered what Helene would think of her Western husband. I was soon to find out.

When we docked at Catalina, the skipper told me that he left at seven o'clock sharp Sunday morning. He emphasized the seven o'clock, and I told him I would be on time; and then he said, if you change your mind and want to go tomorrow, it will be at the same time. I thanked him and told him I would see him Sunday.

It was close to midnight when I arrived at the desk in the Saint Catherine Hotel. I told the night clerk who I was and asked the number of my wife's room. He gave it to me and, apparently having seen some of the publicity pictures that I had taken with Doug, started to kid me about my changeover from flier to actor. He asked me how I liked horseback riding compared to flying. I told him there was a slight difference, mainly in the tail surface.

She was on the second floor. The elevator was too slow. I went up the stairs three at a time. I was so excited that my hands were perspiring. I forgot where I was. I didn't knock, I just opened the door, and it opened. I wanted to make the surprise complete, so I stole down the little inside corridor to the bedroom that was dimly lit. Not too dimly. The light came from the lamp on the nightstand. One bed was untouched; in the other were two figures entwined in sleep. Christ, I had the wrong room. One of the dim figures turned in its sleep. It was she. I never got so goddamned mad so quickly. I ran to the bed, he awoke and started up. He didn't get far. I hit him and he fell back with a groan. This awakened her, she sat up staring at me, not believing what she saw. She pulled the sheet around her to hide her nakedness. For the first time, she looked just like her mother. I did something I had never done before or since: I hit her. She let out a shriek like a little dog who's had its tail stepped on, and she crumbled up and fell back, naked. I left them the way they were when I came in, sound asleep.

I spent the night in the water taxi with the skipper. He could tell something rugged had happened to me, but he didn't ask any questions, just broke out a bottle, and we drank ourselves to sleep. You meet the nicest guys in the strangest places.

It was midmorning when I arrived at what was my home. When I came in, the old shrew was as usual in the kitchen. When she came out to greet me, she was attired as usual, robe, slippers, and the nightcap with the fake curls sticking out like little angry black tongues. She greeted me, as usual, nastily.

Where have you been? You might let me know when you're not going to be here. I told her that I didn't think she would miss me. She said she didn't, but at least she could take care of me for her lovely daughter's sake. I told her that I was sure she would appreciate that now. Then she asked me the sixty-four-dollar question. Where will I tell her you've been? Oh, just tell her I have been to see an old whore I knew. This unstuck the horn, and I went upstairs to pack and get the hell out of there for good. She went back into the kitchen and took it out on the pots and pans. I went into my room, packed quickly; and on the way out as I passed by her boudoir, I got a novel idea. I sneaked in to her dressing table, found her wig in one of the drawers, a pair of scissors in another, and I retired to the bathroom, gave it a butch haircut over the toilet, pulled the chain, and went out of that den of horrors as happy as a lark.

Once again I was homeless. Not broke but bent a little, so I found me an inexpensive room and bath in a house on June Street in Hollywood. It was within walking distance of Doug's studio; and since I had no idea of going out on the town to drown my sorrows, it suited me to a T. My landlady was a lovely little thing, spoke so beautifully and so quietly and not too much, yet I felt she was a little worried about me. I told her I was a very normal young man, had a job as an actor with Douglas Fairbanks, and did not smoke in bed. She said she was not worried about me, just about my horse, then laughed a merry little laugh. Thank God she had a sense of humor.

I roughed her in on my prowess as a cowboy, that I had been in the air corps and was now trying to make a go of it in a strange land. I did not mention the disintegration of my nuptial knot. It all ended with a cup of tea. I had me a happy home.

It was Sunday. There would be nobody at the studio—yes, there would, my horse, so I took off to commune with my dumb pal. The picture started tomorrow, and another session of riding would help me. I was supposed to look as if born on a horse, but after one short week of photographic tests, makeup tests, wardrobe tests, Bernie Ziedman (the publicity hound), and a few hours on a horse's back, my birth must have been a hell of a fast one.

On the way to the studio, I started to think about last night. It was a mixed-up kind of thinking. I would get terribly angry, first at her, then her mother, then at me, and then at somebody bigger than all of us. Who the hell that somebody was I didn't know. Then I'd blame lover-boy. I don't know why. She could have said no. It's a very short, rugged little word when used bluntly.

Then my anger would subside, and I became sorry for myself. The anger is bad enough, but feeling sorry for yourself is suicide. Next thing I know I will find myself in mid-channel in a water taxi on my way back to my wife to beg her to take me back, to give me another chance. It's happened, many times, but by God not by me.

I was thinking big now, but it only lasted a few moments. Then I started to think of getting somebody to intercede for me. Some man friend who could plead with her and say the things that I couldn't—you know, like, darling this is just a big mistake. You are beautiful and so desirable that you just got swept off your feet. You must realize that you are destroying a man that you loved enough to marry. You must learn to curb your emotions, to funnel them in just one direction, to—Christ, I've got to stop this kind of thinking; my friend is going to get there himself. If I get drunk? Oh, God, no, then I might try and swim over.

I rode and rode, then walked around to rest my posterior, then rode again. All afternoon I strived to look as if I were born on a horse, but I wasn't. I was born in a big four-posted bed at Lindon Place in Brookline, Massachusetts. All afternoon, I tried to stop thinking of her.

I didn't accomplish either but was getting tired. Maybe that's the answer. Get tired. Get so tired that you'll fall asleep the minute you hit the bed. Say your prayers while undressing, so you will have nothing on your mind when you lie down.

How am I going to get tired? I looked up at the hills. That's it. I'll climb them, and climb them I did. I overclimbed them. It was a long way getting there, but much longer getting back.

I got home just before midnight, pooped, so much so that I had a tough time getting undressed. I just said half my prayer, stumbled into bed, and fell sound asleep as I was pulling up the blankets. I didn't think of her.

Three days of: In makeup at 7:30. On the set at 8:30. Finish shooting at 6:00 or later. Shooting everybody but me, and you get paid for sitting around doing nothing but watching. I told the assistant that this was getting boring, and he said consider yourself very fortunate. This is Doug's way of breaking you in. You don't know how lucky you are, and I didn't. I apologized. One thing it was doing for me, at least during the day: I wasn't thinking of that other business. I wasn't walking around like a modern Atlas with the world on my shoulders. Nighttime was not so easy. I eased things a little by helping the cowboys bed down the horses and then drinking beer and eating with them. This usually took a couple of hours, and I didn't get home until around ten o'clock. I was tired physically, but not mentally or imaginatively. I was having a rugged battle on June Street. One night it rained, and I thought I would go crazy. Rainy nights are such wonderful nights if you are in love and together, and so lonesome if you are alone.

Maybe they are arguing about who forgot to lock the door. Maybe they have had a big fight over it. So what? It's a little late, isn't it? Or maybe they were so excited that they just didn't give a damn whether it was locked or not, whether they were in Catalina or on the grass behind second base in the Dodgers' ball park, deserted or filled to capacity, floodlights on or off. They had a little aphrodisia to get rid of, and to do it well required unbroken concentration, superb control, and a complete absence from worldly existence. I better start thinking of something else. If you can't think it, talk it, softly or my lovely little landlady will think I'm nuts, which is not far from the truth. What to talk about? Makeup.

The toughest thing for me to get accustomed to was this make-up ritual. A makeup man slops this yellow crap on your face; at first it feels kind of slimy, then it dries, and your face starts to pucker up. The first time he did it and I looked at myself in the mirror, I thought he was kidding me. That wasn't me I was looking at, it was my younger brother, but I haven't got a younger brother. Christ, I looked like a baby. It's true that I wasn't very old, but there were a few wrinkles in my face, and I liked them. I got them the hard way, flying in an open cockpit, looking into the sun, in rain and snow, crack-ups and fracturing my skull, getting a handful of teeth knocked out and a hum in my head, getting scared, and coming back from Catalina in a water taxi.

Now I am learning to put the stuff on myself, and I don't care for it at all: too much mirror gazing. If I make this my career and keep on looking at that son of a bitch, one of two things is going to happen: either I fall in love with him or I get to hate him. The only time I look at myself is when I comb my hair, and then it is to comb my hair. I even shave in the shower.

Finally my big moment arrived. It came late on the fourth day. It was a long shot and included Doug and me. Just we two, the star and the jittery juvenile. It was a very simple scene. He passed by me some fifty feet away and waved at me. I was supposed to wave back. We didn't even rehearse it. Then they lit the lights, the director yelled quiet, camera, action, and Doug passed by and waved at me. I saluted him. Everybody thought it was a gag and laughed like hell, everybody but me. I just stood there like a dope with a dead pan, and they thought *this* was very funny. So they took it again, and believe it or not I had to fight myself not to salute.

That finished the day's work, and I damn near blew my debut as an actor. It was really difficult for me not to salute Doug again. I couldn't figure it out. I guess the stretch in two armies did it, unhinges you a little.

The picture really started moving, and I worked every day. I got a little better as time went on, didn't salute when I should have waved, began to look as if a horse and I were not total strangers. There were even days when I thought acting was a pretty good way of making a living, but I couldn't get used to that yellow stuff.

The direction fascinated me, so I spent all my idle time watching Albert Parker and trying to figure out what he was doing. I got lost, and I think he did, too.

My nights were still on the restless side, but I was hanging on pretty good, until one night I went walking and deliberately steered myself to her house. I knew it was a foolish thing to do, but since I had no intention of going in, I sold myself on just a little saunter past to appease my curiosity. That was a mistake.

There was a sports car parked outside, and of course I wondered who it belonged to. Probably some actress friend of hers. Who you kidding? You know damned well it isn't, so I went across the street to find out who the new gallant was, sitting in there staring at that fakey nightcap and listening to that torrent of talk and getting his reward.

I looked at the license. She's doing all right. He was bigger than the Catalina cavalier. This guy was a top star. I have never met him, and he doesn't know anything about me, unless of course the horn had become stuck. What can I do? Go in and get in an argument with him. Over what? Over something that's lost?

I thought maybe I would slit his tires or scratch up the paint job or screw up the engine. What good would that do? Wouldn't do me any good, so I went on my way. I was a little proud of me. I could see slight signs of me growing up. I didn't hurt his car, all I did was piss on it.

I didn't feel like going home. I didn't want to be alone. I wanted somebody to talk to, someone to confide in, so I went to the little bar the cowboys hung around. There were just a few of them there. I didn't recognize any of them, then I saw him, old Tex off in a corner getting lonesome loaded. I went over to him, asked him if I could buy him a drink. "Never refused one in my life. Sit down, young fella, and have one with me." We started from there. An hour later, we both were completely relaxed, and I asked the old boy if he would listen to a very sad tale and perhaps give me a little advice on how to lick myself. He said fire away, and I did, from the start to the finish. Old Tex never said a word, just drank and listened. When I finally finished my tale of woe, I ordered a couple of more drinks. Tex said no, not for me. Gotta have a clear head. A clear head? He had enough while I had been sitting there to put an ordinary guy under the table, but I guess he knew his capacity.

Old Tex: "I tell ya what ya do, young fella—it's very simple. There is only one cure for this brand of pizon that you're suffering with. Lots of fellas have had this sickness, you know. It's quite common. I've had it myself, a couple of times. God-damned near drove me loco until I learned the secret."

I started to say something, but he stopped me. "Now you just sit there and listen, an' old Tex will straighten you out, by God. You're ridin' a wild horse now, so just listen carefully. You go get yourself a little willing filly. Tomorrow. Now you crawl right in there, boy, and pull the zipper right over you. You don't even come out for air. You get in there and hibernate. Yes siree, you get yourself a eager little filly and all that pizon will skedaddle right out of your system. It's that simple, boy, and it's very titillating. Now I'll have my drink."

I got me a filly, an eager, willing little filly. It did the trick: I forgot about *her,* my nights were not lonesome, and when I felt like sleeping, I slept soundly. Tex was right. It was very titillating.

Everything went along beautifully, the picture, the titillating, putting away a little dough for that rainy day, even my acting improved—of course there was a hell of a lot of room for it—but it didn't come from the heart. I still detested the yellow stuff and all that went with it.

I could see that Doug's life was not all his own. He had to share it with all kinds of people and obligations that you acquire when you work for the public. I wouldn't mind working for them behind the camera, heard but not seen. I made up my mind that if I ever made the grade as a director, I would never have a publicity man. I think I was right. How very few directors have been real box office on their names alone—Griffith, DeMille, von Stroheim. It is the stars the public pays its money to see. Maybe a very small percentage appreciate the excellence of the picture, of the photography, of the music, but damned few go home raving about the direction. In Hollywood, yes, but in Paducah, no.

Doug was a servant, a well-paid one, but everything he did or said or thought had to be screened, carefully blueprinted to suit the tastes of the great American public.

Maybe the actor or actress loves this sort of adulation. I got it in a small way when I first came home in a blue uniform. I played it for all it was worth and got nothing but a heartbreak and a demotion right back to an ordinary Joe, confronted by a tough world to lick all over again, and now a new crisis. A good job, good money, and a chance to really amount to something as an actor, but how far can you go doing something you hate?

The last day of the picture, the day of the stunt, not a too difficult one, but you can get hurt, so they saved it for the finish. It was the end of a chase. For the last three days, Doug had been chasing me on horseback all over Chatsworth; and at last, he was to catch me, dive off his horse at full gallop, and knock me off mine. We were to roll on the ground into the camera, and Doug gets up. I stay down, knocked out—and I wanted to be sure that I was acting.

I have been body checked by Ramie Skelton in ice hockey, Bill Brady and Van Tassel in football, all 230 pounds, rough-playing boys, but never off horseback. Doug was very honest and told me what to expect. Evidently the secret was on the way down. Whoever landed on top had a human cushion. The cushion could get hurt. I was not to look back, so Doug was going to yell Geronimo as he took off.

Parker yelled camera, action—and in I came with Doug on the faster horse gaining on me. He timed it just right; and as we got into the correct position for the camera, I heard "Geronimo," and boy did he hit me. I flew out of the saddle with Doug all over me, and on the way down, I twisted like you do on skates when you have been checked into the boards in a hockey game. It kept me from being the cushion. Doug was less fortunate. He got everything out of the way except one arm. He didn't break it, but it was badly bruised. When the scene was over, he looked at me and said, "Boy, you're all right"; that was all, and it is probably the nicest compliment that's ever been paid me.

This was the last scene of the picture. A party, laughs, and good-byes; and when I finally came to the next morning, there was a message for me to call Mr. X, my wife's lawyer. I did, and he said that he would like to get my views on the divorce that Mrs. Wellman wanted to get. I told him it wouldn't be too soon for me.

My introduction to an important motion picture legal beagle was one for the books. Since I had nothing and nothing to lose, this was going to be fun. Undoubtedly he had been filled in with a complete detailed portraiture of me by my neurotic mother-in-law, and I was curious as to how much they had confided in him. Did my wife tell him that I had propelled her into dreamland, and why? Did old baldy tell him about her no-show haircut?

Mr. X will see you in a few minutes. That is what his secretary told me twenty minutes before, so I got up and strolled over to his Miss Busy-business. She knew I was standing in front of her desk, but her work at hand was too important to pay any attention to me. She was typing, and as the whatever-you-call-it slid over and was about to snap back, I reached over and stopped it. She of course loved this and was about to tell me how charming she thought I was, when I told her not to get upset but that since I had grown a little tired of watching her making a little something out of a lot of nothing, and since I was on time and that time was twenty minutes ago, I was leaving and to please give this message to your Mr. Clarence Darrow. Tell him that he wanted to see me, not I him, and I started out. She came running after me and asked me to please just wait another few minutes and then disappeared into the inner sanctum. She was gone but a few seconds when out she came and waved me in as if I were the pope.

Mr. X was immaculate as was his oversized office, immaculate and flashy, fleshy and smelly, sweet smelly. Mr. X didn't shave in a shower.

We shook hands, the fish-type shake, and he asked me to sit down. He sat down and clasped his hands over his well-fed paunch and stared at me, didn't say a word, just stared. I got sick of it and broke the spell. "What the hell are you looking at?"

He said, "You don't understand, Mr. Wellman, I suddenly realized what a terribly important crisis this could be in your life, and I don't want to hurt you, not the kind of man that has fought so valiantly for his and my beloved country."

"Listen, Mr. X, the war is all over, so let's cut out this bullshit and just tell me what this is all about. What her highness wishes. How much she and her charming mother have told you and what you intend to do about it. In other words, how much of a patsy must I become to get you your fee, me my freedom, and how big a spread of publicity do you intend to brew?"

"Now, Mr. Wellman, you are misjudging this and me completely. There are ways of doing things simply, aboveboard and quietly, provided the parties concerned understand and agree."

"I have not misjudged you, the 'this,' I know nothing about, so I am withholding judgment on that. What am I to be accused of? On what grounds is she to get this legal hereafter?"

"Well, number one, you struck her."

"That's correct. Did she tell you why?"

"An ungovernable temper."

"Did she tell you what made it ungovernable?"

"No."

"Maybe you better ask her—just for your own curiosity—

because it's out; and when you tell her I said it was out, she will agree. What's next?"

"You mistreated her mother."

"Not her mother, her mother's wig. Didn't they tell you about that?"

"No."

"Mr. X, if I were you, I would get together with my client and have a heart-to-heart talk. If you are telling me the truth, they are treating you very shabbily. The whole deal is liable to be most embarrassing, particularly to you.

"To cut this thing short, let me make a suggestion. Get it on desertion. This she won't like. It will offend her ego. A beautiful blossoming picture star deserted by a lousy ex-flier who has been unable to fit into the humdrum of everyday life, but this is what it's got to be as far as I am concerned. I refuse to have my lovely little mother think that her son goes around bopping beautiful women, and I don't want that nonsupport branded on me indelibly for the rest of my life. This is a give-and-take deal, as rugged for me as it is for her."

"Well, I will have to take this up with my client."

"While you are at it, take this up too. The content of my letter of marital resignation."

My dear wife:
The merry rhythm of the tinkling bells has changed key, lower and slower, a funeral beat, and I can't dance anymore. That one unforgettable trip to Catalina made me realize how much you loved what you were doing and how little it really meant to me. It took a short time of misery for it to sink in, but eventually it did, and now *I* want out.

You are young, beautiful, talented, and ambitious. I am young, not beautiful, nor particularly ambitious, and if talented it has only shown itself in the air, so up there I go again.

A wonderful screwball named Merian Cooper is fighting the Bolsheviks, and I have been invited to the party. This sounds less dangerous than coming home each night to the promiscuous charms of you and the wiles of that bald hatchet woman.

My short adult life has been spent hopping from one unsuccessful venture to another until flying rescued me. It was my first and *only* love.

Your beauty can be found all over the world, in every country, city, and hamlet, in the frozen north and the hot south, in the crowded east and the vast west, but the beauty of flying can only be found up there where it's peaceful and, lonesome, just you, not even God; he is too busy below.

I don't think I have robbed you of anything that is not replaceable with but one exception. I'm sorry, I forgot, you lost that long before we met. Please don't misunderstand me, this is not meant as a criticism. I have always been bored by virgins. Virgins are babies' toys or old men's dreams.

In closing: When you are in love with someone, it is always best to remember that there is something inside that love that can cut it off, if you are not very careful. This is what happened to us.

I looked at Mr. X. He still sat with his hands folded on his paunch, and he was still staring. I asked him one question: "Is that nasty enough for you?"

He said rather quietly, "That will do."

All I said was that I had just finished playing the juvenile in Douglas Fairbanks' *The Knickerbocker Buckaroo,* and I got a part, a raise to four hundred a week and a four-week guarantee. I was a British juvenile this time, a young lieutenant in the queen's own something or other.

There is no need to go into the gruesome experience in any great detail. As it proved to be my swan song, histrionically speaking, the shorter the better.

I was costumed, inspected, and okayed. With a white wig, legginged feet, and red and white uniform, you can be sure they had fairies in George Washington's time.

We opened the picture on the beach at Santa Monica. The first scene was mine, a very wet one.

I had to wade out through the breakers, which were very small, and pluck the leading lady out of a boat and carry her safely to the shore. She was very pretty and very tiny; and you get paid for this?

Camera, action—

I waded out, plucked the star from the boat, and started in with a bundle in my arms that was as light as a feather. Despite the closeness to the salt water and all the fishlike odors that go with it, she had a boudoir sweetness about her that was very entrancing.

I was young and strong and she felt it and liked it and showed it. This walk in the ocean might lead to something very interesting; and as I squeezed her a little tighter than was necessary and she cuddled up to me a little more than before, I kissed her and stepped into a hole and we both disappeared from view.

I was a good swimmer; she couldn't swim at all, and she lost her head. This lovely sweet-smelling little treasure became a maddened minx, a fighting, snarling minx under water and above. She made it so tough for me with my water-filled British uniform and my goddamned waterlogged leggings that, for her own good and mine, I had to subdue her, so I did; I cold-cocked her, swam in, and deposited her sleeping little body at the feet of the director.

I thought I had done a hell of a job. He didn't. He fired me and turned on his heels and walked away, leaving me standing there with his star at my feet gasping for a breath of waterless air. I noticed that he had a pair of binoculars hanging from his shoulder.

When I turned in my costume, I asked the wardrobe man, who seemed like a good Joe, what the hell it was all about. I haven't got eyes that can see five feet down through the water of the Pacific, especially if those waters are bounded by the Santa Monica pier on one side and the Venice pier on the other. That's asking a little too much; there's a little flotsam floating around.

He said that's not it, buddy. That little gal you went diving with is his wife, his new wife, his very young wife. You get the picture?

I did, and I guess Mr. Director did too, magnified, through his binoculars.

So I got it on the first scene of the first day of a four-week guarantee. That's not too bad, sixteen hundred bucks for stepping in a hole with a little sweet-smelling possibility in my arms.

Tonight I am going to sneak out and see me in *The Knicker-bocker Buckaroo*. I would rather take a licking, but I have got to do it sometime, and it might just as well be right now while I am healthy and can stand the shock. I want to see how the public reacts to my stupefying personality. I want to clock the times they laugh at me when they shouldn't. Frankly, I want to see how I look to me.

If only I could divorce myself from that juvenile up there on the silver screen and look at him objectively, maybe I could make up my mind on a lot of things. I want to get somewhere, but I want to get there fast, and I know it can't be done if you don't like what you are doing. It has got to be more than just a liking; it has got to be something you are willing to fight like hell for, and offhand I don't think acting will ever stir up such an emotion in me. I am not sure, but I will be in another two hours.

I stuck it out through half the picture and then ran home trying not to think of what I had seen until I got in my room, took a shower and a belt, put out the lights, and crawled into bed. There in the dark and the quiet, I pillowtalked with that young fellow I had just seen in *The Knickerbocker Buckaroo*. I didn't want to hurt his feelings, but I am inclined to be rather frank. It might be a little hard to take, but it will be sincere and honest. I decided to give them both barrels. It is easier that way, easier and quicker and less painful.

I am going to handle this the way old Tex would, so I took another belt. You, the actor, are not going to say a word. You are just to lie there and listen. I will do all the talking. Get yourself ready, sonny boy, because here it comes. There is no frosting on this cake.

First of all, you looked like a sixteen-year-old boy from Fessendon (that's a *very* private school outside of Boston), with an omelet for a face, a vertical omelet.

Secondly, you are undoubtedly the first actor in history that hoped the camera would stay off him.

Thirdly, the only reason they didn't laugh at you? They weren't looking at you.

You made some pretty good mounts, but of course you have had plenty of practice climbing into Nieuports.

I have to say something for you, at least you walked like a man. Uh oh, here comes that limp. Christ, haven't you forgotten that yet?

The only acting that you did well, you should not have been doing. The leading lady was supposed to have been your sister, but the way you acted it looked like a little bit of incest, just a touch.

You have the most active face I've ever seen. Your ears are constantly wiggling, your nostrils dilating, your eyebrows teetering, you have a lip-licking tongue and the smile of a gargoyle, but there is one thing about your head that is good: the back of it.

In some of the long shots, you are not so bad; uh oh, look out, here it is again: a medium shot of you and Doug. Maybe you will get away with this one; it isn't too close, and they will be looking at Fairbanks anyway. Here comes the close-up. You're lucky, it's on Doug. If they will only keep it there and not pay any attention to you. Too late—it's a big close-up, and it's on you, and it goes on and on—cut *cut* CUT. Oh God, I'm sick, and you are starting to laugh—a big silent silver screen crater-mouthed laugh. I got up and walked out on me.

I threw the covers back. I was hot and sweating. I lay there for a few minutes and cooled off outside and inside. I had felt this way before in the air, in a dogfight with a son of a bitch on my tail. I had lost a lot of altitude and was too close to the ground, but I kept missing the trees and the little hills, and I lost him. I was safe and sound and alive.

Tomorrow I would go to see Doug, ask him just one more favor. Get me a job, any job, in the production end of the business. I want to learn to be a director.

I said good-bye to my lovely little landlady and took off for Culver City with my one suitcase and dufflebag. Doug had understood my feelings completely and had gotten me a job at the Goldwyn Studios in the production department.

On the way to the office of the production manager, I passed a big signboard with the names of all the directors and on what stage they were working.

What a list, most of the great directors of that time—Reginald Barker, Clarence Badger, Harry Beaumont, Jack Conway, E. Mason Hopper, T. Hayes Hunter, Clarence Brown, Tod Browning, Robert Z. Leonard, Frank Lloyd, Maurice Tourneur, Ernst Lubitsch, Victor Schertzinger, Sam Wood. I wondered if I would ever get on a list like that.

He didn't shake hands with me or ask me to sit down, just asked me whimsical little questions:

"You were married to Chadwick, weren't you?"

"For a short time."

"Does she know you are working here?"

"I don't know."

"She is becoming very important, and part of my job is to keep things running smoothly—all kinds of things—so I guess we had better find out about this little joker right away."

He stopped talking and started to go through some papers on his desk. I thought he was through with me, so I started to leave.

"Don't be in such a hurry, Lieutenant." (Here we go again.) "You got in here through the front office. There is not much I can do about that, but there is a great deal I can do if you don't toe the mark. The war is over, you know."

He picked up a blue interoffice communication and read some of it aloud.

Quote—he apparently is now interested in the production end of the business—unquote.

"Didn't like acting, huh? Why not?"

"I didn't care for that crap you put on your face."

"Now, don't get smart."

"I am not getting smart. That's the truth."

"Couldn't stand looking at yourself, huh?"

"That's right."

"Well, I hope it isn't catching. You can go now."

Just as I got to the door, he fired this at me without even looking up. "Oh, by the way, what did you get as an actor?"

"'I got four hundred a week on my last picture." (I didn't tell him that was for one day's stepping in a hole.)

"Four hundred a week, huh. Well, here you are a messenger boy, and you get twenty-two dollars a week."

There was a smirk on the bastard's face that I would have loved to wipe off. Later, boy, much later.

I knew where I stood, and I added one more name to my shit list.

I met all the other messenger boys. Boys? Not a one under age. All striving for something big in this kaleidoscopic mishmash of fun and frolic.

The head messenger boy, old Jim, was old enough to be my dad. He was married, had kids of all ages, and I wondered if they ate and, if so, how often. He explained my job, route, etc., and gave me a detailed map of the studio and told me to spend the rest of the day going over it on foot. This I did, and it was a magical afternoon. I knew nobody and nobody knew me. Whenever I arrived at a stage or location where a company was shooting, I took my time and lingered, watching the different directors and how they worked. I felt so happy and sure of myself that I wanted to go to the big directors' billboard and plant my name on it. To hell with the four hundred bucks: my job didn't require makeup; I didn't have to look in a mirror unless I wanted to; I didn't have to look like an omelet.

With the help of old Jim, I got me a room, an inexpensive

143

room with two meals a day, breakfast and dinner. I could get by if I didn't go out at night; maybe a picture Saturday nights, but no carousing. I sure as hell had been demoted, broken right back to a second-class soldier. *C'est la guerre.*

Early next morning, I was given my sack of mail and my route. It included my wife's dressing room. As I went out the door for my first patrol, old Jim whispered to me that he was very sorry. I understood: "We were going to find out about this little joker right away."

With my sack of mail, I passed by the directors' board on my way to my first stop, or maybe my last, her dressing room.

I looked up at all those big names that were doing what I hoped to do someday. What had they all within themselves that made them successful directors? There was no school for directors, no particular education that was necessary, no college degrees, just the complete know-how of the making of a picture, great desire, unending work, and the great privilege of having lived unusual and exciting lives.

I seemed to fit into that pattern: no college degree, great desire, willingness to work, and, for a kid, I had lived a couple of lives already.

Now all I needed was patience and that great equalizer, luck, good luck. That, I think, you can earn.

I knocked on the door. It opened, and there she stood, in bedroom slippers, dressing gown, and, so help me, a towel around her head with a few brown curls sticking out. She looked like her mother, only her horn was not stuck. She was speechless with surprise and confusion.

I broke the spell as I handed her a big bundle of fan mail.

"Red Arrow messenger bringing tidings from your growing public—congratulations." She tried to pull herself together and stuttered four world-splitting words:

"Well—how—I don't—"

"You don't have to say anything until the end of my small talk, and I hope you don't. I got sick of acting, or acting got sick of me, or I am just a sick actor, so I got Doug to get me a job in a production department and unfortunately it was here. I am starting, as you can see, at the bottom, way down. I am a messenger boy. My very personable boss .is worried about what your attitude might be on seeing your outgoing husband grazing in your green pastures. This is his method of finding out, as it is mine. Of course your lawyer has described in detail my feelings on the demise of our bastard romance, and they will remain that way as long as we don't interfere with one another. Is that acceptable to you?"

She stuttered three more words.

"Yes—of—course."

"Thank you, that makes it very titillating."

"Very what?"

"Titillating. It's a musical little word I learned from an old cowboy friend of mine. Means satisfaction, fulfillment, peace of mind—the bears do it too."

I picked up my bag of goodies and started on my route whistling, "I Left My Love in Avalon."

She closed the door slowly and softly, and on her deceitful little face was just a trace of remorse—not much, just a little wisp.

In the following weeks I messengered myself to death. The directors' board seemed to disappear like a zoom shot in reverse. I tried to hang around important places, the sets, even when being constructed. The casting office, with the never-ending hordes of hopefuls. The cutting rooms, the heart of a picture. I stole scripts, new ones, old ones, and pored over them, always from a director's point of view. *The Big Parade* was *the* picture of the year, and I begged, borrowed, and stole from my small reserve and saw the picture twenty-two times, until I knew every cut and. I thought, every reason for it. I lay in bed and tried to figure out how I could have topped King Vidor in his direction. I had no success.

I delivered to Jack Gilbert, Renee Adoree, Tom Moore, Mabel Normand, Barbara Castleton, Ramon Novarro, Marion Davies, Greta Garbo, Lon Chaney, Helene Chadwick (o-o-ps, pardon me), and, thank God, Will Rogers.

For weeks he paid no attention to me; I came in, put the mail where it belonged, took a good look and a better listen to a great star, and went on my way.

One day, early in the morning, he spoke to me. "How ya, Bill; crackin' this morning?"

I was dumbfounded and stood there like a big goop. How did he know my name was Bill?

"This ain't quite like flying, is it?"

I *looked* questioningly, so he continued—

"Saw *Knickerbocker Buckaroo* last night. I thought you were pretty good. Why did you stop acting?"

I answered simply and directly—

"Because I want to be a director."

He stopped putting on his makeup for a minute, reached for the telephone, and asked for Jimmy Flood.

"Hey, Jimmy boy—this is Bill—ya got your assistant yet? Come on over, I want you to meet him." He turned to me—

"Sit down, Bill, I want you to meet the greatest property man in the business, Jimmy Flood."

Jim walked in; we shook hands. He looked me all over, and I him. We liked what we saw. I became an assistant to an expert, and I learned more from Jimmy than from anyone else I came in contact with in all the forty-odd years of my experience in the making of motion pictures.

At long last, I was right in the middle of the shooting of a picture. A big star, good stories, expert everything, and the directors' board became stationary again, my pillar of ambition.

Six pictures, big important pictures, and I was still an assistant property man with a head full of dreams. Then it came like a bolt out of the blue. Word from the front office for all the ex-servicemen to report at the front gate at noon, twelve o'clock sharp.

We were all there, grips, electricians, painters, construction men, assistant directors, property men, cutters, musicians, animal trainers, cowboys, messenger boys, but no actors. All wondering what the hell it was all about, and suddenly Mr. Vice-president appeared. This was important.

He said that he would take but a few minutes of our lunch hour and then announced the arrival the next day of a very important general and that he wanted all of us in uniform, to form a line down which the general was to traverse to the promised land, the stars. Nobody cheered this proclamation, and the deadly silence angered Mr. Vice-president. He continued: "Of course you all realize the importance of this; so, to put it in military terms, this is an order." Again silence, whereupon he decided to find out what the score was.

"All those who will be in line in uniform at twelve thirty sharp tomorrow noon raise their right hands." Slowly and reluctantly hands were raised, all but mine.

I was standing directly in front of him, and he singled me out for a blast.

"Wellman, we particularly want you, in the blue uniform of the French Flying Corps *with* the medals; gives the welcoming ceremony an international flavor. Why is your hand not raised?"

All eyes were on me, and once again I was on the spot. This little unpretentious derby-hatted vice-president of a motion picture company had suddenly become a monster of memories. He looked like a despicable little drill sergeant who made my life miserable at Avord. There was that about him that reminded me of four-letter Fleming of the Butterick Lumber Company, of the insufferable foreman that I scaled soles at in a shoe factory; and, by God, if he had nothing on his head, including hair, he would have looked like my ex-mother-in-law. In short, I didn't like him.

"Well, Wellman!"

This was a big decision to make and a fast one. If I told him to stick it, he would have kicked me off the lot, and the directors' board would crumble all around me. Everything that I had learned from six rugged pictures would go by the boards. I couldn't go to Doug again and ask him to get me another job. To hell with it, I will try one bit of acting, throw one lame excuse at him, and maybe it will work; but at least I will keep my job, and the directors' board will remain intact.

"I am sorry, sir"—that "sir" damn near killed me—"but my blue uniform has everything but a seat in the pants; it is so worn and torn that I can't wear it anymore."

I didn't get to first base.

"You in production now?"

"Just preparing."

"Splendid. You go get your uniform, take it to the wardrobe, and they will rejuvenate the seat of your pants." He thought that was very funny and laughed like hell, dismissed us, and I went home to dig into the dufflebag once more.

Twelve thirty, and everything was in readiness: the long sixty-five-man line, at the end of which the stars and, of course, Mr. Goldwyn. It was the most bastard-looking line I have ever seen —soldiers, sailors, fliers, marines, coast guard, from doughboys to gobs up to a few second lieutenants. All the uniforms looked as if they had just awakened, that is all but mine. Mine had a fresh press and I stood erect, very erect. Mr. Vice-president reviewed the line and gave me a smile of satisfaction and a compliment.

"What a soldier."

Soldier my foot, I was a broken-down ex-flier with a half-soled ass. I stood erect because I didn't dare bend over.

The sirens, the iron gates swung open, and in came the cars. Out of the first one stepped the general, and by God it was Pershing. I snapped myself into attention, as they did all the way down the line. This general was *the* general.

He looked over at this motley lineup of ex-everythings, with not a particularly happy expression on his face. He was much more interested in what was gathered in a sweet-smelling handful at the end of the line. But it had to be done, so he started shaking the sixty-five hard-worked calloused hands to get to the lovely, soft, well-manicured ones that awaited him.

I, the international flavor, was first in line. He shook my hand, then the next and the next, then he turned back to me and said, "Where have I seen you before?"

"General, I had better not say where, right here."

He snapped his fingers and said, "That's it," came back to me, started pumping my hand. "How have you been, it's good to see you—been a long time."

I said, "Too long," and we quieted down a little bit. Then he asked me how I was really doing, and I told him "Not too good." He thought for a moment and then very sincerely asked how he could help. I told him "By making me important in this hotbed of fakery."

He said, "You're damn right, what do you suggest?" I suggested that he take me under the fig tree right behind us and talk to me for a few minutes.

He did, and it worked like a charm. The next day, I was called into the vice-president's palatial office and taken into the president's superpalatial office and introduced to Mr. Goldwyn, who shook my hand and said in perfect English that I was the type of young man he wanted working for him, then turned to Mr. Vice-president and shouted an order. Make him as assistant director to start with; and then he turned to me and asked me to sit down, that he wanted to hear all about me.

Sit down—I goddamn near fell down. He started asking me questions, but for a moment I didn't hear a word he was saying. I was thinking of the general: you meet the nicest guys in the strangest places.

SIX

9/17—2:45 A.M. Four green hornets in last twenty-four hours. This is waiting until the last minute, when pain gets so bad you begin talking to yourself. I fooled around, tapping my back, found where root of pain seems to be—*show the doctor!*

The pain stopped, and I went tiptoeing into slumberland hand in hand with Mike, my little fella.

She was a wonderful cook, and she hadn't been with us very long. She was leaning over the sink washing dishes. Little Mike sneaked up on her. Charming little Mike goosed her.

I have never seen anyone take off as she did: for one fleeting moment, this big, awkward woman suddenly became the personification of grace; for once in her humdrum life she was the consummation of the ballet, the Pavlova of the kitchen.

I told her this, but it meant nothing. The spell broken, she lumbered off into her room, packed her clothes, and left.

Mike had just gotten rid of a cook.

Mike had taken over, my sleep was a fitful affair, awake, asleep, half awake, almost asleep, not quite awake. It was very disconcerting, but Mike appearing every time I slept or half slept made it a wonderful few hours, spent with the only boy I have left. Bill and Tim graduated a long time ago into the upper class, manhood. They now have their own lives to live, their own problems to solve, and I enter into the relationship purely on a financial basis and then but occasionally.

How quickly you lose your kids. Don't think about it, it's frightening. The boys have a deadline. It comes just as their voices are changing, just as they start thinking about little girls as they are meant to be thought about.

Mike's present relationship with dames is purely that of a

spectator sport. He shows off in front of them, and they think he's nuts. This makes him very happy until he gets tired of it, and he often dismisses them in various ways, like pulling their hair or pushing them down or, if possible, turning the hose on them. The real problem and the deluge of questions he saves for me.

A few years ago, I stumbled on what was called an article but in reality is a monument to a boy. Any boy, your boy, my boy, all boys. I framed it and hung it head high just over my relief bin. I put it there because one never realizes how many times during the night and day one relieves oneself.

Since a man does it standing up, he is not as relaxed as is a woman. Consequently he thinks of nothing, but concentrates on hitting the mark, which of course is silly, because he has done this thousands of times before, sober, half drunk, half asleep, and as long as he remembers to take it out of his pants has no trouble in doing it where it should be done.

The artistically inclined will trace bubbly initials or spell out a name or draw a one-line sketch of a house he is building or, in my instance, an airplane. I have a constant urinal plane: a Nieuport.

After I hung up this magnum opus to a boy, I stopped tinkering and spent my relieving periods reading and rereading what had become a never-ending ritual to me. When you are blue and discouraged, just read it and you are happy again, that is, if you have a boy. If your boy has been a bad boy, read it and you will understand why. If the whole world makes you sick, read it and you won't feel so bad, not with the thousands and thousands of boys just like this that will grow up and make your mistakes a best-forgotten slice of a hideous history.

The article is called "What Is a Boy?" from the January 1950 *Reader's Digest*; reprinted from an article by Alan Beck in New England Mutual Life Insurance Company house magazine (copyright 1949).

I don't know Alan Beck. I wish I did.

> Boys come in assorted sizes, weights and colors. They are found everywhere—on top of, underneath, inside of,

climbing on, swinging from, running around or jumping to. Mothers love them, little girls hate them, older sisters and brothers tolerate them, adults ignore them and Heaven protects them. A boy is Truth with dirt on its face. Wisdom with bubble gum in its hair and the Hope of the future with a frog in its pocket.

A boy has the appetite of a horse, the digestion of a sword-swallower, the energy of a pocket-size atomic bomb, the curiosity of a cat, the lungs of a dictator, the imagination of a Paul Bunyan, the shyness of a violet, the audacity of a steel trap, the enthusiasm of a firecracker, and when he makes something he has five thumbs on each hand.

He likes ice cream, knives, saws, Christmas, comic books, the boy across the street, woods, water (in its natural habitat), large animals, Dad, trains, Saturday mornings, and fire engines. He is not much for Sunday school, company, schools, books without pictures, music lessons, neckties, barbers, girls, overcoats, adults or bedtime.

Nobody else is so early to rise or so late to supper. Nobody else can cram into one pocket a rusty knife, a half-eaten apple, three feet of string, an empty Bull Durham sack, two gumdrops, 6 cents, a sling-shot, a chunk of unknown substance and a genuine supersonic code ring with a secret compartment.

A boy is a magical creature—you can lock him out of your work-shop, but you can't lock him out of your heart. You can get him out of your study, but you can't get him out of your mind. Might as well give up—he is your captor, your jailer, your boss and your master—a freckle-faced, pint-sized bundle of noise. But when you come home at night with only the shattered pieces of your hopes and dreams, he can mend them with two magic words—"Hi Dad!"

Mike went on his merry way, and I drifted back to the magic land of the apricot brandy. We were now a happy family, Dan, Virgil, and yours truly.

The rooms were no longer bare of furniture. They were overloaded with an indescribable hodgepodge of Early American, Renaissance, Empire, Oriental, Chippendale, and Modern pieces, all of which we had acquired from the various sets at the studios where we had been working. There were curtains on the windows, they were kinda long, hung like a kid wearing his old man's bathrobe. We almost got an upright piano over the back wall of one studio. Almost!

Dan sat beside an Oriental teakwood table pockmarked with circular designs of coasterless drinking glasses. Dan's apricot brandy not only tasted good, felt good, but was also a good paint remover. His western-booted feet rested on an Egyptian piece, a chest inlaid with fake gold and fakier ivory, supported by two carved rats. In it he kept his jugs full of aging juice. Sometimes the juice got the tittups and exploded. The inside of the cabinet looked as if it had been camouflaged.

He sat in a borrowed director's chair, which we had lettered "Mule Director," mine was "People Director," and we had a frilly-looking job, "Little Girls," and a big-seated leather one we had corralled from Andy Devine, "Big Girls."

Right behind Dan was a Chippendale cabinet with glass-enclosed shelves. There were no dainty cups and saucers on display, no silver porringers or time-dented silver baby cups, just a pair of Dan's western boots, his best. There was something mysterious about the boots. I had never seen Dan wear them; and once I started to take them down to see how they fitted me, and Dan yelled "Leave 'em be"; that was all, and believe me I let 'em be. Once or twice he took them out and shined them; they sparkled.

Virgil had just finished a picture, and we were celebrating. It started in Virgil's living quarters, as Dan called them. Never the barn or stable, that was for horses. Dan didn't curry old Virgil; he brushed and combed him as gently as a mother does her little one. He overfed him, hugged his head, and came and sat down beside me. We broke open a jug, and Dan told me some more wondrous tales of faraway places—all with Virgil.

Virgil would take a mouthful of hay, raise his head and chew, always looking at Dan. I swear he understood what Dan was saying. I saw him nod once or twice.

We just sat there drinking and watching old Virgil, Dan

153

talking and I listening. Time flew, and it got dark, and we got loaded. Virgil got drowsy, and Dan said good night to him, so we staggered out and let old Virgil go to sleep and dream of all the wonderful memories that Dan had reminded him of. Memories of strange costumes and customs and stranger tongues, and through it all the love and care of a devoted master.

We were on the second jug, and Dan started to sing. Some few times before, we had enough to warm up his vocal chords, but he always sang western songs. Now his singing became a strange chanting, in Indian. It was an echo of a voice of a hundred years ago, an organ in the middle of the desert, like a wild wind blowing from all directions at once, full of the sound of sand, the howl of a coyote, the bloodcurdling rattle of a rattler, and a sudden deathlike silence. It was unpredictable, in a lonesome, dangerous way.

We both sat there in a kind of reminiscent daze. Old Dan with his thoughts, me with mine, both so different yet sounding the same—the guttural grunt of the explosion of an antiaircraft shell, the wind singing through the wires of a too-steep diving Nieuport, the angry whine of an off-pitch prop, the awesome silence of a dead stick landing. Same difference; one by land, one by air.

I poured us a drink—Dan bottom-upped his, so did I. I shook all over. We snapped back to reality. I asked Dan how come he never talked about gals. Didn't he have any? He said some.

"How many is some?"

"Five that I kinda cottoned to, got their pictures, too."

"Why didn't you ever show them to me?"

"You never asked to see 'em."

"I never knew you had them."

"What the hell's the matter with you? Did you think the only fondness I ever had was Virgil? I'll show ya five very special gentlewomen." Dan got up and reached for the shined boots in the cabinet. He brought back one of them, dug into it, and came out with a handful of goodies. A murderous-looking knife, a couple of blue ribbons, a pencil with a hawk's claw stuck on the end of it, and a beautiful western silk kerchief, which he carefully unwrapped disclosing five well-looked-at pictures. He proudly showed them to me, one by one, with his own inimitable description of each.

Number One—a big muscular Amazon with dungarees almost hidden by hip-high boots. She had a chair in her left hand, a whip and a revolver in her right. She was looking into the yawning mouth of a big tiger. She scared the hell out of me, and even the tiger with wide-open mouth, full of huge white teeth, didn't look too enthusiastic. He was faking.

Dan: "They called her the Tiger Lady—whipped the livin' daylights out of me once. All the lions and tigers got mad as hell; I was stealin' their stuff. Damn near chewed the bars to bits, had bites all over her body, wasn't a bare spot left for me."

Number Two—a rather jolly-looking lady, all smiles, with snakes curled around her neck; made you shiver.

Dan: "A big mistake, especially in the winter. Her goddamned snakes used to get cold at night and crawled into bed with us. She liked me to call her Medusa, and I asked her who the hell Medusa was and she said she was the beautiful head of a headless Greek dame with snakes for hair. I took off for Phoenix. We were playin' the Winter Garden."

Number Three—an athletic-looking girl with a slim, boyish figure standing on the broad back of a galloping white horse; she looked exciting; she was.

Dan: "The principal rider in the resin-back act, you know, the one that runs and jumps up on the well-resined horse's back. The resin keeps her from slipping. I go to bed one night tired, and she ain't tired. She feels real frisky, so she gets ready for bed, and just as I'm going to sleep, she takes a run and a jump, stark naked, and lands on top of me, and I ain't got any resin on and I'm dead. Hits me in a place ladies ain't supposed to knock on—never could understand that girl, always hurtin' something she liked."

Number Four—a gal way up at the top of the top, hanging on to a whirling mouthpiece at the end of a leather and steel strap by her teeth. Looked like a pit bulldog with a death grip on a spinning rotorooter.

Dan: "My love name for that little gal was Little Spinner. She liked it. When I got mad at her, I called her swivel mouth. Once, just for a joke, I barbecued a shoe sole, covered it with my own special sauce. She ate it without battin' an eye. You know, she could have done me a serious injury if she ever clamped down. Lost my nerve, skedaddled."

Number Five—looked like a corkscrew with a woman's head, a contortionist.

Dan: "Funny thing about this little creature. Said she was a maenad. What's a maenad? Never found out, you know what 'tis?"

"No, but I got a dictionary in the dufflebag." So I went and got it and read to Dan what a maenad was:

"Any frenzied or unnaturally excited woman." This left old Dan speechless for a moment and then with a wicked little smile on his face:

"Goddamn, she sure was."

Dan repacked his treasures, put the boot back with its mate, came back and sat down.

"I'll bet you had a variety of lovemaking with that brood."
"Could be."

Dan was still in another world. He stayed there for a couple of minutes and then very softly and with great reverence, "Maenad. Goddamn, she sure was—pass the jug."

Old Dan took a man's drink—in memoriam.

We sat there for quite a while, Dan trying to remember, I trying to think of some new venture I could get him on. It came to me.

"Dan I have been meaning to suggest this to you for a long time. Now don't misunderstand me, this is in no way a criticism of Virgil or the wonderful way you have trained him, but I just think you could go one step further and really teach him to be like a human being."

"What the hell are ya drivin' at?"

"Housebreak him."

"You crazy? How the hell are you going to do that?"

"Bring him in the house, wait until he does it, and then treat him the way you train a dog. Rub his nose in it and put him outside. Virgil is smarter than any dog I've ever seen. He would catch on after one mistake."

Old Dan didn't say a word, just poured himself a quick one, got up, and said, "Let's go."

We staggered back to Virgil's quarters. We woke him up; and as Dan was putting on the halter, he gave us one of those accusing "drunk again?" looks, and resignedly fell in step behind us as we staggered back to the shack.

The old boy knew something was up, and he began to be a little wary. We had a tough time getting him in through the front door, but once inside he quieted down and became very curious. This was a new experience for him; when Dan took the lead rope off and we sat down to await the big moment, he started an exploratory trip around the room.

It was the first time I had ever seen a mule act like a dog. He not only looked at things, he smelled them. He turned up his nose at one of the half-empty jugs and threw an accusing look at Dan. Dan put his glass down and didn't take a drink the rest of the evening. I have seen and have been the recipient of this mental telepathy between wives and husbands many times but never between a mule and a man. I took another drink. It didn't seemed to offend Virgil, for after all, we weren't as close.

I swear he looked at the pictures on the wall. He spent a long time studying one of himself. He was asking himself if this was a true likeness. Maybe he spotted a little bulge around the middle, a little broadness in the rear, or perhaps a little sagging of the jowls. I asked Dan if he thought Virgil knew who the hell he was looking at. Dan said, sure thing, there's no other mule in the world that's as photogenic as my Virgil. Virgil gave Dan a shy little look.

Waiting for Virgil to make good was like waiting for your wife to make up her mind and have the baby. Finally he did it. He lifted his tail and deposited a round brown braided rug on the floor. Dan leaped to his feet and the fight was on. He bulldogged Virgil and tried to rub his nose in the braided rug. Virgil was not a rug lover and carried the struggling Dan into the kitchen end of the living room. Dan strained and grunted and goddamned him out into the center of the room again. Virgil started to fight from both ends. His tossing head was taking care of Dan, and his kicking hind feet were demolishing the borowed pieces in the room. There was a musical accompaniment to his devastating kicks.

The Chippendale cabinet was the first to go, with Dan's nicely shined boots landing very close to Virgil's contribution—the kerchief flew out and unwrapped the precious pictures, one of which settled down in Virgil's round brown braided rug like a family crest.

The Egyptian piece was the next to go. It took off like a missile, knocking over two of the director's chairs en route, and crashed into the wall spilling two exploding jugs of our precious nectar all over the floor.

Virgil threw a right head followed by two straight left heads into Dan's heaving midriff, and Dan ended up in the middle of the remains of what was a minute ago the Oriental teakwood table. Dan was really mad now, and he bulldogged Virgil once again. The Renaissance and the Empire pieces crumbled as had their emperors of long ago. Virgil's ears were not the horns of a bull, and Dan couldn't get a good hold on them. Around and around they went. Dan looked like the whirling girl in an adagio dance. He was dipping down and up and around, his body skirting the floor until finally he lost his grip and ended in an exhausted heap in the midst of the splintered director's chair with its lettered backrest, Mule Director, emblazoned across his sweating forehead. The whole room looked like an abandoned battlefield, with the victor standing amid the debris with arched tail dropping another large braided rug.

I looked over at Dan, expecting him to blow his top; he didn't; he just got up, brushed himself off, picked up the lead rope, went over to Virgil, hugged his head, and said, "Come on, Virgil, let's get the hell out of here and go back to your room where its peaceful and quiet and tidy and there's no drunken flier trying to tell ya how to run your business." They started out, and just as they got to Virgil's braided rug, Dan stopped and looked down at the picture. He shook his head sadly and almost whispered: "The little maenad. Always told her that's where she'd end up."

9/30—3:00 P.M. Took twenty minutes in the sun—showered with nobody to help me but little Mike as a watchdog and foot-wiper—into bed to try and stop hip pain. Maybe this is screwy, but I seem to be getting stronger, able to do more things, more freedom of all movements, and *more* pain—is this one of the many peculiarities of this ailment, or am I slowly going nuts—have been lying here for an hour like that old possum, in one position, not even stirring—pain has gone, but I know the minute I get up it will come back again. What a hell of a future. Hallelujah, saved another hour—I think I have licked the green hornets.

Mommy came in and lay down on her bed to get some well-needed rest. What a gal; never complains about anything. Cooks for this brood because she likes to cook and because she can cook. Makes clothes for the kids because they look better than those you buy. She can buy anything she wants, anyplace, anytime, but the kids are very proud of the things she makes for them. That is the real reason she does it. She is teaching them so that when their time comes, they will be ready, but she teaches by example, not by words.

We lay there for a few minutes, she in her bed and me in

159

mine. I thought she had gone to sleep, but she hadn't. She was resting with her eyes closed and that lovely face turned toward the ceiling. What a beautiful girl. Freckles and a sensitive mouth and long black hair. That had been all mine for thirty years, and I was as much in love with it now as ever. I never got tired of looking at her, and it was always best when she didn't know.

Then out of the blue she told me that she loved me; it was that simple: "I love you, Bill."

That was the way she was, she started at the peak. She could have asked me how I felt, but she knew that I felt lousy, or what did the doctor say, have you taken your medication, did you go to the bathroom today, how was your appetite, has it been too noisy, a thousand and one usual questions but not my Mommy. She hit the high note and on key.

Now with me, it is different. I will eventually get to the I love you, but not until I have made you realize how deeply I am suffering. What agony I go through all my waking hours. What great pictures I might have made. What a fortune I have lost by doing what I thought was right and suffering because of it. I was the biggest hero in the world to myself and the most blatant liar. I didn't join the Lafayette Flying Corps because I thought it was the right thing to do; I joined because it was the farthest place from Boston and because it was the only way I could learn to fly, and many a time I thought I had made a tragic mistake. The only good thing I can say for myself is that I had the decency to stick it out and the good luck to come through, so I changed my usual pattern of patter and answered Mommy as truthfully and sincerely as I knew how.

"Listen, Mommy, loving me is like being in love with a seashell—put it to your ear and you hear the echo of an exciting life, long past."

She didn't like that but realized that sometimes my thinking was a little warped, so she answered me by coming over and gently massaging my neck. Her hands were so dainty yet so strong, her fingers so soft and soothing, that for the thousandth time under all kinds of conditions and for every reason imaginable, including just good old-fashioned love, I was lulled to sleep by this little wishbone of my life, my wife.

This is what this goddamned stuff will do to you. I dreamed that my wife was a little egg-cozy; that is a little covering to keep a cooked egg warm, in other words to keep one's husband happy and interested and eager. She is small, has a beautiful figure, everything in proportion, and one can imagine her being a perfect egg-cozy, not slopping over anywhere, just fitting tight and right.

A pretty girl with an exaggerated bust won't make a good egg-cozy because when she covers the egg there are two parts of her that will slop over and give the egg two bulbous peering eyes, and it will be a little scary. A big girl has everything going against her. One cannot imagine her being a little egg-cozy; she has got to be a big egg-cozy which means she can't cozy a hen's egg—it's got to be an ostrich egg, and who wants to eat an ostrich egg?

New faces, people that I hadn't even thought of for years, appeared as clear and well remembered as yesterday. Harry Cohn and a picture I made for him in three and one-half days and nights. I can't remember the name of it. I can remember the uplifting theme of its story. Old man takes dose of castor oil, leaves home for office, things start to move; and we got six reels out of that; by borrowing long shots of big scenes in other pictures, by building corners of the sets and cutting our close shots into them, by rewriting to fit what we had or could steal, to give the picture production, by working so long and so hard that you could sleep standing up or sitting down, or lying on the floor or in your car with your feet sticking out. This was making them the rugged way and learning the tough way, but *learning* how to put a jigsaw puzzle together quickly, cheaply, efficiently, and presentably; and TV directors squawk because they only get five or six days to make their hour-long cartoons. I can even remember the hardworking cast—Tom Rickets, Ethel Wales, Dorothy Revere, and Forrest Stanley.

B. P. Shulberg, who was then an independent producer, saw

my three-day wonder and made me an offer; Cohn beat it and Shulberg bettered that. I signed with him at big money, $225 a week. I wasn't what you could call a high-paid director, but I was working and eating.

Shulberg pulled the deal of the year. He had a little dynamo under contract named Clara Bow, and with her he rode into Famous Players–Lasky as head of production. I went along as a questionable asset.

My first effort was a thing with a powerful title, *The Cat's Pajamas*, starring Betty Bronson, with Ricardo Cortez and Daddy Roberts. Roberts was the great character actor of that era. He died shortly after the picture, and I often wondered if he had seen the finished product. It could well have hastened his demise and might have caused it. It was indescribably atrocious, and the powers-that-be took a look at the picture and accused Mr. Shulberg of false representation. He had not sold them a director, he had presented them with an idiot, and they demanded a rebate.

He had a sneaking hunch that my exit might well include him, so he fought like hell for one more chance for his young protégé. I am sure he thought I was a bust; but this had to be a shot in the dark, so they reluctantly gave me another picture.

My defense had been a very honest one. The story called for the Peter Panish Miss Bronson to look and act like a woman of the world. She tried so hard, but all she succeeded in doing was to look like a little girl who had just wet her pants. They didn't need a director, they needed a magician.

My last chance was called *You Never Know Women*, a story of the Russian Chauve-Souris. I had a wonderful cast: Florence Vidor, Clive Brook, and Lowell Sherman. The gods smiled: it won the artistic award of the year, and the bum got a twenty-five-dollar-a-week raise and *Wings* for his effort.

Wings took a long time to make, over a year. Most of the exteriors were shot on location at San Antonio, Texas. We stayed at the Saint Anthony Hotel and were there for nine months. I know that was the correct time because the elevator operators were girls and they all became pregnant. They were replaced by old men, and the company's hunting grounds were barren.

Victor Fleming was making *The Rough Riders* at the same time and was staying at the same hotel. San Antonio became the Armegeddon of a magnificent sexual Donnybrook. The town was lousy with movie people, and if you think that contributes to a state of tranquillity, you don't know your motion picture ABCs.

Saint Anthony the Great was a Franciscan monk, a patron saint of the poor, but he had very little work to do in the months that San Antonio was infested by the two picture companies.

There were, however, two members of the *Wings* company that needed his help: a struggling young actor named Gary Cooper and a brash young director named Wellman.

Wellman had run across the tall, gangling, and secluded Cooper, who had just finished his first role in a Western with Ronald Colman, liked him, and gave him a small but important part at short money.

The studio had Wellman forced upon them. He had made one stinker and one successful picture for them, and he was the only director in the motion picture business with actual combat flying experience, so they took the big gamble and gave him the job of directing the first flying picture (a two-million-dollar item) to be made by the erratic motion picture business at the jumbo salary of $250. a week.

The legend of *Wings* told properly would take a thousand carefully and beautifully written pages, and for what? To recount all that happens when a company of well over two hundred are taken away from their homes and families and dumped into a strange locale? It's rough on the company and rough on the locale. The fires that start burning are burning in every neighborhood in the country. The only difference being that we who lit the match are in the movies. We are monkeys in a weird cage.

There is something unique about us, and only we know what it is. Maybe the closest to us is a doctor. His business is human beings, sick ones. Our business is the same, only our beings are not suffering, they are acting suffering or acting happiness, success or failure, excitement or boredom, life or death—everything that can happen to a human being, every thought they possess the actor echoes, the writer writes, the director directs, the cameraman photographs, and every other department has a share in.

Day in and day out, year after year, you are crying or you are laughing, you are tense or relaxed, your emotions are turned on and off like a spigot, and you must be careful not to become so calloused that when the real thing happens it hasn't been robbed of its vitality. A motion picture company lives hard and plays hard, and they better or they will all go nuts.

To begin with, all the young actors in *The Rough Riders* and *Wings* fell in love with Clara Bow, and if you had known her, you could understand why.

This presented a problem to both Vic Fleming and me, but a far greater problem to Miss Bow. She took care of it—how I will never know. She kept Cooper, Rogers, Arlen, Mack, and a few whose names I can't remember, plus a couple of pursuit pilots from Selfridge Field and a panting writer, all in line. They were handled like chessmen, never running into one another, never suspecting that there was any other man in the whole world that meant a thing to this gorgeous little sexpot—and all this expert maneuvering in a hotel where most of the flame was burning.

This hocus-pocus of love was erased by a growing hatred between the two services, the army and the air corps.

We had at our disposal all aircraft at Brooks Field and the other fields whose names I can't remember, and the pick of their personnel. The best of the pursuit pilots from Selfridge Field.

We had the army too, thousands of them, infantry, artillery, the works, and in command a general who had two monumental hatreds: fliers and movie people.

He met me, the director, and immediately disliked me. This has happened to me many times before, but never so quickly.

I hardly drew a breath and I was in the doghouse, for three hatreds: I was an ex-flier turned motion picture director and I was only twenty-nine years old and apparently anybody under forty was to him ungrown.

We had a couple of very hot vendettas, and I could get nowhere with the old boy until I gently reminded him that whether he liked it or not he was working for Paramount Pictures and that I, despite my age, was the director of the Paramount picture called *Wings*—and brought a copy of the orders from the War Department as a convincer. It convinced. The old boy was still in the army.

When you have been through a big picture from its inception to the king-size opening, with the lights, the stars, and the gagaing public, many of the real important things that happened are forgotten. The little ones, the more personal ones, are those you remember, and suddenly they prove to be the milestones of the whole adventure. It is they that are written indelibly in your ship's log, and after thirty-eight years they are the ones you can recall just as they transpired, with no exaggeration, no rancor, no particular joy, just a memory, good or bad.

The night of my arrival at the Saint Anthony Hotel, a big dinner had been arranged in my honor. The great director was to come face-to-face with the assembled military who had been ordered by the War Department to place themselves at his disposal. The generals and their wives, the colonels and their wives, the majors and their wives, the unending brass and their neverending wives, all curious and anxious to meet this mature genius of the art of motion pictures who was to guide *Wings* into immortality—and in *I* walked.

I was tucked in between John Saunders, the writer, on my right and Lucien Hubbard, the supervisor, on my left. Mr. Biggest General, seeing us enter, had started to stand, and all the other officers at the tables, in true army fashion, followed suit. When Mr. Biggest General saw me and realized that I was the only one of the three that he had not met and must be the director quickly sat down, as did the others, some fully erect, some caught halfway up as if in a crouch, others who had just moved their feet. They all sat down noisily and looked at this gossoon with the long hair, as if the world had just played a dirty trick on them.

I wasn't mad, and I wasn't embarrassed. I just felt as if I had suddenly been embalmed.

I was led to the slaughter of introductions. First the big man. He had to rise, rather reluctantly, to shake my hand and introduce me to his wife, to the other wives and their husband-generals, all of which was accomplished with a minimum of handshakes and a maximum of curt bows. I was as welcome as a psychiatric trauma, and I had to do something to offset this wave of resentment that was slowly enveloping me.

The introductions over and everyone seated, Mr. Biggest General reached for his fruit cocktail, as did everyone else. This was the time. I bowed my head and mouthed a silent grace. It caught everybody by surprise. Saunders damn near slid under the table, Hubbard stared at me unbelievingly, and the fruit cocktails remained untouched. I held it long enough for all to see, finished my prayer, and started on my dinner as if nothing had happened, but I saw that it had hit home with a few of the ladies. Some kept looking at me for an added moment, two or three whispered to their husbands. At least I had some of them going in a different direction.

I turned to Mrs. Biggest General and told her things that I wanted relayed to the big man via pillowtalk. I said that I hoped they all would forgive me my age, implying that age cannot be counted in years but in what those years had lived. I spoke of flying pals gone, of Pershing and Teddy Roosevelt and Tommy Hitchcock and how badly I needed help in this the biggest, most important, and most expensive flying picture the entire motion picture industry had ever attempted.

She was lovely and seemed most interested, and I felt sure I was acquiring a valuable ally.

The dinner was over, the welcoming speeches of the three

top generals, that of the infantry, the air corps, and the head man of the whole shebang, and it was my turn, the sacrilegious grace invoker.

I started right out by telling them that the correct thing to say would be that I was very happy and honored to be here. That is the correct way. The truthful way is that I am not happy and not honored to be here, but since there seems to be great doubt of my ability because of my age, I would like to defend myself on this point-at-issue by telling you how old I really am and then perhaps you will reevaluate this whole situation, and I will be viewed in a more flattering light.

I was born on February 29, 1896, leap year, which makes me seven years old. For one so young I have lived a tremendously interesting life. I have been married, not once but twice, I have flown at the front with some success, I have been in two armies, including the Foreign Legion, I have made moving pictures, and I know Clara Bow. I was also invited to break bread with the officers, high and low, of the services that have been ordered by the War Department to take part in a motion picture called *Wings*.

Perhaps the most prosperous producing company in the motion picture business is the Paramount Pictures Corporation. The idiots that have been so successful in the development of a multimillion-dollar industry have appointed a seven-year-old to guide the destiny of this, their most important project. Quite naturally, one so young must be considered in the category of genius and because of his infancy must be given unending help and encouragement. I stand before you as that young prodigy and in all humility request the decency and the support that is due him; and I sat down.

It was very quiet. Then Mrs. Biggest General started to applaud, vigorously, the old boy took it up, vigorously, and then everybody in the room, including the waiters, vigorously. It was thunder, and it was honesty, and the little old gal took my hand and squeezed it and she said, Mr. Genius, I want to ask you one question: "Were you really saying grace, or better still, can you say grace?" I looked her straight in the eye and said *no*.

There was a lovely understanding smile on her face as she said, "You are an amazing young man, and I like you." She turned and left. I stood, watching her go, the wife and strength of a big man, and I wondered if amazing was the right word. Maybe it should have been phony.

Cooper's big scene was in a tent, so I had the tent lugged everywhere the company shot scenes. It traveled all over San Antonio, was unloaded and put up in the morning, taken down and reloaded when work was finished. This was a traveling tent, an emergency set to be used when all else failed or at my discretion. My discretion was influenced by a growing fondness for this awkward, lovable guy. He was broke, needed a break, and the longer his engagement on *Wings,* the more important his part looked to those back in Hollywood.

His part was a very short one with one big scene. He played the veteran flier and had as tentmates two youngsters just arrived to start their training, Dick Arlen and Buddy Rogers.

He the veteran always carried a talisman when he flew, and on this particular flight forgets his good luck piece and is killed. The audience are the only ones who are conscious of this forgetfulness as Coop stops just outside the tent and throws a salute and a smile back at the freshman kids watching him as if seeing God.

This sounds very simple, but it is not. To be remembered, Coop not only must salute and smile, but he must have something unusual about him, that indescribable thing called motion picture personality, to make it that effective that quickly. Don't ask me what it is or how you get it, because I don't think you can get it. If you have it, it came with you, and you're lucky as hell.

Gable had it, Colman, Cagney, Tracy, Bogart, despite his

lisp, had it, and there are a few more, but there are a lot of fine actors that haven't got it and never will have it. Cooper had it.

Time eventually ran out; and on the night before his big day I called Coop up to my suite, and we rehearsed the scene. It was very simple, because he was very natural and very good.

The next day, we shot it, just once. It was perfect. I yelled cut, print it, and Coop's face dropped. I thought it was because he knew this was his finish in *Wings*. Tomorrow he would be on his way back to Hollywood, and I would miss him, so we reloaded the tent for good, and I started to work on another sequence.

That night just before dinner, I was taking a shower, and there was a knock on the door. I yelled come in and went out with a towel around me, and there was Coop. I thought he came up to say good-bye, but he just stood there sort of embarrassed and didn't say a word. As a matter of fact, Coop didn't talk very much anyway, so I said, what can I do for you, Coop? He piddled around some more, and finally it came out, it was almost like a faltering recitation: "Mr. Wellman"—he always called me Mr. Wellman—"you know I appreciate everything you have done for me, and I'll never forget it, and, and, and I haven't any right to ask this but, but, but couldn't I do that scene over again?" I asked him why, and he said, "Because I just, just think I could do it better," and he breathed a sigh of relief. He had gotten it off his chest.

I didn't want to hurt Coop's feelings, but I told him quite frankly that I was the director and was supposed to know my business, and I thought he had done it beautifully, and asked him just what there was about it he didn't like.

And then he told me—"Well, you know right in the middle of the scene, I, I, I picked my nose and, and—"

"Just a minute, Coop. You keep right on picking your nose, and you will pick yourself into a fortune—and just one more thing, always back away from the problems, from the heavy, and, above all, from the girl. Make them pursue you. Never, but never be the aggressor."

He stood there for a hushed minute and then gave me that goddamned funny little smile and said, "Thanks, Mr. Wellman, for everything."

He knew I was right, I knew I was right, and you know I was right. For a seven-year-old, I was gazing into the crystal ball of the future.

It was all there. Hills in the background, first-line, second-line, third-line, and communication trenches, all down to depth, all done in precise army fashion. I didn't need all of them that perfectly, but when you play with the army, that is the way you get them. It seemed a shame that we couldn't transplant some of our enemy here and fight out our differences. It looked exactly like Saint-Mihiel.

We had been rehearsing with 3,500 army personnel and 65-odd pilots for ten days. Camera positions on one-hundred-foot parallels erected at the apex of a triangle and at various distances down either side. Seventeen first cameramen and crews plus positions for twenty-eight Imoes electrically controlled. It was a gigantic undertaking, and the only element we couldn't control was the weather. That is what I thought.

I had positioned myself on the seventy-five-foot level of the main parallel at the apex of the triangle and had an organlike board with push buttons that controlled and positioned the creeping barrage that preceded the advancing wave of doughboys. This I had practiced until I could do it in my sleep. I insisted on being alone so that nothing would disconcert me when the big time came.

The day had been set and arrived. Everything was ready, everything but the weather. We needed sunshine, bright sunshine, because in those days we did not have the fast film of today. We were in the lap of the gods.

To add a little spice to the dilemma, the air corps had served us with an ultimatum. Since we had unfortunately two crashes to our credit, resulting in minor injuries to the two pilots but major ones to the aircraft, one more and they were to withdraw their participation, and the whole damned picture would go down the drain.

You can imagine my position and the condition of my not-to-be-trusted stomach. I was sick, couldn't keep cooked cereal down. I was on the threshold of being a seven-year-old has-been

As a topper to this spider web of trouble, the three imposing financial giants of the Paramount Pictures Incorporated were expected in momentarily. The railroad siding had been lengthened so that they would arrive within a hundred yards of the battle of Saint-Mihiel. The three great magicians of the buck were, in order of importance, Otto Kahn, Sir William Wiseman, and a gentleman who owned among other things a leading cigarette company, a William Stralem.

All morning long, we waited, everything in readiness. The barrage to gouge its creeping devastation and noise, the troops to plow through God knows what, and the cameras to record the countless number of rehearsed bits of battle business. The planes on the runways ready to take off and circle to my right of the battlefield, to swoop down on their strafing assignments, and the camera planes at different altitudes to photograph the air view of the maze of confusion of a battle.

I had been a sky-gazer for a long time and for good reason: at the front, just before taking off on a shooting-up-an-enemy-airfield assignment, to try to figure out how long the low overcast might remain. To get over the objective just as it started to break up and take advantage of the mousetrap holes to dive through, do a little fast shooting, and zoom up into the protection of the blanket of safety. Shooting exteriors on a Western, when sunshine was needed, and a wagon train was stretched out in the long distance waiting to be called in.

The big three arrived, and I saw Lucien Hubbard, God bless him, take over and explain what was supposed to happen, at a moment when talk wasn't as necessary as prayer, or as easy.

Then it came, a little streak of flimsy brightness fighting its way through the cloud layer. It faded in and out like a faltering

171

heartbeat. There it was, my holy grail. I felt like Sir Galahad, only I wasn't a Knight of the Round Table, and I wasn't noble and pure. I was just a lousy moving picture director with a hell of a problem on his hands, and one bad decision or a false move or a push of the wrong button and somebody might get hurt, badly.

I ordered the planes in the air. It didn't take long for them to arrive overhead, in the right formations, at the correct altitudes, and in the chosen positions, circling like soaring hawks waiting to pounce.

I know that Hubbard thought I had gone crazy. The look of anguish on that poor man's upturned face.

One of the aides, a captain of the infantry, came tearing up to the bottom of the parallel. He forced his way through Hubbard and the moneymen and yelled up at me:

"Wellman, what are you doing?"

"What the hell do you think I'm doing? I'm getting ready to shoot the scene."

"But you need the sun."

"That's right. You get your big ass back and get ready!"

I looked up, and by God my little rift was widening, and the sun was just beginning to shine through.

Five minutes. That's all I needed. We had timed the rehearsals, and the scene took exactly five minutes: a lifetime.

I yelled for everybody to get ready. I took my position with my fingers on the board, readying myself to play the loudest, most exciting cacophonic solo of bedlam that has ever been wrapped up in five minutes.

I yelled, "Camera." They heard my voice in the lobby of the Saint Anthony Hotel fifty miles away.

The first barrage going off was the signal for all the action to start, on the ground and from the air. I pushed my number-one button, and the first barrage blasted. Chee-rist, it goddamn near blew me off the parallel, and all hell broke loose, advancing infantry, diving planes, falling men. I kept the barrage creeping just ahead of the first wave. I couldn't watch anything else. I didn't know what the hell was happening around me, just what was going on directly in front of me, and it was majestic.

I was up to button number eight, nine, ten, the sun was still out and strong. If it would only shine for one more minute, we were in, eleven, twelve, only six more to go, and some son of a bitch spoke to me. I pushed the wrong button, and a couple of bodies flew through the air. They weren't dummies.

I didn't take my eye off any more of the buttons, just kept playing the right tune, with no more sour notes, and watching some crazy pursuit pilot knocking the helmets off the advancing waves of doughboys. The bastard was going nuts, he was slowing us down, screwing up the whole carefully planned advance, and then I saw him crash, and his plane rolled over and over, and I was almost glad.

I yelled to somebody who was standing behind me, keeping one eye on the few remaining buttons, the other on the action—

"Get down off this parallel, you goddamned idiot, or I'll break every bone in your body."

The sun was getting dim—two more buttons to go—seventeen, eighteen, and it blacked out, and the scene was over, and I was limp.

Cheers broke out. Everybody was running around hugging each other. Cameramen were yelling up to me, how sensational it was. What wonderful shots they had gotten. Generals were clustered around my parallel chattering like magpies, and I was watching the ambulances picking their way to my big mistake.

I started the long climb down. Lucien grabbed me in a big bear hug, somebody was pumping my hand. I broke loose and started to run to the ambulance. I got there, all out of breath. Nobody was killed, but two were badly hurt. How bad? Don't know. One is still unconscious. Oh goddamn—I started for the crack-up, slowly and alone.

When I got there, the plane was demolished, but the pilot was leaning against an ambulance with a bandage around his head. He was dazed, but not from the crash, and I suddenly realized that in all my planning I had forgotten one terribly important factor, the human element. This pilot had flown at the front. He had been decorated. He had flown missions just like this one. For five minutes it was not 1926 to him; it was 1918. He just stuck his hand out and said, "I'm sorry." *C'est la guerre.*

Alone at last. Maybe this isn't home, but this suite will do for a few belts and a shower and a "to hell with everything and everybody" for a few no-decision hours. I locked the door, told the operator not to ring the room if the pope wanted to speak to me.

My first drink was a mischief-maker, it encouraged a second, which introduced me to number three. The goddamned drinks became push buttons, and the creeping barrage was the roar in my head.

The five minutes was apparently a huge success. The army was raving about it, the air corps paid no attention to the crack-up, and we were still shooting a picture. Hubbard was in happy land, the three wise men from the East duly impressed, and the two casualties were going to recover.

The only screwed-up one was the wrong-button-pushing director who was pinning on a loner and was getting to feel sorry for himself, which is almost as insufferable as being a reformed drunk.

Even in my cups, I knew why the medicine men from the East were here. I was way over budget and prior to the battle of Saint-Mihiel had sat on my butt refusing to shoot the dogfight unless there were clouds in the sky to give it beauty and a sense of speed.

The studio had sent one of their executives down to force Wellman to shoot the dogfight under any conditions. He declared himself, and I gave him two choices, a trip home or a trip to the hospital. He chose the former. Wellman was a dirty name around the executive offices at the studio, and I wondered how much dirtier it would get when the moneylenders voiced their opinions.

All the principals had been long gone. The only thing that remained now was the dogfight, and I was the only one who knew how to stage it. So help me, for a lousy $250 a week, I was going to get it right. I was going to give Paramount the ride of their life. Mr. Wrong-Button Pusher was drunk and blazing, and the hate hangover was going to outlast the alcoholic one.

A muddled train of thought choo-chooed through my befuddled brain. The button I missed was number thirteen. I counted and recounted just as I remembered doing during the actual scene, and the son of a bitch who spoke to me did it after the twelfth button. Thirteen has always been an unlucky number for me. On the Friday the thirteenths that have come up during my life, I have never left the house, been careful how I walked downstairs, took the phone off the hook, sat down gingerly, nursed my way through the gruesome twenty-four hours, and always uttered a prayer of relief on the dawn of the fourteenth. As a matter of fact, why blame it on the thirteenth button? All my life, I have been coasting along under full sail and doing pretty well, when for no good reason I push the wrong button, and then pain. Already I have pushed wrong matrimonial buttons, wrong business buttons, wrong friendship buttons, and wrong sexual buttons. I am habitually a sometime wrong-button pusher, and I'm loaded and alone and dirty, so to hell with it. I'm going to take me a shower and maybe I can hot-and-cold myself into not being a button pusher and become a pussy pusher, at least nobody will get hurt, not even the little pussycat.

Never has anybody enjoyed the shower as I did. Each bubble of water, hot or cold, seemed to snap me out of my button-pushing complex. I staggered into the shower, but strode out of it almost a sober man. It had cleansed me of the last few dreadful hours, and I was once more nothing but hungry. The button pushing was forgotten, and the pussy pushing but a moment of alcoholic daydreaming.

There was a loud knocking at the door. Bathrobed and slightly tipsy, I answered it.

I opened the door, and there they stood: the unholy three.

I asked them in and poured them a drink. I did not take one my-self. They sat down, all but Mr. Kahn. He started to pace the room, and I knew I was in for it, but what a hell of a way to go out. I had just shown them five minutes of unbroken mad-ness, and I don't think they would ever forget it as long as they lived.

I sat down and waited for the ultimatum. It came fast and concise.

Mr. Kahn: "Wellman, we like you"—I goddamned near passed out—"and furthermore you stay here as long as you think is necessary to get what you believe is best for the picture. We have complete confidence in you, and the picture is in your young capable hands." I excused myself and went into the bathroom to vomit.

I did a good job, kneeling on the floor gazing into the relief bowl, when there was a very polite knock on the door and I heard Mr. Kahn asking: "You all right, Wellman?"

"Yes, sir, all right and getting sober," and he continued: "*I* was that goddamned idiot who opened his big mouth at the wrong time. I am terribly sorry, and I apologize." I heard them go out and the door close. I lay down on the floor and cried.

At long last, we got the clouds, and I got a breathtaking dogfight. It was the night before my home-going. A small dinner with all my pilots, those from San Antonio and the boys from Selfridge Field.

Contrary to what you might expect, there was but little drink-ing, no speeches, just a bunch of guys getting together to say good-bye.

When dinner was over and the coffee was on, someone passed me a silver platter. A simple, plain silver platter, with the lone letter "W" inscribed in the center. Around it, in their own handwriting, their nicknames. They were in no particular alignment, just sort of spotted here and there: Pop, Bill T., Bill P., Ris, Bill I., Burdie, Van, Whick, Robbie, Si, Barry, John I., Carl J., KH., Rod, George, Buck.

They were the best, and they are mine to treasure the rest of my life.

My homecoming could hardly be called triumphant. There was a very noticeable lack of enthusiasm at the studio and in my own home at the sight or sound of me. It was a suspicious attitude at the studio and a very bored, tepid one at home.

The domestic one, so help me, is like an unsolved jigsaw puzzle in my codeinic sixty-three-year-old brain. If I went through hours and hours of research, asking friends if they remembered when such and such happened. If I dug into stored-away boxes of canceled checks and spent long hours interrogating my business manager, turned the safety-deposit box upside down reading papers of divorce and settlement, maybe I could piece this matrimonial disaster together and get the true picture of the whole best-forgotten mess.

To hell with it. It would bore me and the few foolhardy that might read this hanky-panky postcard of a life in Hollywood. There were a few high spots that I remember.

She fell out of love with me. I had been so busy, so completely wrapped up in my work when I found out, I didn't care. The lawyers were retained and whatever there was that jingled, most of it would go their way.

Meanwhile, at my other nook of comfort, the studio, two acts of God had taken place. Number one: They didn't take up my option, and I was off salary, but still working. I hadn't been barred from the studio; they still needed me in the cutting room. Number two: I signed with a new young agent, Myron Selznick. How lucky can you be?

When I told him my story, with no blue pencil, he said he had a couple of keeps for me to do—keep working and keep my mouth shut—that he would take it from here and then asked me if I needed any money. I told him no, and he said if you do, let me know. I became the second client of the agent who became the commander in chief of them all, and he made me a well-heeled young man.

New wonderful things were happening to *Wings*. I got the screwy idea for a wide screen on the takeoff of the dawn patrol. A brilliant man, the head of the special effects department, Roy Pomeroy, made it work. We had special effects for the dogfight *behind* the screen. All the sounds, the firing of guns, the diving of planes, even the scream of a Hun killed in the air. Despite this and good preview reactions, the powers-that-be were still dubious. One bet me a hundred dollars (which I have never collected) that *Wings* wouldn't play for more than three weeks on Broadway. It played for over a year and a half at top prices. It ran at the Baltimore in Los Angeles for six months. It won the first Academy Award for the best picture of the year. It made a fortune, and I got $250 a week and a so-called bonus of $2,500. That is what I got in actual money, but that isn't all I got.

After a very successful preview in New York (to which I was not invited), the front office began to suspect that they might have a pretty fair picture on their hands, so I was called into the head man's cave. He greeted me as if I had just turned up from the dead. It was so insincere that I got mad wondering if he really thought I was dumb enough to swallow it. I guess he did, because he never stopped his inane barrage of hollow-sounding lickspittle. He made excuses for our differences of opinion. Lauded me for my tenacity, which he pronounced tenisity. Complimented me on the excitement and beauty of the dogfight and ended by telling me I was to direct the first Gary Cooper starring vehicle, a flying picture, right up my alley, titled *The Legion of the Condemned,* which was my own story. I had tried to sell them on doing it before I started *Wings,* with no success whatsoever, and he had forgotten all about it.

When he finally ran out of breath and came to a welcome stop, I said nothing. This took what little wind was left out of his sails, and he asked me very apologetically, "Aren't you happy?" I said, "No." Then I gave him the twelve-inch prod. I told him I had been working here for nothing the last six weeks, since they had not seen fit to take up my option. He said that was ridiculous, probably some clerical oversight, and called the business manager of the studio.

He had one of the first interoffice communication boxes on his desk. You could get other people on the gadget, but you couldn't cut off their voices:

"Mike—Wellman is in here and he says we forgot to take up his option—"

"Wait a minute—you remember, you said tell the son of a"—and the headman cut the truth idiot off: he remembered.

Then the sales talk took a new turn. Now I was obligated to Paramount. He recalled the Bronson picture but never said a word about *You Never Know Women*. He told me what I had meant to him, that I was like a son, yeah, but he didn't say what kind of a son. It got boring as hell, and I finally said two words that he, being a big gambler, knew well, "No dice," and started out of his nest.

At the door, I turned and told him who my agent was. A freshman named Myron Selznick and that he was in the outer office and would be tickled to death to talk over my remarkable talent with him, bowed low and retired.

I winked at Myron, he smiled back, and the intercom came alive: "Send Selznick in." (He forgot the Mr.; it was a bad mistake.) Myron got up, stretched, yawned, and told the secretary to tell God that he will call him in the morning, that he has an appointment for Mr. Wellman (emphasized the Mr.); we are late now. The nervy little bastard.

When we got out in the corridor, I said to Myron: "Jesus, do you think you did the right thing?" and Myron's answer was typical. "If he wants you now, when he and that other nincompoop get through their dogfight, he will want you more; and when I finish talking to New York, he had better."

Myron came in the next afternoon, and all I got out of it was a thousand-dollar-a-week raise, a seven-year contract, at the end of which I was getting paid in figures I couldn't count, and the first picture was my own *The Legion of the Con-*

demned, starring Gary Cooper. Mr. Selznick had established himself at Paramount.

The contract was well publicized—too well.

Eliminating all the abracadabra, it represented but one conversation piece of my estranged spouse, the dollar. This she fought for, like a tigress defending her whelps, a beautiful, sadistic tigress with long, lovely, shapely legs.

Her lawyer was the best, mine the next best. When her legal crackerjack called me to the stand, he asked me but one question: "Mr. Wellman, what is your weekly salary?" I had to answer. I did, and he dismissed me. When I went back to sit by my perspiring legal beagle, everyone in the courtroom, including the judge, hated me. I was mistreating a beautiful, ex-follies showgirl, clothed in a tight, but *tight*, fitting dark suit with a figure that made you wince.

My perspiring mouthpiece made the horrible mistake of calling her to the witness stand. She didn't walk to it, she glided with just a little shimmer of the rudder. She sat down, crossed her legs at the judge, and I was penniless.

That kept me in line for a short time. One year to be exact. It takes that long in California to get the so-called final decree. I was then again lonesome. I needed a wife and the quiet of a home. The love of one beautiful girl, so I married an aviatrix.

How crazy can you be and not be confined? I knew fliers; I was one of them, not too reliable, on the goofy side, hard to handle, impossible to control, and not good to live with day in and day out, so I married one. The only difference was in the sex, and that proved no difference at all. Two married screwballs can murder each other. It didn't quite come to that but got awful close, so she crossed *her* beautiful legs, and I paid through the nose once more, only she didn't get so much—there wasn't much left.

Old Dan was my marriage vane. Whenever he started coming around, I knew that something was going to blow sky-high, and that something was always that so-called marriage bliss, matrimonial harmony, meant for each other, divine couple, ideally suited, God what a couple muddle, and I paid and started smelling around for that apparently unobtainable luxury that was not for me. I have seen hound dogs nose-to-ground tracking a bear, and they reminded me of me, always nose-to-ground, tracking a wife, never satisfied with a good-looking stray, had to go all the way. Must be some kind of a disease, and I had it bad. It was inoperable.

Dan never said he was sorry for me; he just looked it. I knew Dan had the same sickness, so we broke open a jug and tried to find some other kind of madness.

Dan was one of those unfortunates who always looked dirty. He wasn't, he was as clean as a whistle, shaved, showered, scrubbed his fingernails, all the normal processes of cleanliness, but he still looked dirty. Maybe it was his hair, it looked greasy, or maybe his heavy black beard or the smell of a barn about him. Whatever it was, I in my cups decided to solve this puzzling mystery.

Months ago, I had my bathroom enlarged, and instead of the usual tub, a small-size swimming pool, all in black.

It was a magnificent hunting ground. Said pool had echoed to the sounds of the hunt, the tracking, the chase, the treeing, the kill, and the drying out of the pelt. This was a most unusual game preserve, for poaching was legal and it was always open season.

I was sitting in one corner of my large living room, and across the room in another corner sat Dan, midway sat the jug breathing its last. I told Dan that he always looked dirty. I knew he wasn't, but I wanted to be sure, so I suggested that we retire to the black super-tub and I would give him a bath. I would soap and scrub him the way you would a dog. He was very unreasonable and objected, so the fight was on. We made merry and tore our clothes and the room to pieces, and finally I nailed Dan in his soft underbelly, bumped him down the stairs to the bathroom, disrobed what was left, placed him not too gently in the scrub tub, and went to work. It was like bathing a bear, but I got the job well done, took off what remained of my clothes, bathrobed myself, went upstairs, took a lusty one, and went to sleep in my chair in the corner.

I don't know how long I was in slumberland, but when I awoke, there he was, sitting in his corner across the room, looking like a dirty old fluffed-up owl.

Somebody was bathing me, and I came to. It was Mommy. She said I had been very restless and was yelling in my sleep, so she thought it best to awaken me gently and get me out of my bad dream.

They weren't dreams, they were codeinic jogs of the memory, little twitters of the past, good and bad, adult pain and laughter, sophomoric actions and reactions, a life of too many faults and failures and an overabundance of rabbit-foot luck. From my insane kaleidoscopic walk on earth, I end up hand in hand with Mommy. Let some Chaldean of the couch explain that.

I have now committed the cardinal sin. I am cheating on myself. It was done exactly like sneaking a drink and breaking the pledge. Then you had only your breath to cover, so it was always vodka followed by a brushing of the teeth and a smoking of the pipe. One brush and one pipeful per one drink. They couldn't detect it by smell, just by sight. Your eyes did funny things, and you wouldn't contain your released vocal chords, or if you did, you just sat there in a funk, suspicious of your friends and waiting for the inevitable accusations and the blasphemous defense that got you nowhere but admitted your weakness and made a bum out of you once more. My poor wife lived in terror during the nonalcoholic days and weeks and, some few times, months, just waiting for the inevitable. That fearful moment when the eyes slept and the tongue babbled and the home became a wilderness of false promises and the wagging tail of patience was pointing, out!

I was suspicious of the doctor. Maybe he had counted the green hornets. Maybe he didn't believe my nurse's report, so one morning when Mary was vacuuming my bedroom, I spilled the green hornets all over the floor, and we searched for each and every one, but I told Mary two were missing.

I reported the disaster in my nurse's report and gobbled two of them hours before I should have. It was wonderful, my pain left me, I went to sleep happy, until I came back to pain two hours later. I reached for the nurse's report, made my usual entries, amount of exercise, movements, appetite or lack of, and, since it was the correct time, reported the taking of two green hornets. I went to sleep again very proud of my ingenuity. I fooled them, outsmarted them. I was on again, and I felt comfortable.

When I awoke from my codeinic binge for a moment, I thought I had just arrived home from the hospital. Little Maggie in the same spot gazing down at me in the same loving way. What a wonderful little face, full of freckles, red hair, and that dainty turned-up nose. Some lucky guy is going to go nuts about her someday, and he better not be like me.

"How do you feel, Daddy?"

"Fine, darling, feel much better," but I didn't tell her why. Then Maggie took the floor.

"You know, Daddy, Mommy told me all about those horrible green hornets. How they help you when you are really hurting but what what's in them does to you unless you're strong like my daddy. We are very proud of you, and I love you." Then she kissed me gently, and I felt like Judas.

I got out of bed, put on a robe, and Maggie and I went for a short walk in the play yard. As we started out of the room and down the stairs, she buried her little hand in mine. How small yet how strong it felt. I began to get ahold of myself, no silent promises, no vows, no words of honor, just that little hand in mine. It won't always be there, won't be there when I want to cheat again, but when that ugly green hornet starts to look beautiful, I'll feel it, with all its love and stickiness, I'll feel it.

SEVEN

Hal Skelly—tall and skinny with an enormous appetite for fun and frolic, a very close relationship with John Barleycorn and a rented estate in Beverly Hills. Add to this a superb skip-tracer named Ben Gimbel and another disciple of the depraved, me, and you have an unholy three who made their mark in the years of the riotous Caliente.

Caliente had everything: the hotel, the cottages, the pool, the gambling, the music, the food, the longest bar, the crookedest dog races, everybody from Hollywood, including Skelly, Gimbel, and Wellman, and beautiful women just waiting to take their hair down.

Skelly's greatest success was on Broadway in *Burlesque* with Barbara Stanwyck. Paramount made it into a picture and signed Hal with an option for two more, which I directed. That is how I met the one and only irresistible, screwy, skinny Falstaff.

It was a Saturday night, and the huge barroom was loaded, and so was everyone in it. The bar six deep with actors, actresses, jockeys, doctors, lawyers, and an Indian chief from Oklahoma, loaded two ways, oilwise and fire-water stupid. It was so noisy that anyone wanting to be heard had to yell, and everybody had the floor. Sounded like the floor of the stock exchange, only they weren't buying stocks, they were buying hangovers.

Tucked in one corner was Falstaff and his two rapscallions, plus a pal from Hollywood, my assistant, a miniature demon, short, stocky, strong as a young bull, and full of flit. He was one of the most beautifully built guys close to the ground that I have ever seen. He shall not be nameless: Charlie Barton. We occupied our position of importance only because we had been there since midafternoon. We had intended to do our drinking in a box at the dog races, but a something far more important had been thrust upon us. We had spent the early part of the glorious afternoon playing poker in Falstaff's bedroom. The reason, not poker but the gentleman who was lying under the bed hiding from a Chicago gangster. This hidee had been straying in the big boy's pasture with his girl, who was acting(?) in one of his pictures. Said girl was in the hospital having her profile repaired. You see, this frightened, perspiring, shaking under-the-bed man was a very important producer. He had landed in the middle of the room from nowhere, blurted out his agony, and begged to be rescued. The Chicago Mephistopheles wasn't kidding; he was out to get our prowling oversexed friend, and Falstaff stuffed him under the bed, called for cards, and we started a boring afternoon of poker. Hell, we could have done that in the Beverly Hills Hotel.

All the time we were playing, Hal and the bedridden one were making plans for his escape from Caliente, and we were the messenger boys running between the base of operations and his friends.

At long last, it was all arranged, the place, the pilot, the car, and the prisoner of loose love left our bungalow, attired as a Mexican chambermaid. The funny thing about it, he looked just like one, even had falsies that Charlie had borrowed from a mock-chested girl friend of his. Charlie said he was through with her. He wanted all and got nothing. He seemed rather disillusioned.

This really wasn't very much for Caliente. All kinds of interesting little blackouts happen every minute. Caliente was most refreshing.

We retired from the bedroom to our corner in the bar and began drinking, not to our escapee producer's health, but just to catch up. We had lost a few precious hours, and as we drank more, Skelly became more and more disgusted with himself.

Why the hell should he act as a savior to a Judas who would double-cross his own mother?

"Gimbel, why the hell did you and that bufuddled ex-flier friend of yours let me get involved in that blindman's bluff?"

"We are not your keepers, slim man. Why don't you stop complaining and keep drinking?"

Skelly thought that was an excellent idea; so did we all.

The cantina was so noisy and so jammed that it looked as if it might blow up, and we all felt so good we couldn't have cared less, when suddenly a voice pierced the wall of sound like a clap of thunder. It was the baritone voice of the big musical star, rich in quality, perfect in execution, and spellbinding. The hoi polloi became strangely quiet. An alcoholic silence is so hushed you can hear people breathing, which means it isn't quiet at all, it's frightening.

The voice had a sardine-packed audience, and in the first row center a concentration of open-minded, pearly-teethed, drink-heated female slaves hanging on his every note and wishing to devour him.

This got Falstaff's goat, and he addressed most of his displeasure to Charlie, and I wondered what our mirth-minded man had up his sleeve.

"Look at that, Charlie, that big buff's making an ass of himself. You going to let him get away with that?"

"Why me?"

"Well, just look."

"I am and listening too. He's in good voice tonight."

"But just look at him."

"I am, can't you see I'm looking at him? He looks all right to me, needs a haircut, lot of guys his age are losing theirs."

"No cracks now, Charlie. Mine may be getting a little thin, but I'm not making an ass of myself in front of a lot of drunken bums."

"Aw, the hell with him. What do we care?"

"Well, I do, and you should too."

"Why? Just give me one good reason."

"He's not only making an ass of himself, he's making an ass of our profession, yours and mine. Haven't you got any sense of decency about your calling?"

"Goddamned right I have, but what do you want me to do?"

"I want you to go up there and stop him."

"Why me? Why not you or Ben or Mr. Wellman?"

"Because nobody knows you, you're the shortest, you can mole yourself up there, knock his needle off the record, get back into your furrow, and come home to your big father. Now be a good little David, and go get Goliath."

Charlie just stood there weaving a little, saying nothing, carrying on a pantomimic conversation with himself, made up his mind, shrugged his shoulders, and disappeared in the crowd. It was as if he had been drowned in people.

The voice was rising to the high note. He hit it with such power that the rafters shook. He held it, when suddenly there was a dark flash across his upturned face, and the voice was cut off like a knife. He slumped out of sight, a woman screamed, and bedlam broke loose. We all looked for Charlie, but with everybody yelling and milling around it was impossible to pick him out. Then all of a sudden here he was, with us again. He seemed to come from nowhere, just popped up like a little prairie dog. He looked up at Hal with a proud smile of accomplishment on his face:

"How did I do, Pappy?"

Hal gathered him in his arms. "Charlie, you hit the highest note you'll ever reach and right on key. I'm proud of you, sonny-boy. Now we can drink in peace and quiet."

You been to parties where they play games? Charades, the game, password, and such? This delightful Falstaffian clown really played games. He didn't have any particular name for them, and they had a same sort of pattern. They looked unusual and different, good clean fun type, and they always ended in a fight.

Men fights are interesting, but ladies shedding their femininity is an event to watch and remember. I dare not mention these two gals' names, for they are still very much alive and, although nudging sixty, most attractive, and they wouldn't like it a bit. I am sure they would voice their displeasure either legally or forcibly, and since I have seen them in action, I much prefer the guessing game. Now, who could they be? Well, let's see, who were the big stars of that era? Yes—yes—yes, such a long list. They don't have anything like that today. Oh, but it couldn't be her, she was such a lady—well, that's who it is.

We had a junior Caliente at our home in Beverly Hills. It wasn't really our home, it was Falstaff's western playhouse, rented. Ben and I were men-who-came-to-dinner. We were there all the time between pictures and on weekends, during the shooting of a picture. The bar wasn't as long as the senior one in Mexico, but the action was just as fast, just limited to fewer players. We had a superb cook, a magical houseboy bartender, and Falstaff's affinity for fun. We played games. Hal's kind.

One in particular, a favorite of Mr. Skelly's, was played with a pillow and kneepads. He called it pillow polo. The stadium was the huge living room, beautifully furnished when Hal moved in. In order to play the game expertly, one must have a championship course, so all the furniture was removed except a few standing lamps. There was such a great wealth of big impressive pieces that most of them had to be stored in the patio. Since it was the dry season, Hal felt that no harm could come to them. He forgot to figure on the dew and fog.

The gridiron was now the empty living room, the goals in the middle of either end of the room, lined in white paint about the size and depth of an ice hockey net. There was a white-painted line that divided the room in halves. The surface of the playing field was a very expensive, highly polished, pegged hard-wood flooring. Painting white lines on it was almost like ravishing your sister.

The game: Can be played with teams of one, two, three, or even four if well inflamed. The pillow is dropped between the teams lined up as in a football scrimmage. Each player is on his or her knees with hands clasped behind them. With their heads they try to fight the pillow through the goals. If a player unclasps his hands or rises above a kneel, he or she is disqualified. The prize? The satisfaction of victory.

The secret of the game is in the choosing of the contestants. Get people who don't quite like one another. Never have close friends playing against each other. It then becomes a game, and the results just a pillow being pushed through a goal with gales of merry laughter—you know, good clean fun.

Now, the people who don't quite like one another, who have never expressed their feelings openly: they make the game rugged, they explode. The minute they kneel facing each other and clasp their hands behind them, you can see the whites of their knuckles. This is no ordinary clasp, it's a clench; and as they wait for the pillow to drop, look at their eyes. They are glaring at each other like a couple of bullmoose in the rutting season, waiting to lock horns and twist each other's necks into a corkscrew.

We spent hours figuring out who to invite to our Saturday night fights: not how pretty or loose she might be, not if we like him or he us, not if it might help us businesswise or if we owed someone a dinner, but just if they would be good for the game. We were as nosy around the studio as was Harrison Carroll. He was looking for news, we were looking for suppressed hatreds. We came up with two dillies.

Number one: a big, big star. Her present secret undying love had just pooped out, a well-known leading man, and she was carrying her sorrow in a very extravagant lonesome manner, but we knew that the seclusion was due to her fondness for alcohol.

Number two: a big star whose sexual desires were questionable.

We thought this might make an interesting bout, so we invited them to our Saturday night tourney. Just these two and we three.

Five kind of screwy people, not too happy, not too sad, just living a little too much. I have often wondered if perhaps the ever presence of the still struggling has-beens, the as-good-as-you-but-not-as-lucky, the day after day of trying to amuse gives you a fatalistic attitude about life in general, makes you want to be doing something all the time, usually for laughs. A couple of bad pictures and you are through. There is a sharp impatient scimitar curving around your neck, just waiting to be tripped.

The victims were late. When they met, it was surprise, a cold fencing duel between two experts. They were good, but cautious, sports about the whole thing. Lady number one cast some killers at Falstaff, but they warmed up after a few drinks, and the party got off the ground.

The dinner was delicious, the wine flowed freely, and Ben kept the conversation away from shoptalk. He is an amazing man in finding out what the guests liked to talk about. Number one was crazy about paintings, the old masterpieces. She discussed at great length the works of the masters with Mr. Gimbel, who seemed to know more than she did, which encouraged her to try and top him; apparently she never did.

Hal and I and number two had become long lost. I did, of course, recognize some of the names such as Michelangelo, but the particular painting that they were discussing, called *The Creation of Adam,* I had never seen but gathered that it was a painting of two very expressive hands. She was demonstrating their positions with her own, and it looked like deaf and dumb gobbledygook. *The Creation of Adam,* two hands both busy, that figures. Rembrandt, Pablo Picasso (not a favorite of mine, although I have tried very hard to understand him; his works still look like my kids' early drawings). *The Last Supper,* by Tintoretto, I knew. Once long ago, I was going to duplicate it for a set in a picture I never made. I decided not to use it. It was much too busy. I thought it looked like some secret fraternity function with huge big-busted women serving the boys hard-boiled eggs. Skelly entered into the conversation at one point. His favorite was *The Lion Hunt,* by Rubens. He couldn't remember Rubens' first and middle names, but he thought a candy bar had been named after him. Number two, the questionable one, got her two cents in. She liked *The Dance of the Nymphs,* by Corot. Skelly winked at me. My favorite was *Stag at Sharkey's,* by George Bellows. I didn't express myself. We were angling for our own blitzkrieg. Number one's pet was the *Mona Lisa,* by Leonardo da Vinci. Skelly thought it would be much better with Bill Fields' face. That sort of cut off any further discussion of the great masters, and we paid a little more attention to the grog. Both of our guests were loosening up, now even willing to listen to a few of Ben's slightly off-color stories, whereupon Falstaff lost his patience, made a plea for everyone to stop being a snob and take their hair down, told the dirtiest, funniest story I have ever heard, and everybody rolled on the floor. This got us from the table to the ballpark.

Ben and I played a carefully planned game. Hal explained in great detail the rules and incidentally mentioned a few of the more famous ladies of the cinema who had taken a whirl at pillow polo. We three had really become proficient and handled ourselves as do the wrestlers. We grunted and groaned and quarterbacked each other. We had signals as to when the head would be raised, and the other could sail the pillow across the room with a twist of the neck and a blow of the shoulder.

I forgot one very important rule: A player can unclasp his hands and use all fours when chasing the pillow, but immediately the head is on the pillow again, the hands must again be clasped behind one's back. While using all fours the player can get off his knees but must keep one hand and one foot on the floor at all times. No leapfrogging. This prehistoric animal position is very titillating as far as the ladies are concerned. One gets an entirely different viewpoint of the feminine figure, especially if it be a well-rounded one, fascinating I calls it. Sex can rear its pleasure-seeking head from the damnedest positions.

Ben and I put on an expert exhibition, not too rough, with a great deal of clowning, and our sacrificial artistes became so enthused that they almost got into a fight cheering us on. They were about to be hooked, when Ben made a fast recovery and sent the pillow skimming through the goal. While our rooters were still hot and excited, we suggested a lesson before playing a game. This met with their approval, so Hal took number one and I took number two.

Now came the first personal touch. The putting on of the kneepads. It was done most carefully and not too quickly, with a goodly display of lovely legs as far up as we dared. We of course overdid it, but they didn't seem to mind, so a part of our journey had been successful.

I started giving my pupil her first lesson in the art of pillow flipping. I showed her how to bring her shoulder under when swiping at the pillow with her head, how to raise it a little if she wished to make a mistake and sock her opponent in the temple. We practiced the different feints to make your adversary raise her head and give you the opening to sail the pillow goalward. Then, of course, we practiced the monkey walk. She was very good at this, and I had her do it, over and over again. She had a very seductive stance.

Along with his lesson, Falstaff was doing a little improvising. He told me later that he now knew how an anteater propositioned a dame.

At last everything was ready for the main event. Our two well-drilled pillowpushers (pillowpushers seemed to fit them so well) had been rested and recharged with a long, spiked cool one; the kneepads, although in perfect position, had been carefully checked and readjusted, and they were at the line of scrimmage.

Frankly, I felt sorry for the lover of the masters. Her lesson had been amateurish compared to the professionalism that the questionable one displayed. I was afraid it was going to be a walk-away, that number one could not and would not take it. I was never more wrong.

Hal, the referee, called ready, and the two Valkyries kneeled in the takeoff position. I looked at their eyes and saw two wildcats, two mad animals glaring at each other. I looked at the clasped hands; they weren't clasped, they were clenched, and the knuckles were a pale white. This was going to be a donnybrook.

One pillow and two heads hit the floor at the same time. It sounded like a cork being shot out of a popgun: they didn't even notice it. They were lined up head to head like a couple of billy goats. They pushed and pushed; and to my surprise, number one was the stronger pusher. Number two began to give ground, when suddenly she pulled one of our practiced feints; number one raised her head, and my baby let her have it. Her head zipped the pillow across the room, and the slightly raised shoulder belted number one in the temple. It staggered her, but she used her head and instead of monkey running after number two, she cut across between the pillow and her goal, intercepted a well-aimed shot, and sent the pillow back in the direction of the enemy's goal. The race for the pillow. They got there together, their heads again on the pillow, and the hands reclasped behind them. Then another pushing duel while regaining their breath.

The reaction on us three was most unexpected. We had envisioned a sloppy, amateurish, pratfall type of performance, full of laughs, some growing anger, and a hoped-for, easy-to-break-up bit of hair pulling. What we were getting was a professional exhibition of two players who could well have been playing the game for years, that plus a quiet deadly anger. We started to cheer them on, yell directions; it was as noisy as at ringside in the tenth round of a rousing fight. It was contagious, and these two gals, bless them, kept at it hammer and tongs.

The pillow had dusted back and forth the length of the gridiron, and the two billy goats were directly in front of my fighter's goal. They had slowed up and were having a tough time breathing. I suggested to Hal that we call the fight a draw, but he didn't have to answer; there were muffled negatives from the pillow, so we let it go on.

They were head to head, just holding the pillow in a set position. Their hands now clasped, the clench gone out of them, they didn't have strength left. My cheating little wildcat was heard to compliment her opponent, "Darling, I never liked you before, I do now"; and as number one raised her head to thank her, the pillow flew into the corner, away from the goal, and the monkey run was on again, this time to an accompaniment of four-letter words that made Falstaff hold his breath in awe.

They banged together in the corner, each fighting to get her head on the pillow. From our point of view, one could see but two very active female behinds. It looked like a couple of hungry dogs fighting over a bone. Then something happened; what it was we couldn't tell, but my number two was flung against a lampstand, the shade came tumbling down, just as she sat up, and lit on her head; for a brief moment she looked like Hedda Hopper. Number one came struggling up, and my wildcat made a tragic mistake—she crowned her with the lampshade, not gently. The connoisseur of the old masters looked like a surprised prairie dog with its hole on its head.

This did it, she tore off her crown and hit number two with the prettiest left hook I have ever seen. This got them to their feet, and before we could jump in to break it up, she had landed two left jabs and a straight right that stretched the questionable one out cold. We had a winner, but the pillow remained so firmly crumpled in the corner that it seemed to be exhaling to straighten itself out.

The game had suddenly been switched, and we now had two jobs on our hands: restraining a tigress who had gone berserk and bringing back to consciousness a defeated ex-pillow-polo player. I took on the tigress, being most careful to get her from behind, for I had just remembered that she at one time had six months of sparring with a middleweight champion. He lost his title shortly after.

When we got everything straightened out, and Ben had taken the abject one home, I left. At the doorway I looked back on a very quiet, domestic scene. The great lover of the masters was reclining on a divan, drink in hand, slave at feet with the white of her thighs showing. Falstaff was removing her kneepads.

Once during that first year, when everything was so wonderful and crazy and we just had each other, we decided to go to San Francisco. There is nothing unusual about that, except the time. It was three o'clock in the morning, so we got up and drove to San Francisco.

This was, and still is, the fun town of the world. We went everywhere, ate cracked crab until it was coming out of our ears. Cracked crab, beer, garlic bread, a young, strong stomach, and friends you meet that you haven't seen for years, and always that one more hot spot. Early in the morning, waiters pushing and stacking chairs and tables to the sides so clean-up time can start.

They left one table and one occupied chair in the middle of the floor. This was a big spender with a case of acute alcoholism, and he was sad and lonely and enjoying it immensely. A big picture star pinning a big one on; and he had, according to him, a big reason.

He spotted me and yelled like a banshee Indian.

"Hey, Bill, come on over and have a drink, bring all your friends with you."

Boy, was he a torch; the place was deserted, all my friends were little Mommy.

We made the big mistake: we sat down with him, and he told us all about it, how big he was, how fairly big she was, and what a hell of a dynamic fusion it had turned out to be (this was a new one on me, but I guess he meant that he had made the grade). Two of the great artists of all time finding each other (location unknown). How much great personalities meant to each other. The humdrum of the populace would never understand, because they could never reach such heights. (He could have said depths.) It was one of the greatest performances without an audience or a mirror, on or off the screen. He cried, he laughed, he burped, he said things he shouldn't have, he made a complete alcoholic ass of himself, and this was a man that little girls write fan letters to.

For hours, he told us about it, he acted it out and damn well. In the café, in the taxi, on the way to his hotel, and in his suite, until it was no longer dark in San Francisco. The sun was out, so was my Mommy, on the couch.

He and his celebrity bedmate had met in San Francisco, to get away from his wife and her husband and Los Angeles in general. Of course, nobody in San Francisco knew that they were there, not during the heat of the day, but in the cool of the evening, when the pangs of passion had been appeased and the call of their public rang out, they sneaked out to *the* place to dine; and the whole town woke up, and the clicking tongues and the nasty innuendos started, and our hero started overdrinking.

This her ladyship objected to strenuously, but to no avail. Buster was going to play; and Bacchus, fresh and strong, had just kicked the hell out of an exhausted Eros, so he got himself on one, and she got herself on a train and went home to the serenity of the City of Angels and the dull safety of her husband's unexciting arms.

At last, he ran down and said he would see us tomorrow, and we left our love-sick friend sleeping like a baby. The breaking up of the great affair had really torn him to pieces. You could tell that by his untroubled snoring.

I was chased out of San Francisco and back to Los Angeles by my doctor reading aloud, yet softly, my nurse's report to Mommy:

"Awoke bent over with arthritis—hip pain not too bad—have not taken any medication for thirty-two hours and still going strong—prior to the thirty-two-hour mark, had gone nineteen hours, twenty minutes—this last stretch despite the knock I gave the hip on the bed yesterday—it is rugged when you bump into something."

Then in a very subdued tone:

"He is doing very well, but I am afraid he will have to learn to live with his arthritis."

Mommy: "There is no real cure for arthritis?"

"Not as yet," and I could have added that there was no cure for the common cold either, and that I have lived with everything else, why not arthritis.

They went out, and I lay there thinking of all kinds of things, not codeinically inspired, but with as clear a head as I ever had. I just lay there thinking, because there was nothing else to do.

Did you ever think of how many things you think of when you are thinking, and how different and rapid they are? Money, sex, you, the world, life, business, licorice, toilet paper, TV, pencils, dirty diapers, bad pictures (yours), flying, crack-ups—oh, nuts. So here I go on an uncrazed trip for a change.

An interviewer came out to heckle me once long ago; and as he tossed me one questionable question after another, I took a little more time to answer these snide little bombs and tried to figure out what the hell he was trying to do. I had known him for a long time, but had never been particularly fond of him, nor he me. He had a reputation for being a real rugged guy, and I wasn't a sissy. We had never crossed swords, and whenever we met, which was infrequently, we tossed a how-ya, fine-thanks at each other and went our way.

He was getting real clever about the questions. One would be pretty naked and the next rugged but passable, such as: "I got ahold of the story you wrote, you know the one you sold to hopalong Selznick—what the hell was the name of it, I can't remem—"

I cut him off. "The name of the story I just sold to Mr. David Selznick, the greatest producer in the motion picture business, including Thalberg, Mayer, Zanuck, Cohn, all the Warner Brothers, and Mr. Goldwyn, all of whom I have worked with or for, is *A Star Is Born,* and there is a son of a bitch of a publicity man in it played by a magnificent actor named Lionel Stander who reminds me of you—don't get me wrong, it is not Lionel Stander that reminds me of you, it's the way he plays the part that reminds me of you, who could very well *be* you."

Silence, then: "You got me all wrong, I didn't imply anything like that, I just thought that you write like a guy who never got out of high school; you may have a little odd way of describing some things." I told him I thought he was wrong and right. Wrong in thinking that I never got out of high school; I was thrown out in my senior year for being a bad boy. Right, I am an "it's a man," not an "it is a man" type of writer. In other words, either my education has been limited or I'm (not I am) just an ornery old bastard. Take your pick, and you won't be wrong either way. He ran out of gas, but not for long. The next question was a dilly.

"Can you remember what your wives were like? Let me be a little more explicit: Do you remember what your first wife was like in bed?"

"Yes, she was charming."

"No, I don't mean that; you know what I mean." I got up and went to a corner of the room, where I have a sand wedge— I like to swing golf clubs. I took ahold of it, adjusted my grip, and started taking practice swings, full swings, and each one got closer and closer to Mr. Nasty. He didn't say anything, and he didn't move until the last one, which I swung right between his knees, and he felt a splattering of sand as it zinged past his jaw. I started another swing a little closer, and suddenly he wasn't there; it was like a streak of greased lightning. On his flight out, he dropped a piece of notepaper on which he had written the questions. I read them all—usual nasty, unimaginative bitchings of a very sick man. If I might indulge in a slight exaggeration, I felt sorry for him.

One of his unquestioned questions interested me. Who is the screwiest guy you have ever known?

Excusing the implication, I would have said it has to be a

toss-up, a flier or a stunt man, and knowing so many of each, it might take me a few minutes to determine who the real champ was. I got it.

Either Harvey Parry, of the suicidal fraternity of stunt men, or Everett T. Buckley, a brother under the skin whose happy land was in the air, but unfortunately there were times when he had to come back to terra firma, and that was bad.

One of those times was in the summer of 1917. He was a pilot in the crack French squadron Spad 65, the escadrille of Lieutenant Nungesser on the Verdun sector. Sergeant Everett T. Buckley, in his fifth week of constant patrols and too little action and spotting a lone Fokker not too far inside his own lines, decided to change the humdrum monotony of formation flying and took off after what was to be his first and final victory. He got close enough to open up on his victim, when suddenly a couple of bad-luck bullets buzzed by his ear, went through the isinglass windshield, and wrecked his prop. He had nowhere to go but down, and this he did too fast, crashing out of control at Dun-sur-Meuse. He was knocked unconscious in the crash and, upon coming to, found himself surrounded by a welcoming committee of smiling German infantrymen.

There were a few minor mistakes that Sergeant Buckley had made: he left the patrol, he went into Germany alone, and, the major one, he forgot to look around like an owl while so doing. The decoy was successful, and a couple of Germans had improved their batting average, and fate had slapped Buckley right in the face.

After eighteen days of bread-and-water diet in a fortress, he was sent to the notorious Karlsruhe "Hotel" for the usual sojourn, while being interrogated by German intelligence officers. He was then sent to a prison camp at Heuberg and escaped two months later, by breaking through the fence.

Caught at the Swiss frontier, he was escorted back to Heuberg and then sent to Donaueschingen to work on a farm. Two days later, he escaped while at work in the fields and was recaptured while trying to cross the Danube. Back he went (under considerable compulsion) to Heuberg.

The hopeful enemy, after giving him time for reflection in solitary confinement, tried farming him out again, sending him this time to Waringenstadt. Here he worked very hard—the first night—with seven other prisoners. They cut the bars out of a window and were well away from the neighborhood before daybreak. All were recaptured and returned to Heuberg. Solitary confinement for thirty-one days, as before.

The fourth attempt was successful. While working in a field, cutting hay, Buckley and a French prisoner made a last break for freedom. They were immediately pursued by a crowd of German farmers, but they eluded them in a wood. Profiting by former experiences in approaching the frontier, they dodged the three lines of German sentries and continued walking until certain that they were well beyond the last posts. Two Swiss musicians first gave them the news of their safety and directed them to the military police, who sent them on to Berne and Paris.

I knew this idiot before he started playing hide-and-seek with the Germans. Trying to escape four times and finally making it and losing some of his marbles doing it proved him to be one of the most bulldogged morons in the world, with a genius at raking up the past—and I was his past. It started in the Folies Bergère, the *the* place of any night in Paris, a rainbow of colors, the men, their uniforms, the women, their attention beckoning, easily removable night sportswear, the wine, the Pernod, the music, and a giant appetite for quick fun. Time was so short.

I had me a little beauty at a corner table, and we were getting to know each other with a few words, a lot of pantomime, and a bottle, when who should barge in but Buckley. I had a couple of drinks with him somewhere in the Avord to Pau to G.D.E. training trip, and that was all; but he greeted me like a long-lost brother, he greeted me but he didn't look at me, he never took his eyes off Olga, sat down, ordered a bottle of champagne, and went to work. He spoke a little French, how well I didn't know, but she was answering him; and as the new bottle got emptier and I got angrier, I decided it was about time to get rid of this son of a bitch, so I pushed the table over on him, not gently, grabbed my gal and hustled her over to the bar, ordered a couple of champagne cocktails, before continuing my pathetic pantomimic lovemaking.

She seemed rather proud of me. I had become jealous and protective, had crowned my adversary with a table, so she was flattered, Buckley was gone, and I made her understand that I would like to go and see her etchings. She took me by the hand, and we were on our way out into the blackout. It was young and exciting and short-lived—from nowhere, I was hit on the button by a beautiful right hand; and as I drifted into dreamland, I heard Buckley—"Come on, he's a baby"—and then everything was stupid. It seemed like a long time, but it was just about a count of five. I picked my dizzy self up and Buckley was gone; so was Olga. Buckley was one up.

New York, 1919.

During a short trip from the coast to see some shows with my then-wife, Helene Chadwick, we were coming out of the Ziegfeld Follies, and Helene wanted to stop in the lobby and look at the pictures of the Ziegfeld girls, some of whom she knew. Naturally I didn't object; and as we started to browse, over my shoulder I saw him, complete with a little gem, Everett T. Buckley happy as a lark, talking like a magpie, and as usual on the make. They were so happy and carefree, it seemed almost sacrilegious to even think of what I was going to do. Helene was very busy gazing as I sneaked around the corner of the theater they were heading for, waited, hoping that he would make a sharp turn. It was a very sharp turn and a beautiful right hand and so quick and unexpected that no one knew what had happened, except Buckley, and he was sound asleep. I strolled back through all the confusion and joined my wife with a big smile on my face. She asked me what was so funny; and pointing at a picture of Leon Errol, I said the rubber-legged pratfalls he takes.

Buckley and Wellman were all even.

Hollywood, 1921.

My mother was visiting me, and we had just finished a wonderful dinner at Musso-Franks. We both had eaten a little too much, so we decided to walk to the Hollywood Hotel, where Mother was staying. It was just a few blocks, and we started on our way. We got almost to the hotel when, from behind a tree, just in front of me, a very quiet voice—"Remember, I had you cold"—and out stepped Buckley. I was about to introduce him; he raised a silencing hand. This was going to be a monologue, a Buckley special, so I kept my mouth shut, but I was ready. "Your Mother; you look like her; hitting you now would be like hitting her in the face; I never liked you, you never liked me; so what the hell." We broke even, and he disappeared into the night.

Mother looked at me in a puzzled little way, and I tried to explain the inexplainable—"Please, Mother, don't ask me; it would be such a long difficult tale; he is just a guy I used to fly with; I mean, we both were in the Lafayette together; he is a persistent kind of an oddball, or maybe I'm the oddball." Mother just looked after him and then up at me and said, "I like him." That was all, and I took her into the hotel, got her key, and kissed her good night.

Everett T. Buckley is dead. I don't know when or where or how, but he was some kind of a man.

Mike, just at the age when he begins to realize that isn't a large white worm dangling down, and he gets bashful in front of his mother and covers up, and she complains jokingly to me:

"I've oiled it, and I've diapered it, and now he won't even let me look at it."

Jack Holt, working for me, playing an old Indian chief in *Across the Wide Missouri,* refusing to believe he was dying.

J. Carroll Naish as Three Finger Jack in *Joaquin Murrieta,* misnamed *The Robin Hood of El Dorado,* pulling a gun loaded with blanks in a scene with Warner Baxter and catching the hammer in his belt, and it goes off just before he gets it out of his holster. It dug into him in the upper inside of the thigh, bad, and he wouldn't look down because he wasn't sure of the location, just gazed at me with a stricken, pleading face, "Bill, Bill, tell me it isn't so."

Ronald Colman and Wellman, an odd combination to say the least. He didn't like me; I didn't like him—the only two things we agreed fully on. The most beautiful voice in the whole motion picture business.

That crazy little English girl that tore into my office unannounced and demanded that I watch her play Bessie Broke in the big scene from *The Light That Failed.* I did, right in my office, and I played Colman; and despite that, she was marvelous, and I gave her the part, and she became a star: Ida Lupino.

I am living with a coward, one so close to me that I dare not do anything about it for fear of inflicting frightful desolation on myself: my pecker is afraid. He never used to be, was one of the guttiest guys I have ever known, nosy, rugged, an adventurer, a real pro, would assault anything big or small, shallow or deep, narrow or wide, search it out, find it in the goddamnedest places imaginable, in airplanes, behind billboards, beneath windmills, standing in a closet, in a vestibule in Boston in the middle of winter, and where it should be found. (Of course, that was before he handed over his sword to the impenetrable pantyhose.) Now he is pouting and curling up, and rather a large curl, but unfortunately he is steering his curl inside where he can be quiet, untouched, alone, and sound asleep. That's great for him, but what about me—say, when I go to take a shower at the club and some guy sees me with a hole in my pelvic arch. Would probably think I had be-peckered myself, or wonder what strange acrobatics took place to get seven kids. And all this without any green hornets? I can hear the clang-clang of the goofy wagon.

Chic Sales, as old Gramps in *The Star Witness,* tough to handle, late on the set, complaining about everything and every-body. I was so understanding and polite and patient and suddenly realized that he wasn't an old man, he was just acting it. He was my age. No one was ever debearded as quick as he was. I told him that if he didn't behave himself, I would put a little age on him in a very unusual way, and it wouldn't be with makeup. He behaved himself.

Kennedy, whom I didn't like until it was too late. Four days in front of the TV set, watching, trying to learn, getting completely confused. Here was a young, attractive, well-educated, smart-as-a-whip young man, loved all over the world and for what? A few self-confessed tragic mistakes and too short a time to determine the outcome of his so-called New Frontier. He was young and daring; maybe that was it. There are so many of us that are old, too old.

I can't project myself into a position of criticism, because I am just an ordinary guy that reads the morning newspaper (mainly because it has Jim Murray's column in it), *Newsweek,* looks at the pictures in *Life,* laughs at the cartoons sprinkled through *The Saturday Evening Post,* looks at and listens to the news commentators on TV (most of whom I can't stand), and ends up in a dither, completely confused, conscious of the slanted propaganda and its effect on others and me, and so with the first two fingers on my left hand I play the goofy tune on my lower lip.

However, there is one thing I do know a little bit about: personality; and this handsome, well-bred young gentleman was chock-full of it. He was fast, unafraid, jarring at times, ap-pealing to the opposite sex (and that ain't bad), and could have been a great motion picture star. I do not say this in the spirit of slander, but just to emphasize what he had so much of.

Those that followed and preceded Mr. Kennedy were no match for him before the cameras. His voice was excellent, his timing faultless, and his sense of well-mannered humor contagious, and he knew his best photographic angles without letting you know he did, and he starred before an audience of millions. He made suckers out of them all.

My politics are kind of eccentric. I am a Republican sometimes and a Democrat others. When Dewey and Truman were battling it out, I didn't cast a vote. I couldn't stand either one.

I abhor extreme rightists and leftists, and I think the worst thing that ever happened to this country was when it was made easy for people to get something for nothing. Initiative and experience went out the door of ambition, hand in hand. A young actor today, with just a fair amount of work, can get himself sixty-three bucks a week for a lot of weeks of unemployment. Some of them are honest about it, and some try to work just enough to keep this welcome cycle of gift money coming in and have a pleasant, easy-living, loafing time doing it.

There are a lot of actors and actresses—at least they call themselves that—who have nothing but an insurmountable wall of discouragement ahead of them and old-age pension, and this muzzy money anesthetizes any desire to work at anything else.

Christ, am I going nuts? Kennedy, whom I disliked until he died. Johnson, who was a slick guy *either* way; and we look for a Lincoln, with the legion of the young going to hell and the hosts of the afraid-to-say-stop. The government is getting to be like that soft rubber-faced plaything we used to have as kids. You can make any kind of a face out of it you want to: irritated, resentful, indignant, provoked, offended, but never really mad; stop squeezing it, and it comes right back to a very negative good-natured rubber face, ready to be made into another face by whomever we have elected to be the principal maker-of-faces, and most of the time we don't know why the hell he chose that particular face to make anyway.

Hank Fonda, perhaps the best actor I have ever directed,

certainly the most dedicated. Six weeks before we started *The Ox-Bow Incident,* he wardrobed himself, had me okay it, and then lived and probably slept in it. The boots, the Levi's, the hat, the shirt, the bandanas, became a part of Gil Carter (the character he portrayed), not Hank Fonda because Hank had become Gil. He looked it, talked it, felt it, and, by the time we were ready to shoot the picture, smelled it, and his performance was perfection.

Mommy and I were the only Republicans there. It was a big dinner, given by a big man for a bigger man, and there were producers and their wives, actors and their wives, writers and their wives, writers and their mothers, the host and Mrs. Host, all gathered to pay homage to the guest of honor, Eric A. Johnston, president of the Motion Picture Association of America and a first fiddle from Washington.

Everything was very charming and very witty, everybody was trying to outbrilliant one another, even the food was charming, and you felt kind of cruel clamping down on it. It was the kind of a meal that should have been absorbed through a straw. It tasted awfully good, but you didn't quite know what it was. Like eating in the dark in a strange country.

Mommy and I were a little out of place; we both felt it, and I looked it. Mommy didn't. Mommy always looked watertight wherever she was.

I had a leak. I was getting bored and angry, and I had forgotten my pipe. What an idiot. I could have laid down a smoke screen that would have at least broken the monotony of this dreary conversation and introduced a few genuine coughing spells and maybe a changing of places and an isolating of Mommy and me.

The long, long feast finally ended; the men furtively slipped a notch or two of their belts, the ladies breathed uncomfortably and sort of shook their fannies deeper into the chairs. I put down my straw, and Mr. Johnston started slipping punches, that is those that needed to be slipped, but of course in this supermarket of Democratic credenda he had little to fear. He fascinated me by his glibness. Reminded me of an African dodger; he wasn't dodging baseballs, but he sure as hell wasn't going to be nailed on the head with a wrong reply.

He was an extremely talented storyteller, and he loved to tell them; in other words, he liked his horn stuck, and he had a ready-made audience. He was big, moving picturewise and politicalwise; everybody was duly impressed, except me. I was getting a little too much of him. I wanted to go home and get something plain and ordinary out of the icebox—an old lamb chop, a chicken wing, or maybe just a piece of cheese and a glass of milk. Jack cheese.

Mr. Johnston's present story was a long baby. It had gone on and on and was still going. It had now arrived at the White House on the fateful night of the firing of General MacArthur.

It seems that Mr. Johnston, who was serving on important management-labor committees for the government, had a problem important enough to be answered by Mr. Truman, whom he considered the greatest of all our presidents. President Truman had just relieved MacArthur of his Far Eastern commands and was exhausted (and I think he should have been); and according to the story, he took Mr. Johnston into another room in the White House just to sort of get away from things for a few moments. In this new, untroubled room was a piano, and on it a picture of Mrs. Truman. The president picked it up and read the note of endearment that the Mrs. had inscribed on it, and when he finished and turned to Eric, the tears were coursing down his cheeks.

Everybody seemed most impressed, especially the ladies, some few of whom were sobbing softly, but not Mommy or me; and being very adept at getting in wrong completely and quickly, I broke the silence and asked Mr. Johnston how that made a great man out of President Truman. Just because he loves his wife, he's a great man? I love my wife, my milkman loves his wife and kids; he's shown me pictures of them taken at birth, and they are now married and have kids of their own. That is a long love-span. A lot of guys love their wives, and just because the president happens to be lucky and loves his wife doesn't make him a great man, just a very fortunate one.

Then the sparrow hopped, and from left field, Mr. Johnston said I suppose you're the kind of a man that would vote for Taft. Maybe I was wrong, but I was under the impression that we had been talking about Bess's message to Harry, but since he wanted to stray into other conversational fields, I'd go along with him. I told him that was a silly way to find out about my political leanings, that if he would phrase his question a little differently, I would be very proud to answer it. He said that was fine, you rephrase it to suit yourself.

So I did.

"If I had within me the power to select the man as a candidate for the presidency of the United States for whom I would vote, it would be General Douglas MacArthur," whereupon the record ran down, Mr. Johnston was speechless (a feat in itself), but not the hostess, who stumbled to her feet and screamed, "Don't you ever mention that man's name in my house again." I repeated "MacArthur" loudly and clearly seven times, took my little wife by the hand, and left the lair of the Democrats with the vital force of MacArthur breathing down their ample necks.

I just saw Robert Kennedy on the Paar program. They showed a few flashes of the ex-president in news conferences. I didn't laugh; to me (a late believer), it was too tragic for laughter. Everything about him was up there doing something he liked doing. If you liked him, you saw what you liked; if you disliked him, you saw that too, but no matter which side of the fence you were on, there was one thing you couldn't take away from him. He was young, vigorous, and attractive. He made mistakes, all kinds; but who hasn't? When you are young, there is an excuse for them, not for an overabundance, but for a fair average; that is, when you are young and mistakes are experiences.

When he went, a whole legion of youth disappeared with him. They were making a few mistakes, but they weren't standing still, and their leader became the most respected and loved worldwide figure in the shortest time ever known.

He must have been a very remarkable young man, and we had better find another like him. Might be right there in the Kennedy clan. That young fella I saw talking to Paar has had a lot of rugged experience. Helped decide a lot of issues, some good, some bad, with a frightful topper to it all.

Maybe through all the ghastly tragedy, his brother's Alladdin's lamp shone on him, and who can tell, he may have the magic ring.

He had it—that Kennedy magic, tragic ring.

It was in 1936; I know because I was making *A Star Is Born* for David Selznick, and I still have the script, old and water-stained, with dried brown spots freckled all over the pages, like senile keratosis on an old man's hands.

It had been through two fires. Up in one corner of page one, in my handwriting, a memo, barely legible—"guild meeting tonight."

I don't remember at whose house or how many members we had then, maybe twenty. Twenty of the leading directors in the business, all making successful pictures, all nurturing a monster who devoured us.

That monster is now called Directors Guild of America, Inc. It no longer has a secretary; it has a national executive secretary. The lousy little handful of twelve or fourteen have grown to twenty-five hundred, two thousand and five hundred members, including directors of *all* mediums except stage (how the hell did they escape?), unit production managers, assistant directors, East and West, live television associate directors, stage managers, and production assistants.

Money in the bank, a big pretentious building on Sunset Boulevard. Tucked in it, a beautiful theater where you, as a member, may be invited, through the courtesy of some asthmatic picture corporation, to a screening of a picture directed by a rabbit-footed member of the Directors Guild of America, Inc. There are fine offices and a big, big boardroom, which occasionally becomes a library where you can read about a dream world that once was.

You can get your life insured and your Blue Cross and a retirement benefit. The wonderful things you can get, all but one, a job directing a motion picture.

Epitaph for the directors who fell at the crossroads of the world; date, long ago: LEAVING IT TO POSTERITY TO KNOW THE TRUTH.

His home was in Oyster Bay, not far from the Hitchcocks, so I was driven there to meet a great man. It's funny, but I don't remember meeting anybody else. I must have, but he was such a titan that it is only he that I can remember. I can't even remember eating lunch, if we ate at all, just sitting on the porch of a spacious home in Long Island and listening to a man that I felt sorry for.

At first we talked mostly of me and how I learned to fly "the Blériot Method," which is a polite way of saying "by the seat of your pants."

Then he asked me about Tom Hitchcock and how he was brought down. I told him it was in a dogfight; that I was there and was so busy taking care of myself that I didn't even see Tom. Things can pass awfully fast in the air, especially if someone's on your tail, and he's a persistent bastard. Oh, I'm so— Never you mind, I understand perfectly. He chuckled a little and then asked me if I thought Tom was still alive. I told him I had no way of knowing, just hope. Sometimes they would let us know; sometimes they wouldn't. I felt that this was a "wouldn't," because of Tom's importance and reputation as a great polo player. He had a good trade-in value. He thought that made good sense. The only time you can be sure is when the flier crashes inside our lines. I knew whom he was thinking of. We just sat there quiet for a minute or two, then he asked me how well I knew his son. I told him I didn't know him at all, just met him once for a few minutes, with Tommy, and that was it. He looked away off as if trying to remember something. He had a strong, powerful face, but there was a sadness in it. He thought of something, and it made him smile, the sadness disappeared. He turned to me and he said, "You know all my kids and their friends were known as the White House Gang. I used to play around with them once in a while, and one day I got word that the gang were preparing an attack on the White House. I sent a message to the kids through the War Department, ordering them to call it off. An armistice was declared." He looked off again into that way-off world of his, and then he said very quietly that you two wild Indians would have had a lot of fun together. I didn't say anything. There just didn't seem to be anything to say. Another pause. Then, how do you feel, boy? I told him I felt all right. A little backache once in a while, didn't bother me much. Don't let it ever bother you, won't do you any good if you do, and if you don't, chances are you'll forget it. That may sound a little foolish, but it isn't. I've always had trouble on my left side. I'm blind in my left eye and deaf in the left ear. People all knew about my deafness, I couldn't hide my ear, but nobody knew about my eye because I wore glasses, and I never said anything about it. I learned to see with one eye as well as a lot of people could with two. It's like a game, doing something better than the other fellow who has more to do it with than you. Wilson had too much more. I can't understand that man. In 1914— Germany, a ruthless, militaristic country, and he wouldn't even start getting ready, just in case; and then finally after we are in it, I ask permission to raise a division of troops to fight in France, and he said no. So I sit here alone. It's peaceful and quiet, but the whole world is so noisy. Theodore Roosevelt died January 6, 1919, of a broken heart.

EIGHT

He once signaled the pilot to take off when I was standing on the tip of the wing, in the middle of the Los Angeles harbor, doubling for Walter McGrail, and I became a wing walker for the first and last time. Bernie considered it an added thrill for his picture. He never had the slightest doubt that I wouldn't make it back to the cockpit. Let's put it this way, we just played rough.

Later on, we were making a Dustin Farnum picture at Yosemite in the off season and living in a little hotel across the river. There were so few people there that practically everything was closed. No water in the pool, no main dining room open, just a gorgeous spot cluttered up with a goofy motion picture company.

Wherever we went, and we traveled, Bernie insisted that I be his roommate. In trains, hotels, indoors and out. It was wonderful, because we talked of nothing but pictures. I learned during the day in production and at night listening. I was getting my bachelor's degree.

It was cold when we got there, but it soon warmed up; we brought the heat with us. We made a quaint entrance. As the bus bearing the stunt men passed by the pool, they all jumped out fully clothed and full of flit and had a footrace to see who got in the water first. Harvey Parry was the fastest and a magnificent diver. He got there ahead of the pack and took off on a beautiful swan dive. At its height and with arms gracefully spread, he looked down and saw no water. It was a little too late to change his mind or his direction. We scraped him off the bottom of the pool, and the hospital reopened for business. We kept it busy for a couple of weeks.

We got there on a Saturday, arriving at midafternoon. We were going to spend Sunday looking over the locations and start shooting on Monday; as a matter of fact, we had hoped to look over a few of the close ones that afternoon, but Harvey, trying to scalp himself, ruined that; and by the time they had him put together again and he was sound asleep, it was time for a very late dinner, a short game of poker, and off to bed.

Bernie and I didn't spend much time talking that night. I asked him a few questions about the sanctimonious leading lady we had to contend with, and his verbal portrait of her was very picturesque: "Don't pay any attention to her bleating; she is like a well-used hand towel, dirty in the middle, but clean around the edges, you know, she goes to church; good night, jerky." And that was that; he had demoted Miss Sanctimonious.

I slept on one side of the room, and Bernie directly across. I awoke early, I have always awakened early; well rested or not, hungover or not, hungry or not, having to go or not, I get up with the birds.

I looked over at Bernie, who always slept on his back as if floating in the ocean. It was hot, and he only had a sheet over him; but this morning, old Bernie had himself a tent pole and it wasn't a pup tent, and by the smile on his face, he was enjoying himself immensely.

This was the time that the Murad cigarettes were sold in a neat little pocket-fitting can. I had my can on the chair beside me. It only had a few cigarettes in it, so I emptied it and kept looking at Bernie's tent pole. It was a helluva temptation. The chances of my hitting it were very small, so the hell with it, I took aim, fired, and scored a bull's-eye. I quickly faked going back to sleep but just for an instant.

Bernie grabbed his wounded tent pole, leaped to his feet, and started charging up and down the room yelling like a stuck bull. He not only awakened everybody in the hotel and for blocks around, he frightened them, frightened the hell out of them and me. If he found out that I had bull's-eyed it with my fast Murad can, Harvey, in his hospital bed, had better move over and let a mortally wounded man crawl in.

I made believe coming out of a heavy sleep and asked: "What the hell was wrong?"

He grunted, "I don't know."

"What do you mean, you don't know, you're yelling like a madman."

"I don't know."

"Running around hanging on to your—"

"Shut up, goddammit, something's happened to it," and I thought, holy mackerel, if he ever finds the Murad can, but I couldn't see it. Maybe it dropped down on the floor on the other side of the bed. Maybe I was lucky.

"What do you think, Bill, this goddamned thing's killing me."

He was suffering a little more quietly now.

"I don't know, Bernie, I can't figure it out unless maybe in your sleep you bit it."

By God he sneaked a look at it.

"You silly bastard, there's no teeth marks on it."

"Maybe you took a punch at it."

"Maybe you better shut up."

"Seriously, Bernie, perhaps you could treat it the way you would a sprained thumb, the hot and cold water bit."

"Where am I going to stand, in the bowl, or just kneel in the tub? You think I'm a goddamned contortionist?"

Bernie just looked at me with disgust and marched into the bathroom, still hanging onto his outraged tent pole, and slammed the door shut. The hotel trembled.

I felt a little ashamed of myself, not to the extent of admitting my guilt, for I honestly didn't think I could hit it. I went over to the bathroom door:

"Listen, Bernie, everything is going to be all right. That persuader of yours is just like the tail of a lizard; it will wiggle for a couple of days after you're dead."

He didn't appreciate my trade-last at all and came storming out of the can, but I was way ahead of him. I got out of there in nothing flat and hid in my pal Campeau's room. Frank was in such good shape, he didn't even know I was there. He was the only one within miles who didn't hear Bernie in his moment of misery.

I had been with Bernie for eight pictures, crammed full of excitement, laughs, the unexpected, and learning. He was a tough taskmaster, would excuse you a mistake, but never a repetitive one.

He was the big man, but when he was directing, you took everything else over; and if somebody didn't like it, that somebody was your responsibility, to be handled the way you saw fit, but that way had better be *the* way. Right or wrong, you were always right with him in front of anybody, from Charlie Bird who ran the studio right down the whole parade, actors, extras, the troop, even the star; but when he got you alone, if you had been wrong, he let you have both barrels, loaded, and you never made that mistake again.

The thing that amazed me most was that during all those pictures, under all kinds of stress and emotion, he never gave in to that sickness that was supposed to possess him. True, on a few occasions, he imbibed a little, but nothing that ever made him lose a single minute of work. The only drink he habitually overindulged in was chocolate ice-cream sodas. Three whoppers at a sitting and never bat an eye or add an inch to his waistline or a pound to his sit-down.

Then the explosion. We were in San Diego doing some air sequences on North Island, staying at the Grand Hotel. I was very happy, because I was in my world and Bernie's, and my

nights were taken up with our own problems, the flying sequences, and I was answering the questions and Bernie was do-
pupil.

It was two o'clock in the morning when the telephone rang.
ing the asking for a change. Bernie was proud of me. His teaching was paying off, and I had been an eager and gratifying
It was Bernie, and he asked me to come to his room. It was Bernie all right, but it was the voice of the once-in-a-while bastard.

He was sitting up in bed, wide awake. Frank was sprawled
down in an easy chair beside the bed, sound asleep. There were
a couple of dead soldiers lying around and a half empty that
they were working on.

I stood at the bottom of the bed. There wasn't much to say,
so I said it: "Hi, Bernie." His head was bowed, and for a long
moment he didn't answer me, he didn't even move. It sounds
kinda crazy, but he looked like an overgrown boy who had just
been sent to bed for wetting his pants. When finally he did
raise his head, there was a look of remorse on his face that I
will remember as long as I live.

His voice had changed, his tongue was too big for his mouth,
but his brain was alert. He didn't get words all screwed up.
He knew what he wanted to say; it just sounded strange and
bewildered.

"That 'Hi, Bernie' is all I want you to say, Willie—has come
now that periodical point of time for which you got your brains
knocked out long ago. For the last two years, I have said my
say, and there is nothing left. With great pride and complete
confidence, it is yours, Mr. Wellman, and I don't want to see or
hear from you until it is all wrapped up. Don't turn the light off
on your way out. I don't want to be completely in the dark."
And he lay down and went soundly to sleep.

I looked at this amazing man, drunk as a lord, and the only
way you could detect it was by a little thickening of the tongue, a
slight flush to his face. There was no slobbering at the mouth,
no conversational wanderings, no loudness, no me when loaded,
yet he was a slave to whatever you chose to call it and would

rest in this alcoholic hibernation for a week, just coming to often enough to replenish the burning wick.

I went out. I left the light burning.

I yelled cut and that was it. I had finished my five days' shooting, with the fliers and the troop working their heads off to help me make a go of it. We had even cut a full day off the schedule. It had been easy and exciting, and I didn't know how I could go back to assisting again.

He said he didn't want to see me until I had it all wrapped up, so into his suite I went, and there he was, fully dressed, cleanshaven, immaculate; and, believe it or not, he looked rested. His bags were all packed, and he was ready to leave. He was going home.

"Hi, Willie, you're all through, huh? Saved a day. I knew you would do it. You bring the company in, will you? I've got to get Campeau home, he doesn't feel very good—I'll see you in the projection room," and he started out. Just as he got to the door he turned; and with that big Irish smile on his face, he said two words, two beautiful words: "Thanks, Bill."

That's all I wanted. I once said them to Tommy Hitchcock for saving my life. I hadn't saved Bernie's, but I got news for you—I would try.

It seemed as if we had been in the projection room forever, looking at all my rushes, Bernie, Mr. Wurtzel, Mr. Sheehan (the two Mr. Bigs), and the perspiring secret director: That it was still a secret was a compliment to Bernie. Nobody in the entire company would ever let him down.

At last it finished, and the lights went on. Bernie, wasting no time, untangled himself, stood up, and asked the two powers-to-be how they liked it.

They both were most enthusiastic in their praise. They told Bernie that it measured up to everything else he had shot in the picture.

Bernie just stood there with a proud little smile on his face, looking at me, then he answered them:

"You know, Sol and Winnie, I got a little tale to tell you. This one is on me. While in San Diego I went on one of my pilgrimages to the land of nod, and I was gone for five mislaid days. You should be very thankful that I took the tour. You got a better picture. This is the young gentleman that did it; and if I were you, I would make him a director. Dusty is nuts about him and, incidentally, so am I," and he walked out, and I became a director again.

I ran over to Bernie's office—just as I had two years ago, looking for a job as an assistant director—to thank him. When I got there, I couldn't say a word; but Bernie cut my moment of embarrassment off by ignoring it and gave me the key to a successful directorship with Dustin Farnum.

"No need to tell you that I think you have everything to become a great director, everything but good luck, that you acquire by hard work, and you love work. It's that simple, you're in, but every once in a while there is a little gimmick that pops up that can't be ignored. With Dusty, you have that little gimmick, his toupee. Never, but never, allow it to be dislodged. When you hire your actors, their ability isn't as important as their allergy to that forelock, especially in fight scenes. One misdirected punch, one dusting off of Dusty's dustcloth, and you will be back assisting me and waiting for another battle of the Grand Hotel. Keep Campeau and Conklin in your pictures, they have been well taught; and *remember*."

"I remember, Bernie, haven't made one mistake."

Bernie thought for a moment, and then very seriously: "Now, even more than before."

I got my assignment, a Dustin Farnum picture, and Bernie got his, a big expensive special with an all-star cast to be made in New York. He had a lot of work to do on the story before going to New York, and mine was ready to go, so I started shooting the first of the Dustin Farnum pictures I was to direct.

For the first three or four days of the picture, I didn't see Bernie. Then one day, he came visiting, asked me how I was doing, if I needed any help. I told him no, that if, after two years with him, I couldn't handle a picture, then I got to get back in the air again. He patted me on the back and left, a big smile on his face; he had given me the confidence of a pit bull-dog and he liked it.

A few more days passed and no Bernie, when suddenly I saw him, way back, half hidden, just watching. I didn't let him know I had seen him, but it made me feel very happy. The master still cared.

Once in a while, I saw him at lunch or crossing the lot, and again he came on the set to tell me Wurtzel's reaction to my rushes. I thought that maybe it was my imagination, but he seemed changed. It was hard to define. He was a little more quiet, seemed worried, didn't carry himself as erect as usual.

We were going to Lone Pine on location the next day, so I went over to his office to say good-bye to him.

"I want to say good-bye to you, Bernie; we are leaving for Lone Pine in the morning."

"How long will you be gone?"

"About a week."

"I'm leaving for New York Monday."

"How long will *you* be gone?"

He didn't answer for a minute. Looking at him now, I could tell that he had changed; he didn't laugh anymore.

"Long time, Bill."

He meant longer than the picture, much longer. I felt like asking what was wrong, what could I do for him, but there was nothing, or he would have said so. It's no fun seeing trouble when you can't do anything about it and that trouble is your friend's.

"Good luck to you, Bernie."

"You too, Bill," and I left him. I never felt so helpless in all my life.

We were in Lone Pine, and this was the last scene of the last day. Pedro Leon was doubling Dusty and was about to ride away into the sunset. My assistant came up and whispered to me, "Bernie is dead!" That was all. The king of terrors had reached out and grabbed him, and Bernie was not ready to die.

I yelled "camera," and Pedro rode off into the sunset. It was a pale horse and the rider was death.

You don't have to write an epitaph for Bernie. Bernie was his own epitaph. It has been some forty-odd years since he died, and I still think of him constantly. Maybe a few weeks or even a few months pass by, during which he is buried in my memory. Then a reminder—a well-delivered blow, a wild ungovernable display of temper, a simple act of helping some poor unfortunate, an example of respect for the opposite sex, young or old, or a tall, slim, handsome faultlessly groomed athletic young giant with a walk like a panther, then again I think of Bernie.

A *réforme* is a man, usually an old one, who has done his bit and lost something in the doing, like a leg or an arm or half a face. They are used behind the lines in some sort of menial work. Pierre took care of Hitchcock and me. Part of his job was to get us up in time for patrols or to find us if suddenly needed. This particular "suddenly needed" was very early in the morning, early enough to still be dark.

Old Pierre had a novel way of awakening you; it may not have been sanitary, but it was effective. He got his *réforme*ship by having his leg blown off from the knee down, and he wore a peg leg. He had been a fine athlete before the war and was the most agile wooden-legged man I had ever seen, and the noisiest. You could hear old Pierre's hippity-hop blocks away; it was the drumbeat of doom. If you were asleep when he came in, he gently nudged you on the chin with his wooden persuader. If you didn't awaken right away, the nudge became taps; and if that didn't work, he might rap you into a deeper sleep.

It was very urgent, so we got the tapping treatment. We responded quickly, and he told us—or rather Tom, because Tom understood and spoke French—that the captain wanted us in the pilotage immediately. My vocabulary was limited but picturesque and concerned only with the land of hobby.

The captain wanted us immediately, and we got there immediately. We dressed with the speed of a couple of freshman firemen.

The pilotage was full of pilots, the captain, and two tall piles of pamphlets. For some strange reason, they seemed to be waiting for us. We apparently were the guests of honor. We were.

The minute I closed the door and the black blanket shut in the light, the captain started to talk. He was not a very voluble man under ordinary conditions, but this early morning he let his hair down. He talked and talked and got more and more excited, and the assembled pilots became more and more electrified, and they kept looking at us. The room was full of white heat, and Tom's face was a mask of emotion. Suddenly, the captain reached the climax of whatever the hell he was saying, and an ear-splitting cheer shook the room like a quake. I timidly asked Tom what the hell has happened, is the war all over; and he said no, it has just begun—America has declared war on Germany. I outyelled everybody.

The pilots were kissing us—and not on both cheeks; they weren't being choosy. I have never been kissed in so many places by so many lips; and, this early in the morning, it would be kind of rugged, even in bed with a bevy of beautiful dames.

A couple of mechanics came in and carried out the pamphlets, and all the pilots followed them, talking like speeded-up Mickey Mouses. The captain was walking and talking to Tom, every once in a while glancing back at me, who was the last man out. I had a hunch I was going to be the first man in. Thank God I had an interpeter. I would find out the score as soon as the captain stopped bending Tom's ear.

We crossed the road to the hangars. There were two planes on the line being warmed up. Tom's and mine. I was in whatever the hell it was. A couple of the mechanics were tying the pamphlets into small rolled-up bundles. Finally the captain dismissed Tom, and he came over to give me the picture.

"How do you feel, Bill?"

"A little lost. What goes?"

"The pamphlets are President Wilson's message to Congress announcing our entrance into the war."

"That's great—so?"

"They are translated in German and are to be dropped in the front-line trenches."

"Shouldn't take long with fifteen pilots."

"There are not going to be fifteen—just two, you and me."

"What have we done to deserve such a great honor?"

"The captain thinks we would be insulted if anyone else was given the privilege of dropping our great president's declaration of war into the hands of the enemy."

"For Christ's sake, he's nuts; if he thinks it's a privilege to go out and have those bastards throw everything at you but their helmets, he's got a hole in his superpatriotic head."

"Come on, snap out of it; it's got to be done, so let's go. I'll toss you for choice of half the sector."

I won and took the easy one, from Vosges to the Forêt de Parroy. Tom got the rough one, down to Pont-à-Mousson.

We were flying Nieuports, a little bitty job with a rotary motor, the LeRhone, and one Vickers machine gun synchronized to shoot through the propeller, sometimes it went out of sync and did just that, shot right through the prop, and then you had a very interesting glide home—or as close as you could get.

In the cockpit there was no room for anything but you, so the trick was to put a bundle of the pamphlets under each knee, hedgehop to your own lines, sneak over theirs, put yourself into a vertical virage, throw the bundles down, kick your rudder so the prop wash wouldn't cause the bundle to hit your *gouvernail de profondeur,* and the pamphlets would become disengaged and fall like a king-size snowstorm to be picked up and read by the eager Hun. They weren't waiting with outstretched arms to catch this manna of the mighty; they were throwing everything they had at you, and you got out of there *tout de suite.* You couldn't cheat, which of course I wouldn't have

222

done, because the balloon observers and the military outposts were watching you with eagle eye.

You got a bang out of the first two or three sorties, but then it became boring and dangerous—and that is an ugly combination for a long life. Compared to poor Tom, I was having a very easy time, and I was giving myself a little added incentive between sorties. Nothing hard, just a little cognac, but it was early in the morning, and this was going to last for a handful of very long hours. Each "just-a-little" became just a little more, and I was getting crocked. It didn't bother my flying, but I was getting awful brave and having the most interesting conversations with me.

At long last, my final sortie over the Forêt de Parroy, a very quiet sector inhabited by the gray beards of the *poilus* and the ancients of the enemy. They had even been accused of fraternizing. When I sneaked over their lines, it was so peaceful that I felt like an airborne newsboy about to deliver his papers, so I decided to do it with some style, to perform a little aerial ballet of the bottle for them to gaze upon. Instead of going into the usual vertical virage, I pulled up into a loop, at the top of which I would throw my stack of newspapers straight down at them. This is not a difficult maneuver, the only danger being in my proximity to mother earth and in losing a wing or two.

On the top of the *manche à balai,* or control stick, is a little coupé contact button. When you want to cut the motor, you push the button; when you release it, the motor starts again. At the top of the loop, it is best to push the button, or you will stop flying and start plunging, because you won't have any pretty silver wings: they will be floating down behind you like graceful tails to your wingless kite.

Just as I was about to push the button, surprise, a tappet or tappets broke and sprayed fragments of the protective shielding of the motor tearing through the wings. I cut the motor; and since I was in the embarrassing position of upside down and too close to the ground, I had to work fast to straighten myself out. I just made it, missed cracking up by a breath, and had to make a landing. I had no idea in which direction I was going, into Germany or France, and it was too late to change. Making a dead-stick landing in no-man's-land is not an ideal runway to choose. Shell holes, barbed wire, trenches, a hell of a runway.

There was one little clear spot ahead of me, the size of a dime. I hit it, and went over nice and neat and soft and ended upside down straddling a trench, whose I didn't know. My belt was stuck, and I couldn't release it. I was nailed to the cross, with my soused blood rushing into my befuddled head. My quiet little sector erupted into the goddamnedest battle since the Marne. The quiet fraternizing old men became tigers. I have started a lot of unpleasant things in my life, but I am probably the only man in the world who started a battle by being a drunken, idiotic show-off. With my flying alcoholic wand, I rejuvenated the aged, started the blood of patriotism coursing through their shriveled old veins, and all hell broke loose. A shell hit just to my left and one to my right. This last one got rid of what was left of the right wing, and I knew I was in friendly territory, upside down, stuck and not able to do anything about it. It's a hell of a feeling. I expected the next salvo to get me where I used to be spanked—and then my hero appeared, a bearded old *poilu* with a blade in his hand the size of a butcher knife. He wasted no time. He performed a minor appendectomy on me, and I came tumbling down, landing on my noggin in a pool of mud. He fished me out, and we took off just in time. It was a direct hit, and my plane took flight in little pieces. President Wilson's message to Congress was delivered to the wrong people, by a drunken American postman.

I was hustled through communication trenches to a sandbagged farmhouse. This was the castle of the boss of the regiment. He had no beard, and he looked like Frank Gifford. He greeted me in typical French fashion by kissing me on both cheeks (the French are the kissingest people). He didn't speak any English, and my French is extremely limited; but he cracked open a bottle of cognac, and our pantomimic language became very understandable. I couldn't understand exactly what he was saying, but I think he was proud of my being an American in a French uniform.

A French lieutenant burst in with one of my newspapers and started to translate it for the commandant, who listened enraptured and drank frequently. It made him cry, or maybe it was the bottle, or maybe a little of both, but it sure made him happy. He kissed me again.

The translation took a bottle of time; and when the lieutenant left, another man and another bottle took his place. This jolly gentleman was a member of the Croix Rouge (French Red Cross), who spoke a smattering of English. He was a great help. He entered into the spirit of the celebration so unselfishly that it wasn't long before he couldn't even speak his native tongue.

We had a ball. I went on an inspection tour of the trenches, shot a seventy-five into Germany, viewed the skeleton of the late Nieuport, a few splintered struts, some pieces of silver-covered canvas, a couple of disjointed cylinder heads, and a hell of a big hole in the ground, but no newspapers. They were being translated for the *poilus*. That's a switch for you.

We had dinner served in the sandbagged grogshop, and the party went on and on, and I met, was kissed by, and drank with all the officers of the regiment. Suddenly everything blacked out, and I had forgotten to report in. One of the wire services picked this up, and I was reported "missing in action." How true. My poor mother's hair turned white. The hours and hours that she must have spent worrying about me, and I didn't deserve one minute of it.

My captain came to get me at noon the next day. He was glad to see me hale and hearty (and hungover). The captain, the commandant, and the newsboy journeyed out to the grave of what had once been a pretty little silver pursuit plane. In great detail, with the help of an interpeter, I explained all that happened (practically all). My captain congratulated me on my skill in handling the sudden failure of my motor. I didn't tell him I was upside down when it happened.

MGM—in my office on the phone, listening enraptured as my secretary tells me that Mr. Mayer wants me and Mr. Van Dyke to come to his office immediately, but we can't find Mr. Van Dyke, do you have any idea—"Never mind, I know where he is," and I put the phone down. His "where-he-is" was sound asleep on my casting couch, hungover and snoring.

"Woody, time to get up, Woody—the king wants us in his throne room." Woody wasn't very happy, as he struggled up muttering, "Which king?" I answered, "Mayer." He uttered a remark that fitted the occasion perfectly—"Oh shit"—and I steered him toward the door, asking him if he could see. He said, "Barely." Woody talked a lot.

En route to the bull's-eye of the motion picture business, I wondered why the hell Mr. Extra Big was lowering himself to talk to a couple of lousy directors, even though they were his.

It would be useless to ask my sleepwalking friend for an opinion. I already knew it, the same two words, or maybe Woody would cut it to one.

We were ushered into the sports palace by a secretary who walked like a ghost, so silently it was eerie, the door opened and closed; you saw it but you didn't hear it. Behind a desk that was damn near as big as a pool table crouched L.B., as he is playfully called. He didn't look up because he was concentrating on papers with rows of figures on them, profits and losses, but no scripts—the whole huge room was money. He said, "sit down," not in a particularly commanding tone, not a "please-sit-down" or a "be-with-you-in-a-minute" sit down, just an unusual "sit down"; it had an uncomfortable ring to it. You could well imagine it being transposed to a "Get in bed"— "But I have my clothes on"—"I'll *tear* them off," so I sat down nastily. Woody collapsed in an oversized leather chair. He is skinny and tall, and stretched out he looked like a many-seasoned broken-down scarecrow—as if an artist had penciled him in. He went sound asleep.

While God was still busy bouncing his figures around, I took a good look at the overgrown room, long in length and wide in width and richly overfurnished. Impressive? No. Bad taste? Yes. Big enough to house a comfortable little café, to put wings on and fly first-class, to play badminton in, to cart in rows of folding chairs and have lectures or seminars, or PTA meetings or funerals, and without changing a thing a sporty course to chase dames in and soundproofed.

There are a few more of these racecourses among the leaders of our industry (active courses), but they keep the results within the law; they are not exactly rape, but they sure are one-sided lays.

I don't know why looking at Mayer made me think of a praying mantis—a praying mantis is a carnivorous insect who has a long prothorax, feeds upon other insects, and clasps its prey in forelimbs held up as if in prayer—this sounds kind of normal today, but the sex life of these dainty little creatures is something else: five of these guys go after one poor dame, and you think, good God, this is going to be terrible, a full-blown mantis rape. You are all wrong. Only one of those five makes the grade. You know what happens to the other four idiots? She devours them, while the conqueror conquers.

Why Mayer? He is carnivorous. I don't know anything about his prothorax, whether it's short or long; he feeds on other people, and he holds them up, but never in prayer. As for sex, if only some unbelievably beautiful girl felt like and was like a praying mantis and L.B. was one of the unlucky five. Now I know why looking at Mayer made me think of a praying mantis.

There were three of us, and only one liked Mayer—Mayer. We had him outnumbered, but one of the outnumbering was out, so be careful, baby; all the thunder is going to roll your way.

At last he stopped figure frigging and looked up at me,

a very faint suggestion of a smile, then at Woody. He did a double take that would have made Wallie Beery proud, then composed himself, and the big important whatever-it-is was about to be announced to the breathless world. "I have twelve directors all making pictures, good pictures for MGM. Of the twelve, the fastest and most efficient are the half-asleep Van Dyke and you, Wellman." Van broke wind. "I have presented an idea to my publicity department, which they accepted with great enthusiasm, and as you know, they are at times pretty hard to convince." (Maybe he wants us to do the phone book; I'll take the yellow pages; that crack is as funny as high mass, but I'm going nuts in here.)

"This whole idea can be told very simply and very quickly, proving its value. We are embarking on a controlled campaign publicizing the great gift that God has bestowed upon you two men, that of knowing what you want and being able to shoot it fast. This is secret, and I expect you to treat it as such.

"Directors are very vain men, and I admire them for it. I feel sure that when your brother directors see what a bonanza of publicity you two are getting, they might very well get ahold of themselves and try and ape you." (Christ, he's got us with the monkeys now.) "And that could well mean the same quality of pictures for a great deal less dollars; in short, I am your proud general, and you my two sergeants."

Hurray! This was my out. I got up and walked over to his desk and stood right where I could look down on him, "Mr. Mayer, I have been a second-class soldier in the Foreign Legion, a corporal and a sergeant in the Lafayette Flying Corps, a first lieutenant in the American Air Corps, and when the war was over I asked for and got an honorable discharge, and I never want to be one of them again. I got sick of making my living avoiding having my brains blown out, and if you think by making me your sergeant you are doing me a great honor, you are daffy.

"What did you hire me for, my personality or my so-

228

called talent? If for my charming personality, you are already behind the eight ball; if for my questionable talent, you have a slight chance; but never as a fink."

The soundproof room trembled with Woody's applause. He flew out of his leather nest, and together we marched out of the lair of the Mayer.

> He whom the Gods favor dies young, while he is in his
> health, has his senses and his judgment sound.
>   —Plautus

Gable—never have I known a man who loved to live, to live well, as he did. I made three pictures with him, *Across the Wide Missouri, The Call of the Wild,* and before he became a star, *Night Nurse,* in which he was just one of the cast, played a black-clothed chauffeur who punched the doctor (Charlie Winninger) in the nose and stole food from two lovely little girls. He was trying to kill them through malnutrition. One of the most despicable heavies imaginable, and he did it with such savoir faire that he became a star. The powers-that-be at Warner Brothers liked his performance but decided he was not worth fooling with, not star material: his ears were too big. They forgot to look at his dimples and listen to his voice and see his smile.

We had trouble on *Call of the Wild,* big trouble, on top of a mountain. He wasn't tending to business, not the business of making pictures. He was paying a lot of attention to monkey business, and I called him for it, lost my easy-to-lose temper, and did it in front of the company, a bad mistake.

He was a big man. I am not, but there was a big something in my favor, his face. He made his living with it, mine was behind the camera. He might have beaten my brains out, I don't know, but I do know that I could have made a character man out of him in the process. I think he knew that, and we finished the picture speaking only when necessary and only about business. This carried over for a long time after the picture was fin-

229

ished. Occasionally, we would meet, bow politely, and say nothing.

Then came *Across the Wide Missouri*. I was under contract to MGM, as was Gable. I cannot remember (or did I ever know?) the story of the trouble on the picture. Everything apparently was ready to go, and they came up minus a director. I had finished my contractual number of pictures for the year, and they asked me to take over. I refused, not because of Gable, but because of that demon income tax. They worked the problem out in such a way that I would not be penalized, and I agreed, provided they included all my family from the moment they left the house until they returned. This sounds simple, but it involved a wife and six kids (Maggie was not on the way yet). When I say "included," that means they pay everything. They agreed. This was an expensive agreement, for most of the picture was to be made on location at Durango, Colorado.

I suggested to the big men that they had better query Mr. Gable on this their choice of directors and was surprised to learn that they had and that there was no objection whatsoever; on the contrary he was most enthusiastic.

So I thought to myself, if he is man enough to forget, so must I. We became good friends once more. This was the kind of a guy he was, a nice guy, and my kind, not too nice.

I have always loved dogs, so I reverse the attitude that the liker of dogs has. The liker says that so-and-so reminds him of a sleek greyhound, or that she reminds him of a little bitty chihuahua. With me it's the dog that does the reminding. A little Boston bull reminds me of Peter Lorre. A big bushy-haired, lion-headed old Saint Bernard reminds me of Gable. I guess I just love dogs more than I do people.

Now take Buck, the big Saint Bernard we used in *The Call of the Wild*. He looked like Gable, only with a heavier beard. In the Jack London story he was supposed to pull one thousand pounds a hundred yards, on a snow-packed roadway in Dawson, in the frozen north, in the middle of the winter. In the picture Buck had to make-believe-do-it at the RKO ranch, in the San

Fernando Valley, in midsummer, with fake snow. That's the way we make pictures sometimes, ass-end backward.

Summertime in the valley is scorching, full of females in shorts, males in trunks, and everybody that had pools was in them. Everybody acting in the picture was in mackinaws and fur coats and fur caps pulled down to cover the ears. Shoes full of heavy socks, everything worn for extreme cold, in intense heat. The hospital was full of fainters, men, women, and children. Buck, thick-coated, was just as hot and uncomfortable as all the rest.

We faked the thousand pounds, but the sled was still heavy although loaded with feather-packed sacks. The scene called for him to pull the sled one hundred yards. We hedged on that, and most of my property men were dressed like extras and kept nudging the sled along to help poor old Buck, who didn't like this kind of a job in the heat of a stifling summer's day. He resented it and showed it in the only three ways he knew: by panting, by sticking his tongue out, and by lying down.

His trainers tried everything to make old Buck move, but he just lay there panting. They got tough with him. Didn't mean a thing. Offered him food; too hot to eat. I was getting worried. A thousand extras is a lot of money. All waiting on a dog. We tried and tried, and Buck said to hell with it.

Then I got an idea. I gathered all my prop men and told them to take cars and scour the surrounding countryside for female dogs in heat. Get a bevy of them, and then I called an early lunch.

Lunch lasted longer than usual, but no property men; then in came one with his trophy, a Pekingese in heat, and then one other with a little French poodle, just a little gal with a slick hairdo and a walk like a fast trot. These were the loose women of dogdom. They had them on leashes of big rope, which made the little gals look even tinier.

I called work, and we lined the shot up again, hiding the girls from the panting Buck. I started the cameras, the property men sneaked in the bait, keeping them ahead of Buck and just out of camera range. We started trucking back. Buck saw the girls, forgot all about the hot summer's day; the real heat began to boil in him, and he started after them. The property men had to hold back on the sled to keep Buck from breaking into a gallop. When we got to the finish line and the scene was over, I had the cameraman pan his camera to the two silly-looking little dog-dames, neither one as big as Buck's head. They were marching on, flaunting their flags at full mast, deliberately teasing this struggling, panting, shackled idiot behind them.

There's a lesson in this somewhere, but I'll be damned if I know where—maybe it's the human in the dog that screws up his reasoning.

What has this got to do with Gable? Plenty. Gable of course was in the scene egging old Buck on. Naturally Buck thought he was helping him get to the dames, and when the scene was over and the girls were whisked away in an automobile, he realized that he had been duped, and he blamed Gable, who came to me heartbroken and told me that Buck wouldn't have anything to do with him, growled when he offered him a meaty tidbit as a reward for a great scene. Snapped at him. In all seriousness, he said that was the first time he had ever double-crossed anybody in all his life. Gable was a lover of dogs too.

"How do you want me to say it?"

"Say it your way, baby, and when you say it, think of what you are saying. If I got some actor to play you, I would make him spend hours with you just listening and looking so he would learn how to talk like you, walk like you, act like you, be you. Does that answer your question?"

"Yes, sir."

Then I thought now would be the time to straighten out all the G.I.'s that were working in the picture. Be sure they knew what it might mean to them, to me, and most of all to Ernie Pyle, so I asked their captain if he would get them all together, just the

G.I.'s, and bring them over to a little field across the street from the set. I would like to utter a few pearls of wisdom.

He got 'em all, hundreds of them, and they were all standing out in the field waiting for me. Most of them were kids, old kids. They had been through the African campaign, the Tunisian business, Sicily, Rome, and now were home but not for long. Next stop, South Pacific.

They all knew about me, a retread, hater of infantry, but they had also been tipped off by Ernie of my, shall we say, awakening.

When I got over there, I asked the captain if I could take over, and he said with pleasure. I asked them all to sit down and take it easy. I remained standing.

"Fellas, there's a couple of things I would like to clear up, and a few to explain. I know you all have heard how I got into this, because of one man, Ernie Pyle. I think as much of him as you do, and it was through him that I got the great desire to make *G.I. Joe*. Not just a picture, but something that you, Ernie, and I will be proud of. That's a big expensive job, that's why you are here, that's why actors have been training with you, so they will look like you, handle themselves the way you do. That's also why a lot of you fellas will be playing scenes, speaking lines. I want to make this the goddamnedest most honest picture that has ever been made about the doughfoot.

"I have already picked a few of you to play parts. All through the picture, when a G.I. has something to say, I want a G.I. to say it, not some bastard G.I. You know the story is good, and it's real, and it's beautifully written by a man whose very life is you. Let's give it what he deserves.

"One more thing, that camera is just a camera; it won't bite, but it will pick up everything, and what I want it to pick up is honesty and sincerity. That's up to you. Just do what I ask you, I'll never give you a bum steer; and then maybe with a little luck, when it's all over, you'll see something up there that will be more than a picture of the infantry; it might just be a monument, and I am going to make it that if it breaks my ass. Let's go make a picture, huh?"

And they went to work. I am talking boastfully because the picture was a big success, and all those kids that were in it were great, and they all went to the South Pacific and none of them came home.

How does that make you feel? You, the man that directed the picture, that got to know all of them and liked most of them. How do you feel?

I feel lousy. I couldn't have stopped it, but at least we had some fun together. We were shooting, but they were blanks, and nobody was getting hurt. We had a lot of laughs together, a lot of work, a lot of drinks, and I got them a little extra dough. It all seems so futile now. It's the one picture of mine that I refuse to look at.

There was one thing I will always remember about them. When they weren't working, you could always find them behind the sets throwing knives. We had built a half-ruined Italian village. A big portion of the picture was shot there. It was a replica of the many real towns these kids had taken, defended, and lost. When we shot scenes in the different streets, in front of cafés, municipal buildings, church, or whatever, they went about their business in a deadly sort of a way. There was no kidding, very little laughter, and a great deal of silence. Between shots, they would sit down or lean against a wall, just look around, say nothing; but their expressions spoke volumes; then, when they were excused, they would disappear behind the set and start throwing knives again.

I don't know how to describe the sound of a knife being thrown at a log or a set two-by-four or a telephone pole, but that's what you heard, until I was ready to take a scene and the quiet whistle blew. Then it stopped, and it became strangely silent until the scene-finished whistle blew, and it started again, *whiiiit-thud, whiiiit-thud,* day in and day out. I used to hear this stygian sound at night in my sleep. It wasn't the sound alone that got me; it was its constancy.

G.I. Joe is still on TV, and Mitchum, Freddie Steele, Wally Cassell, Burgess Meredith, and all the rest of the cast were wonderful. The writing, poetry of the doughfoot, cruel poetry but so honest, so tragic, so miserable, so lonely, and so many wonderful kids gone. You can't replace them, ever, but maybe you can stop wars so we don't keep adding to that castigated list. Castigate—"to punish in order to correct." It's a hell of a punishment, and we haven't corrected a thing, and Ernie never saw his picture.

NINE

Crazy bastard is diving straight at him. Why doesn't he dive underneath him and pull up and rack his blind bottom? I could help him, but I can't do anything now but get away from behind him, or that German gunner will miss him and get me. Tom's coming around now to take his turn after me. Oh-oh, too late. There goes Marin's wing, and there he goes. That's the goddamnedest crookedest spinning nose dive I ever saw, and look at that beautiful silver wing drifting down after him like a giant leaf falling in a very peaceful gentle breeze. Poor Marin, let his hate get the best of him. Stop looking at it. It's my turn, here goes. Tom's right behind me just a little to the left but behind, that gunner is getting all screwed up, doesn't know who to shoot at. Straight down, you idiot—keep going—little more—more, now pull up, easy, easy, you can rip 'em off and you'll join Marin, and everybody will say you died fighting for liberty; balls, I'm not dying fighting for anything. I'm not dying. Good boy, you did it, you still got your wings, wait a minute, hold it, hold it—now let him have it, give it to him, more, more, fall off or you'll ram him. That's it, take a look boy, you got him. The Rumplers got just a pilot now and just one gun like you and Tom. Jesus, look at him go, that heavy Mercedes motor and these goddamned light little rotaries. Tom missed, so we'll keep as close as we can. If he levels off, we can get another crack at him, but he isn't leveling off, he's trying to make his lines, wise bastard. Take a shot at him, it's a long one but maybe. Nope, no good. Tom's trying now, can see his tracers. Too far away. Give it everything you got, baby; wish I had a Spad with that heavy

Hispano Suiza, might have a chance to get a few shots at him. Tom's probably wishing the same thing. We'll follow that son of a bitch as long as we can, something might happen. Hey, it has, you can see the way his prop is turning. Tom got his motor. I'm getting closer, so is Tom, so is the ground. Try a couple; still too far away, but getting closer. Pour it on baby, all you got. Christ, I hope this LeRhone stays together. By God, he's got to crash-land, and lookie, the front lines. Tom's getting closer. Getting awful close to those trenches. Give it another try, I'm reaching him, so is Tom, pour it in, we got him. There he goes, baby; Christ, what a crash, over and over; pull up, you dumb bastard, and get out of here, it isn't healthy. Where's Tom? Can't see him. Christ, they're throwing everything at me, hang on, pull it around, atta boy, you're past, you made it; hedgehop now, you're on your way home. You lucky bastard.

That was it, as best I can remember. I always talked to myself in the air, even when just flying along doing nothing. In a fight it helps, makes you think you got somebody with you, that you are not all alone, gives you that little added zip, can pull you through some tight spots. He can talk you into doing the right thing at the right moment. Had a hell of a nice guy with me this time. Wish he was with me more often. Maybe I better get to know this other me. He has certainly been the best friend I have ever had. He seems not only to understand me, but he can stand me too, and that requires a very special technique. That other me is of course my conscience, in my case, a noisy, fast-talking conscience. I call him Peter Larynx, his last name is the same as mine, we are consanguineous.

I don't think he is crazy about me, but I am his job, and he does the best he can. After sixty-odd years of riding around with me, he gets pretty tired and bored, but when I go, he goes, and to the same place; and he doesn't know where it is any more than I do, and we are both a little scared.

Sometimes I get mad at him, and *I* start talking. I think he should do better than he does, with all the experience he has had with me, all the odd places and screwy people and fantastic history he has been subjected to, and in many instances he hasn't done any better than I.

He has one very valid excuse. He claims that he cannot talk out loud under all conditions and in all places, like in a church or a bedroom, when it is best not to be talking at all; if he did, the white-coated men might seize me, slap a straitjacket on, and retire him. If I would only listen to his still small voice, I might get it through my thick head that he is trying to think me into not doing things that make me lose my temper and start him yakking in a loud, blasphemous voice.

He admits that he swears too much, but he never tells a dirty story.

There is something else very commendable about him. He tries so hard and so often and in such good faith, but he is out of his class; he is up against a champion who, if the truth be known, needs no codeine, no green hornets to make him daffy.

You start out like a vapor trail, straight and true and in the right direction; then life butts in, your vapor trail begins to look like a filmy white corkscrew with ever-widening ups and downs; eventually it is all screwed up, so are you. Lately you've been taking divots from your cheeks, the inside, and you get worried about a guy who starts gnawing on himself—arthritic, growing old and bumping into things, stumbling over a pebble; everything becomes a problem—a lunk in a funk.

Tim Wellman was twenty years old; Tom Landis, Tim's pal, the same age; Mike, my youngest boy, was fourteen, a rugged fourteen and a crack shot, the junior champion of California for two years.

Tim, Tom, and Mike are bear hunters or coon hunters or forest-fire fighters or anything that has to do with the great outdoors. At this particular time, I went on a bear hunt with these three young savages. I was in my sixties. I should have known better.

We were to hunt bear around McCloud. That is a region

near Mount Shasta to the north of Los Angeles, a long ways to the north.

Tim and Tom and the pack. By the pack, I mean the dogs, or as Tim calls them, the boys. Two old-timers, Rough and Alfi, and five young fellas, all sons of Alfi. They are hound dogs, bluetick Walkers, big, fast, tough babies. Will fight bear or coon or cats, no deer. They are as hardy and tough a dog as there is. They are also very gentle and lovable, especially with kids. They'll let the kids pull their big drooping ears and their long snakelike tails, and they'll just cry, but never get mad. The only way a lad can get hurt by one of these wonderful dogs is to get in the way of their wagging tails. That hurts; it's like being belted by a club.

Tim and Tom left a few days before Mike and I did. We were to bed down in a motel in a little town near where they were to make camp. They would leave a sealed envelope with an enclosed map to show us their camping site. Sounds very simple, the enclosed map, but how to find it is another thing.

Everything went according to plan. They left, we followed, arrived at the motel, and got the envelope. It took us two days and directions from old hunters, older fishermen, and finally, believe it or not, from a barfly, before we found the base of operation.

It was a camp, so called, but the locale was beautiful: little stream, fireplace, seven dogs roped to seven trees, two sleeping bags—and no Tim or Tom and no jeep or station wagon. They were out looking over the country.

We spent the hours of waiting, fishing with not very good luck. Our catch consisted of three trout, fractions over the catchable size. It got dark; we found the dogs' food and fed them. Had to climb a tree to get it. Looked around for human grub, found none, and ended up eating the three small trout to try and tranquilize two mountain-inflamed appetites. It didn't help much.

I caught Mike stealing some of the dogs' food; and when

239

I told him he didn't know what he was eating, he said he didn't care, he was hungry, and it tasted good. How do you answer that? So I tried it, and by God he was right. I've eaten worse dinners at five bucks a throw.

It got dark and late and no Tim and Tom, so we built a bigger fire and crawled into their sleeping bags and went to sleep.

The bags had no air mattresses. It wasn't necessary. Just carefully chosen pine boughs laid neatly. A mattress fit for an invalid, which I was sure would be my ultimate fate.

How long we slept I couldn't tell. My outdoor alarm rang; it was old Alfi licking me awake. It was still dark, and the three boys had everything in readiness for the start of the big hunt. I got up stiffly and was told to get in the station wagon beside Tom. In the back were the five young dogs, about three hundred pounds of strength, vitality, swiftness, and smell.

With Tim in the jeep that was to lead the way were the two veterans, Rough and Alfi, and young Mike. They carefully extinguished the fire, leaving not even a spark, and we were on our way. There was no talk, no nothing; this was business, and I just sat there trying to keep my skull from penetrating the roof of the station wagon. I had visions of myself going through the woods with my head sticking out like a released jack-in-the-box.

Have you ever been in a real dust storm? This was it, only the wind was not blowing. All the windows were closed, that is, as closed as could be in a 1955 often-bear-hunted station wagon. You could barely make out the five dogs in the back. They looked like restless brown ghosts, and they smelled like hell. I've lived in bad odors, in quickie hospitals, French latrines, seasick staterooms, unwashed second-class legionaries, but none of them ever affected my eyes. This puppy pungency made them water.

This cook's tour of the old logging roads and firebreaks went on and on. The bumpiest, darkest, most helpless, scariest crawl-along imaginable, at the end of which your reward, a bear and a mild concussion.

Tim and Mike were in clover. They just got dust that billowed up from the big-treaded tires of their jeep. We got our own and what was left of theirs. They were most charitable.

It was still pitch-dark, and the headlights were on. The effect of the dust in the beams was cabalistic, but who the hell cares for artistry at this stage of your asphyxiation.

Suddenly Tim stopped, so did we. I ended up against the dashboard, with a covey of sixty-pound dogs on my back. They thought this was the time to play; and when Tom and I got through convincing them that it wasn't, I smelled like a dog.

Tom got out and joined Tim, who was inspecting the headlighted road. They didn't seem to do much, just walked up and down as if looking for a lost contact lens or some sneezed-out uppers, then got back in the cars, and the exhilarating pilgrimage started all over again.

While Tom and Tim were having their directors' meeting, I opened my door to let in some badly needed fresh air. It was fresh all right, mountain fresh and mountain cold, and it didn't get rid of the foul odor; it just froze it, so when we started again and it began to warm up inside, the smell began to thaw, and we had hot stink the rest of the trip.

After enough more directors' meetings for me to become acclimated to the tang of the bluetick sniff-whiff and to look like a high yellah, Tim once more stopped the caravan, and Mike came back and said Tim wanted me up in front with him. He was about to start the hunt.

I changed places with Mike, and Tim got old Rough out and set him down in the middle of the road directly in the lights of the jeep.

It was still pitch-black, except for the long path of light ahead of us, down which old Rough sauntered. We just crept along behind him.

Old Rough had been car-ridden for hours, and for the first mile, he left his identification card on damn near every tree we passed. I asked Tim when does he stop leaking and start tracking. Tim just grunted.

I wanted to find out a few things and asked him what Rough's title was. He gave me the whole lineup without once taking his eye off Rough, occasionally opening his door and looking along the side of the road. I asked him what he was looking for, and he said tracks, that sometimes old Rough would become so fascinated with one side of the road that he would forget to give the other side a nose going-over.

As Tim explained quickly: Rough was the start dog. He starts the track. Tim would listen to his bay; in short, Tim became a human sounding board and regulated the intensity of his baying. If it sounded right and he had a hot track, Tim would release Alfi, who was much faster, and his job was to pick up the track and get the bear moving. Once more, Tim brought his sound board into play, and if the baying became intense enough, he let the rangers out and they picked it up; being faster than both Rough and Alfi, they not only kept the bear moving, but eventually treed him. They were the tree dogs. Simple, isn't it?

Everything went according to Hoyle. Rough stopped his tree mulching and picked up a track. We stopped, jumped out, and I heard the first of the sounds I will never forget as long as I live.

It was just breaking into a dim dawn when Rough's low bay started. It was as regular as the tick of a metronome for a few minutes, and then the tempo increased, and Tim released Alfi. Another baying was added, excited and a little higher than Rough's. We listened, and suddenly Alfi exploded like a bunch of firecrackers; he had the bear moving, and Tom let out the crazy young boys, and off they went, their baying high, sharp, and staccato, bouncing back off the mountainsides and burying themselves in the deep valley bottom.

What a music, the tones low, high, loud, soft, sweet, harsh; the minors, the majors, the trebles, the basses, all blending together in an eerie symphony of the goddamnedest sound I have ever heard.

My sixty-odd years were whisked off me by a magic wand. I wanted to tear after them, but this is not the way it is done, no sir, you just get back in the stink wagon and start the same bumpy, dusty slow ride, staying on top of the valley, out of which rises the cacophony of the chase.

Every once in a while, Tim would stop and get out and listen. I got out with him on the last stop, and instead of looking down at the tree-packed valley, I watched him. It was daybreak now, and I could see him clearly. His eyes were like a sound lens bringing all the baying into focus. They had the bear treed.

He yelled at Tom and Mike and looked at me, a look of the conqueror. "Let's go, Dad!" And down we went. It was the steepest, most treacherous down I had ever traversed. I stayed behind, hell I couldn't do anything else. I slid, fell, rolled, but managed to do them all in the right direction. We got to the bottom. I was perfectly willing to stay there, but the chorus of the baying, the magnetism of its sound, kept me going.

Across beaver dams, tightrope-walking felled trees, wading waist-high through streams, hell they were rivers. Tim and Tom were out of sight, but Mike stayed where he could keep his eye on his old man. God bless him.

We started up again, oh no, but we did. Looking back, I wondered how I did it; but I did, and at long last we came to the tree, the end of a perfectly executed dog maneuver, and there he was up a giant sequoia, the base of which all five of us couldn't reach around joined hand to hand. He was a big one, way up there glowering down at us and the dogs, who were still in good voice.

It was to be Mike's bear. In other words, he was to perform the kill. It was a rugged shot, and it had to be deadly. A wounded bear could kill a lot of valuable dogs. I was a little worried, but I shouldn't have been, because Mike was as cool as a cucumber.

Tim passed him the 30-30, and Mike readied himself, one foot much lower than the other because of the slope of the hill. He took careful aim, fired, and got him right between the eyes. He started to fall like a taut tent flap and suddenly came to rest on three closely outgrowing limbs. There he remained, a hundred and fifty feet in the air, never to become the beautiful bear rug that would have graced Mike's bedroom.

It was a pathetic ending to a successful hunt, full of the noise of victory. Just the noise.

The whole world was there: rich man, poor man, beggar man, thief, doctors, lawyers, and so help me, an Indian chief, and gals, wow! Stanford had whopped California, and here at Ernie Never's house, the invitation to the Rose Bowl had just been received. The action was so wild and rugged and loud that the ballgame was still on. After ten minutes of complete insanity, everybody suddenly realized that there weren't any California people there; they were just kicking the hell out of each other, so they quieted down a few notches, put back what was left of their clothes, and started to do a little honest drinking. My little balmy cluster of buffoons feeling no pain had gathered in a corner of Ernie's study, and there we stayed. Why? Some girl had to go to the ducky so they hand-passed her over their heads, clear across two rooms, and just made it. We were, to put it lightly, impounded.

Suddenly a funny-looking little old head popped itself out of this beehive of madness and looked around for help, its shirt and collar were torn, necktie long gone, glasses askew, and what little hair it had was standing straight up like a scared cat. I reached down and pulled him to his feet; he fell into my arms. The poor little guy was scared to death. He told us he got pushed down to be a football and some big giant centered him, passed him to the quarterback, who tried to forward-pass him, but he got mad and yelled for Ernie, so they put him down and left him on the floor.

"I have been fighting my way through a forest of legs: big ones, small ones, men's ones, women's ones, ugly ones, and beautiful ones—one of which I bit and the owner slapped the man she was talking to—I bit her kind of high.

"My name is Dr. Cricket from Santa Cruz. I am Ernie's

doctor." Well, God bless you, Buffalo Bill, and I introduced him to my wife, my assistant and his wife, my trusty, Spencer Tracy and his keeper, and the real party started. I asked him if he would like a spot of bourbon after that long trip in the leggy forest. "Thank you, that would be very saporous"—that was a new one on me, but I got him a glass, asked if he wanted water or maybe a little ice—"just a very little piece, and do you mind if I pour it myself? I'm always afraid the helping might be too generous for my capacity."

Why, of course, and I passed him the bottle. He poured himself a drink—generous was not the word, awesome, and he bottomed it up. We had us a pro. This unwound him, and he started to tell us all about ourselves. It was very amusing and very frightening—I was the first victim.

"Mr. Wellman, I have met many people who know you. Not all of them like you, but they know you, and that is what counts; good or bad, they remember you or your flying, or your pictures or your wives or something you have done good or bad. You are an interesting man, or maybe you are crazy or lucky, or perhaps they are both sewed together." Could be.

"And you, Mr. Zimmer, I don't know much about you except that you are the great man's assistant. I don't envy you. I don't mean, by that, that Mr. Wellman is a complete son of a bitch, just lacking in patience, which happens to be what is wrong with the whole world. Right?" I beat Zimmy to it. Right, and by God he was.

"I feel very sorry for you, Mr. Tracy—you are a tragic figure, a dealer in emotions, one picture after another; joy, sorrow, fear, love, hate, passion, violence, patience, sentiment, hysteria, on and on and on. It is always a beautiful performance and now it is all over and a new emotion, you got to laugh, be funny, laugh like hell, and it's seven o'clock, and you are excused. You get home, you're pooped, and the real things happen —you don't recognize them, the honesty has gone, the adhesions have set in, the inflammation has been too great."

It must have hit home. Tracy was strangely quiet. So was

everyone else. I didn't know if it was the booze bomb or what, but suddenly Dr. Cricket had a pathetic faraway look on his face and apologetically asked if we would be patient and listen to a funny-looking little guy's story of love; it is very short. He didn't wait for an answer, and after his next few words it wasn't necessary—"Five years, two months, two days, and half a night ago, my wife went to sleep forever. She wasn't beautiful, but to me she was the most beautiful woman in the world. I am not handsome, but to her I was Tarzan—lying in her arms was like being cradled in a beautiful song. Sounds a little foolish, doesn't it, but it wasn't, because that is the way it was."

This odd little guy made me realize how foolish it is to judge anybody by the way they look. This was a wonderful little man, ten feet tall. I wished that I had known his lovely wife; maybe she was even taller.

Dr. Cricket broke the silence again. You know, Cricket was accomplishing wondrous things. We were quiet and very attentive—even Tracy, and that was an achievement. "During this self-imposed requiem of mine, my only real moments of happiness have been when I have entertained friends; old and new.

"Perhaps you would come down and visit me for a few days as the new, and leave as the old. It is delightful in Santa Cruz now, and whatever you want to do I can arrange. What is your favorite game, Mr. Wellman? Golf, I'd like to play golf—you will, with Marion Hollins on her own course. The Pasatiempo, you must have heard of it." I have. "It's yours, and you, Mrs. Wellman?" I want to fish, and the Zimmers popped in with two so-do-I's. "Okay, and that leaves just you, Mr. Tracy—what would you like to do?" After I got over these last few days, Dr. Cricket, I would like to listen to the way you tell the truth; it is very effective, and who can tell, we might be of a little help to each other.

"Hi, Cricket, where you been all night?" And Ernie swarmed all over him. They had a ritual; they clasped hands, and then hand-wrestled; and, inch by inch, the little doctor forced this giant of a man, whose neck muscles were so distended that I turned away for fear of witnessing the birth of a hideous hernia, to the floor. Amazing, done so well you almost believed it; and with Ernie writhing on the floor in excruciating pain and the onlookers cheering and clapping, the little winner accepted his victory, displaying his enormous biceps like a ham wrestler.

Ernie bounced to his feet, threw his arms around the doctor, and yelled at us. "You just met the grandest little guy in the world, my take-care-of-me pal, and you are about to lose him; some more of my friends are waiting impatiently to meet him; Dr. Cricket has autography to do, so will you please excuse us? I will be right back, don't leave," and Ernie performed a ballet lift with the good doctor arriving in an inverted arabesque yelling at us to remember tomorrow at one o'clock, 630 Elm Street, Santa Cruz, 630 Elm Street, cracked crab, beer, and garlic bread—cracked crab, beer, and garlic bread. We chorused back, "Cracked crab, beer, and garlic bread," and the whole crazy roomful picked it up—"Cracked crab, beer, and garlic bread," in perfect synchronization. It grew louder and louder, the clarion call of a multitude of starving Stanfordites, and above the tide of chanting people, a handsome blond head, the arms, and Dr. Cricket glided on like a moving statue as undisturbed as the crest of a powerful wave pressing toward the beach.

Early next morning, three cars drew away from the St. Francis Hotel in perfect funeral formation.

Number one—full of Zimmers and Wellmans, quiet, squirmish, and hungover.

Number two—full of luggage, one overnight suitcase with a dainty little panty that just didn't quite make it, lying at half-mast.

Number three—full of two exhausted sleeping keepers and Tracy, looking fit as a fiddle, taking a morning belt. The car shivered.

We were on our way. There were three stops, beer stops, nothing harder, and we arrived in the village of Santa Cruz at one o'clock sharp—cracked crab, beer, and garlic bread; like hound dogs with nose to ground, we found the scent; it led us right to Elm Street. I started baying like my Timmy's bear-hunting bluetick Walkers as we started down the street; all the rest joined in, and the Santa Cruzites must have thought we were nuts—well? Our baying got weaker as the numbers got larger and the houses smaller, then 630—a lovely little place just big enough to hold our luggage. The door opened, and out poured Dr. Cricket, a crab cracker in one hand and a bottle of beer in the other. During the how-are-yas and the I-knew-you-would-make-its, the handshakes, the hugs, and the kisses, I kept looking at the house, wondering where the hell we were going to sleep, maybe on the floor in sleeping bags, but we didn't have any bags; after all, who is going to second-guess Dr. Cricket? So I told our two helpers to leave the luggage in the car.

Once more the Cricket-inspired festivities started all over again. I am not blessed with women's intuition, but I have hunches, and this one was in the blues, way down.

We gorged, we guzzled, we met friends, the head of the chamber of commerce, Mr. and Mrs. Mayor, and suddenly we were all alone, the Wellmans, the Zimmers, the keepers, a sober Mr. Tracy, and as he said, the most compassionate man he had ever met, Dr. Cricket. Mr. Tracy was being baptized.

It was getting rather late, and I was getting more worried about where we were going to nest for the next few days. I didn't want to embarrass our host by asking him what the next move was, when the amazing little man got up and looked at me with a knowing little smile on his face, as if reading my mind—which he was—and made the big announcement—there just happened to be three empty suites, one for the Wellmans, one for the Zimmers, and one for Mr. Tracy. Miss Hollins is disappointed at not being able to greet you at her guest house this afternoon. She has been out of town and will be home a little too late, but will see you early in the morning—little did he know that this was *the* masterpiece of understatement. So Dr. Cricket took us up to the Hollins guest house; it was beautiful. He gave out the suites—the Wellmans and the Zimmers upstairs, with a balcony that extended the length of the house and looked down on the twelfth and thirteenth holes of the most beautiful golf course imaginable. (I should have known; there was that goddamned number 13—look out, baby.)

Tracy was on the ground floor; he didn't like heights—Tracy was freaky, the bottle never made him high, it always made him miserably low.

Our good doctor introduced us to the housekeeper, the cook, and all the Filipino boys who seemed to come out of the walls at the snap of a finger, and then left to do some doctoring—to pick us up in the morning for the golf, the fishing, and the whatever he was doing with or for Mr. Tracy, who had become completely sober and very quiet. It was almost like the terrifying hush just before an earthquake.

A little chilly, so we all decided to have dinner in the library before a warm open fire, all except the two keepers, who had a suite above the garage and had settled down to a nice quiet dinner in their sitting room and, for the first time in a week, to relax, forget about Mr. Tracy, and watch (would you believe it) the fights on TV. (These two guys were insatiable.)

No drinks, not even beer. The food was excellent, so good that, despite the cracked crab orgy, we all ate heartily, except Tracy, who had not regained his appetite for food, nor lost it for the funny water. He was giving it a battle, and I felt for him.

From nowhere, one of the Filipino boys appeared before Tracy; he was nervous and shy and spoke to him as if talking to God. Mr. Tracy, you are wanted please on the telephone. Without saying a word, Tracy got up from the table and followed the Filipino boy to the telephone in the lobby. It wasn't a happy walk, and we all looked at one another hoping—I said my hope is it is a picture; Zimmy said his hope was that my hope was right; it wasn't.

"No—goddammit, no!" And a door slammed, and the water spilled out of a glass on the table, next world.

Someone was ringing the chimes at the front door and kept

ringing them, and they were getting all screwed up—sounded like the recording of a horror picture, and by God, that might well be. Two Filipino boys racing to the door; the winner opened it, and Clarence stormed in. Clarence was the name of Tracy's keeper, but don't let that fool you, as he went by on his way to his nonpredictable patient, he yelled at us, "What's up?" I yelled back, "He just got a telephone call"; and with an "Oh-Christ-no," Clarence disappeared into Mr. Tracy's blue-fogged spa.

You couldn't tell what they were saying—Tracy's voice the louder of the two, and Clarence's muted, pleading, barely distinguishable at times, but Tracy let you know every once in a while that he was there, with some well-known four-letter babies that had never rung through the house of Hollins.

I didn't know who was on the phone, and I never want to know, but whoever it was set Mr. Tracy off to the races, not the quarter horse or the harness, a full-blown one-hundred-thousand-dollar handicap. Mr. Tracy's baptismal didn't take; he didn't like the water.

The chimes again, the Filipino footrace; this time it was my man, Dan. He rushed over to me, and he also said, "What's up?" (Apparently that's their universal language.) "You better go in there and help your co-worker; he's got a tiger by the tail, a very enthusiastic tiger." He went in, closed the door, and judging by the sound effects of his reception, he damn near came flying back through the door.

The main event started, and I was about to suggest to my little peace-loving group that we retreat when lo and behold, the terrified little old housekeeper, surrounded by three terrified Filipinos, edged toward the door of fury. She knocked timidly. No answer. The groans, the grunts, the pratfalls, the foul language, the something through a window—Mr. Tracy was holding his own. The poor little gal knocked again. Nothing. Then the three Filipino boys stepped bravely forward; they all knocked together, this time loud enough to cause a time-out on the battlefield. Then she spoke her piece: "Mr. Tracy, Miss Hollins would not like this kind of playing going on in her home." And the out-of-breath reply: "I can understand your point of view; you have a job to do, and you have done it; be a good little girl, and go back to the lonesomeness of your inactive little bed. I'll tell Miss Hollins what she can do about this, and in slow motion. I can see the lights in her house from my window. The one that's broken." It was quiet just long enough for Tracy to make it across the room; then it started like thunder. Let's say he was being very choosy with his words; in fact the ones he was using were burning the fairways on their way across to Miss Hollins' house. Tracy was in good voice. The lights in Miss Hollins' home went out.

We stole upstairs and quietly retired to the safety of our suites. Mommy and I undressed in the dark, got in bed in the dark, and it was wonderful in the dark, and then we went to sleep in the dark, but not for long. Tracy was now being funny: He was knocking at all the doors delivering his message, call for Mr. Wellman, call for Mr. Wellman, over and over with no response. Finally he lost his patience and, at the top of his lungs, "Fuck you, Mr. Wellman—what did you expect, a Merry Christmas?"

Next morning, at a quiet breakfast, the Zimmers, the Wellmans, no Tracy. I had a hodgepodge of Tracy-inspired emotions, some few good, many bad, but all very boring. If this strange creature would wake up sober and stay that way, we could all have a wonderful time, but I am beginning to suspect that he is a sleeping belter—has a bottle under his pillow, and when the craving starts, he reaches for, gets, takes, never spills, puts back, and slumbers on peacefully.

Then suddenly she was there, Miss Hollins towering right beside me. This was a strong woman; she frightened the hell out of me. "Mr. Wellman, where is Mr. Tracy?" Mr. Wellman, meekly, "We haven't seen him this morning," and I could have added thank God, "so I imagine he is sound asleep." As she left, she added, "But not for long." This was a condemnation, good-bye, Mr. Tracy. We watched her spellbound as she damn near goose-stepped to the Tracy nest. This was not the little old housekeeper, and she didn't need any Filipino boys with her; This was a champion golfer about to tee off, not on a golf ball, on Mr. Tracy.

She didn't knock politely on the door; she goddamn near knocked it down. It whizzed open, for apparently in the furor of quieting the wild man, they had neglected to lock it.

The sight that greeted Miss Hollins was one that undoubtedly has never been seen, before or since.

All the lights on in the room and despite the knock and the whiz of the opening of the door, three sleeping people—the two keepers in the twin beds and Tracy stark naked, slumbering peacefully on the floor at the foot of the beds with a blanket half pulled from one of them that, by chance, covered his so-called privates.

Miss Hollins never moved from the doorway, which, by the way, she filled. She looked like something carved out of stone. Suddenly her voice rang out, *"Tracy!"* not Mr. Tracy, just *Tracy* —and they were frightened awake, the keepers in bed to sitting positions, Tracy to an erect scrambling posture, trying to cover his naked body with the blanket and ending up looking like a hungover Roman, with a screwed-up toga and just a little bit of a peeking penis exposed. It didn't like what it saw, and on a slight move of Tracy's toga, it happily crept back out of sight.

We all waited for the cannonade to start—it never did. Miss Hollins had been a champion too long; she kept her cool— quietly. "Mr. Tracy, there is a full-length mirror on the wall just to your right that has not been broken; would you mind looking at it?" He looked and saw an indescribable apparition, Mr. Spencer Tracy—Star. He almost threw up, looked back at Miss Hollins, and shuddered one word, "Gruesome."

"Yes, Mr. Tracy, gruesome and frightening." Then, in a very matter-of-fact manner, she informed Mr. Tracy of the expected arrival of Madame Tory, the brilliant and well-loved opera singer—for a week of complete rest and quiet after a very long and successful tour—tonight for dinner. He has ample time to get dressed, packed, and out by noon, with of course his two playmates. She turned and left, closing the door very, very quietly. The room stopped breathing.

Miss Hollins went straight for the front door, not even a glance to right or left. One of the Filipino boys opened and closed it for her. On his way back, he passed by us. Zimmy dropped his coffee spoon, the Filipino with forefinger to lips shh-ed us and, sotto voce, "Madame Tory is coming." He wasn't kidding; from then on whenever a noise, a "Shh, Madame Tory is coming." It became a gag, good for a bundle of laughs and one best-forgotten moment of extreme sadness.

We made it. Are you sure? Certainly she would have included us when she drummed out Tracy and his G-men. Zimmy, you and I are very lucky; we married not two beautiful women, two beautiful ladies—that's why we are still here. Zimmy's little wife wondered what was going to happen to Tracy now. I told her that any guess was as good as mine, that I didn't envy Dan or Clarence, but at least they were being well paid for their chosen vocation. Personally, I would rather take care of the monkeys in a zoo; they don't talk, and they are funny little fellas, *almost* human. I guess that is why they don't kill themselves. Tracy is human. After all, he is in a tough spot, an extremely embarrassing one, and he might remember that last impossible request that he asked me to do, so let's practice golf and get the equipment ready for tomorrow's fishing and be back here in time for lunch. I will leave word at the desk where he can reach me if necessary, which I hope won't happen.

We accomplished everything and were back having lunch; in fact, we were just about finished, and the Zimmers were leaving to take a nap, when a woebegone Tracy joined us. He looked like the wrath of God. I asked him if he wanted something to eat; he said, "No thanks, just a little advice." Mommy started to leave, and he stopped her with a "Maybe you could help, from a woman's point of view."

We just sat there for an uncomfortable few minutes, with

Tracy for the first time that I had ever seen him unsure of himself. Finally he found his way, "I have got to get that blazing woman to call off the war for just a few days, to prove something to her, to myself, and to someone else."

Being a nasty bastard, I suggested maybe you can awaken her sexual desires, if any, after all she saw all of you—just tell her that is not fair, to be successful it has to go both ways. You never can tell, you might talk yourself into something. All he could say was "Jesus, you know, you're funny as hell."

"Well, anyway, you better get up, go see her, and use all your charming charm. It will have to be the best scene you have ever played, an Academy Award performance; good luck. He just looked at me and said, "Yeah, and you could have added 'you son of a bitch.' " I said, "That's right, I did, a silent one." There was a moment's still tableau—this could be it, and we all would be thrown out of the Hollins domain, but Mommy put out the fire. "Don't you think we all are in enough trouble as it is?" She was right; he knew it, and so did I—peace. He had one more thing to say. "You know the only one, male or female, that ever really got me was Dr. Cricket, and so fast he got you too, Wellman; you're no bargain." I threw a half-assed salute at him.

Mommy watched him go out the door; there were no chimes this time. She turned to me with a sadness in her voice, "You really don't like him, do you?" "Nope."

Mommy and I played us a little golf, the Zimmers did a little pier-fishing, and we met for dinner in front of the fireplace, a front-row view of the door, through which would enter the one and only magnificent Madame Tory.

The "Shh, Madame Tory is coming" gags had been so many—some very funny, and some not so funny—that we got sick of them and made a deal. Anyone pulling a "Shh, Madame Tory" gag had to put a buck in the pot. We had eleven dollars. We had another buck in the pot for the mention of the name Tracy. This was my suggestion. The pot was empty. This can be read a lot of ways, the girls not bringing it up for fear of starting something best buried; Zimmy not wanting to mention it because he didn't think it was worth a buck; I didn't bring it up because I was sick of the name, with due respect to O'Brien, Cagney, and the smitten ladies of the past, present, and future. When Tracy came in, he was newborn, clear as crystal, sharp as a tack.

"Good evening, my friends. May I break bread with you and celebrate with a small glass of milk?" This is a new Tracy, awaiting breathlessly the coming of a great star of the larynx.

I congratulated him and said that either he was a magician or she the most patient woman in the world. He smiled a cozy little smile and added—and the nicest.

The big moment was upon us, the spick-and-span Filipinos gathered in the hallway in their assigned places. The little old housekeeper immaculate in her Sunday best, vintage early twenties, and then the flustered Miss Hollins literally out of breath with excitement stopped by our table for just a fleeting moment. "I am so proud to have her here, one of my great favorites choosing my home for her vacation. It is like winning another championship—hi, Spencer," and she was gone to join her group in the hallway.

Hi, Spencer—how do you like that? If he sticks around a few more days, it will become Spence; the "r" will be beheaded and so will I.

Miss Hollins was talking to one of the Filipino boys, apparently sending him on an errand. As he passed by, he shh-ed us, "Madame Tory is coming"; and for the first time in the dozens of times this had been said in beds, locker rooms, stores, bars, ladies' and men's rooms, and wherever, it was *the* time —the sound of cars in the gravel driveway, we all jumping to our feet and standing as if about to hear our national anthem, we heard the chimes, so help me they sounded like the ones Clarence rang.

The door swung open, and there she wavered, Madame Tory, the magnificent, drunk as a lord, arms holding bottles as you would a beautiful little baby. Behind her, a six-foot-six black-uniformed chauffeur, young and handsome and bottle laden.

She bowed at her open-mouthed audience, damn near fell on her face, staggered to the staircase and started up, made it halfway; but the altitude got to her, and she passed out, taking the six-foot-sixer and all the bottles with her and ending up where she had started from, flat up.

The ensuing melee was a thing of beauty, a multiple screen full of multiple Filipinos, Hollinses, six-foot-sixes, breaking bottles, flowing wines, Madame Torys, and one pathetic figure standing apart, the poor little old housekeeper, immaculate in her Sunday best, vintage early twenties, crying her heart out.

Tracy, to no one in particular, "Well, I'll be a dirty son of a bitch." He looked around and spotted Clarence, "Come on, Clarence, let's get the hell out of this nuthouse and get back to good old San Francisco, where the fun game is never-ending." As they started for Tracy's former Hollins playground, Clarence was heard to say beseechingly, "Ah, come on, Spence, you've had enough." *"I never have enough!"*

That was it; Madame Tory had touched the smoldering punk to Mr. Tracy, and he exploded all the way to a quiet retreat in Pasadena.

I am going to end with the beginning, which is really a beginning and an ending.

It was in the year of 1933 or '34 B.O.—before obligations. Mommy and I had not been married very long. All the warnings from friends? The snide quotes from the scandalmongers, the crucifying layout of pictures of my former wives, with the amount of settlement emblazoned above their pretty little heads like inscriptions of great courage, rewards for having lived with an imbecile for a certain length of moneyed time. Above my lovely little Mommy's head, a question mark. That was some thirty-odd years ago, and the question mark is still unanswered. With all due respect to the press, when they climb on your back, you get an awful rough ride.

Mommy was a dancer, a very talented one, and one of Berkeley's best and most dependable. Buzz was the *big* of all the dance directors of that or any time. His career was as remarkable as it was stormy. He had great respect for little Dottie Coonan, dancewise, and otherwise. She was the quickest to catch on to his involved routines, and he used her in all his pictures. She was nineteen, supporting her family, as pretty as a picture—a freckled picture—and the only one of the so-called leading dancers that was not under contract. Think that last one over; it goes a lot of ways.

We both were working on the same lot, Warner Brothers. She dancing, I directing. Buzz was doing a roller-skating number, and one noon on my way to the café for lunch, she skated by, in shorts. I lost my appetite.

You can lose your appetite for various reasons: sickness, too much to drink, disgust of something or somebody, not liking the food, trouble with your teeth, or having a hum in your head. She looked at me as she skated by, no smile, no wink, no nothing, just looked, a long look. I got the hum in my head.

I went to my office, closed the door, and communed with myself. This was so idiotic, so completely me. I didn't even know if she could speak English. Maybe she was one of those dumb kind of gals, you know, the kind that never listen. The watchers watch the other girls to see what they have on, who they are with, what kind of a car they are driving, how they got it, otherpeople's-business watchers. Maybe she was what I called "front office figure work." I sure as hell didn't know anything about any of them. I was still a champion of the Bernie Durning system. I had learned that long-ago lesson well.

I could ask my assistant, he does all right; but no, I don't want to get myself in that kind of a position, especially with him. Oh, balls, I'll go on the Berkeley set and ask Buzz to introduce me to her; there has got to be a first time for everything. Then she can ask the other girls about me, and she won't find out a thing. Might do some good.

So I wandered over to the Berkeley set. It was the right time;

257

they were all returning from lunch, and the work had not started yet, and they wouldn't think I was trying to get a little cozy, the way some of the others did.

Buzz came in, and I went up and said hello. I didn't know Buzz very well. Had a couple of drinks with him at different places, away from the studio. I liked him, and I think he liked me, maybe because I never gave him any trouble, never fiddled around his sets.

Buzz: "Well, Bill, this is an unexpected pleasure; don't tell me you're breaking down."

"Well, not quite—yes, by God, I am."

"Who is she?"

"I don't even know her name. I just saw her, and here I am."

I looked around, and there she was, looking at me, not too eagerly, just sort of questioningly.

"She's that little freckled-face fella over there."

"Dottie Coonan, huh? One of the nicest girls you'll ever know. Hey, Dottie!" and over she came.

"Dottie, I want you to meet Bill Wellman," and he walked away with a little hopeful smile on his face.

"How do you do?"

"How do you do. I have never seen you on a Berkeley set before."

"I've never had any reason to be on one of them before."

She got a little embarrassed, and I didn't feel too sure of myself. I was sure of one thing—the closer you got, the more lovely she became. This was not going to be easy.

"How do you say 'I would like to take you to dinner, some-time, anytime'?"

"You just said it, but unfortunately you are married."

"No, I'm not. I'm just waiting out the California dogma, the final decree."

Buzz's assistant screwed it all up.

"Come on, girls—places, let's get going!"

"You will have to excuse me, Mr. Wellman, I have to go to

work," and she was gone, a little bundle of freckled grace. I had accomplished nothing. The hum in my head was much louder.

I spent a lonely, restless night. That dainty little freckled face haunted me. I tried drinking to erase it. No dice. I was cloud-built. The last thing I remember just before I passed out was the freckles. Thousands of freckles, everything was freckled, the pictures on the wall, the black swimming-pool tub, the ceiling of the living room, of the bedroom, my sheets, my life was a freckled mass of disaster, and now new hope, and it was freckled.

This sounds screwy. It was. A screwball in love with a cute little freckle-faced Irish gal named Coonan; and that was over thirty years ago, and I don't know any more about her now than I did then except a thousand and one things, all freckles.

Next day, I planned a new approach. Directly across from Berkeley's stage was the one they were building sets on for my next picture, a Richard Barthelmess starring vehicle, *Heroes for Sale*.

The script was nearly completed, and I knew it by heart, but I appeared on one of my finished sets, sat me down, and made-believe go to work. I figured out setups and bits of action for scenes that were still three weeks away. I opened the big sliding stage door for light and air, and because it disclosed the Berkeley stage door, out of which poured the dancing girls when excused for lunch or for whatever they might have reason to do, I sat there, feigning work, but waiting for Freckles to appear.

She did, about eleven o'clock, on roller skates. I pounced on her like a hawk diving on a lark. I called to her, but she skated faster. I chased her into the administration building and down a corridor and was stopped when she hummed into the ladies' room. I couldn't go any farther, so I sat down on the floor and waited. She had to come out sometime.

She was gone long enough to get a manicure and a hairdo, but they don't do those things in there, so eventually she came out, and I grabbed her.

"What is so distasteful about me? How can you tell what a bum I am after but a few embarrassed words of introduction? Can I take you out to dinner? Bring your mother or sister, or sisters, bring the whole Coonan clan, but just give me a chance to make your life miserable," and she started to laugh. It wasn't the giggle of a nineteen-year-old, it was a full-throated musical laugh, and when she finished, she said—

"Excuse me, Mr. Wellman, I have to get back on the set. You can pick me up at the gate tonight at seven. We work late," and off she went. The humming in my head began playing music, beautiful soft music.

We dined that night together. It was quiet and comfortable, as if we had done it many times before. It was the first of our ten thousand, nine hundred and fifty dinners (give or take a few) that we have had together. At first, just we two, and then with a daughter followed by a son, another daughter and another son, still another daughter and another son, and finally our last little daughter, and their friends, and our friends, and now the seven grandchildren and more to come!

That's what you get when you sit on the floor and wait outside a ladies' room and the one you are waiting for is on roller skates.

OBITUARY

That is all, and it is high time. Not the end of my troubles but the finish of this short piece of insanity. I have a new kind of pain; it hits like a hummingbird—*whi-i-i-i-i-t* and it's gone, and it leaves you with your mouth wide open! I have a corset that I should wear. I prefer to suffer. I broke the habit, and I feel lousy; I am growing a beard, and I look a little bit like Hemingway, but I can't write a little bit like him. My insides have been buffeted so hard and so long that everything inside of me slumbers;

I wish to high heaven I could sleep as soundly as some of my most important vitals.

What are the most important vitals? The dictionary says —"those bodily organs that are essential to life as the brain, heart, lungs, and stomach." My brain is questionably screwy. My heart beats, my lungs are boisterous, and my stomach is shot. None of these four are asleep; a couple are getting a little drowsy, but it's the sleeping ones that are driving me nuts, so I don't think these four are so top-drawer. There are a couple more that can stand on their own.

The big house is getting bigger and lonelier; Pat and her kids are in Palm Springs, or Colorado Springs; Bill and his brood we see every Sunday; Kitty and hers are very busy, and we see them occasionally; Tim and his live in Morro Bay, and when they get a few days off, he goes bear hunting; Cissy is on her own and lives in an apartment and flutters around as aimlessly as a moth in a sea of bright lights; Mike lives here, but you would never know it except on school nights; Maggie is still all ours, but she is going to Honolulu for the Easter vacation. It has now become a once-in-a-while family. The inside of the big house has been repainted and rewallpapered. Gone are the baby prints, the finger paintings, and the crayoned mosaics on the walls.

My wife is a pretty fifty, and if I die, I am sure she would look thirty. I am sixty-eight and look every minute of it and feel every second of it.

She may be at peace with the world upon my passing, but this will all change when she realizes her importance to the state and the federal government. That bugaboo, the inheritance tax, must be met. The liquid assets must go. The house, the pool, the orange orchard, the whole damned six acres, the thirty-odd years of struggle and dreams dissipated by the death of one old poop—that is, unless she girds her armor and captures some rich pigeon with a strange love for another man's children and their children and eventually their children's children. This could go on forever. I am beginning to think that the minute a Wellman says "I do," he or she is not kidding. It is merely a three-letter way of saying we will be pregnant, soon and often. The only answer to this dreadful predicament presents a destiny even more horrible—*keep him alive.*

I'll die, but I will be around for a long time, with Mommy and all the kids and the grandchildren remembering the happy things about their old man, his love of flying, his pictures, his distaste for producers, his love of golf and the sometimes he played well; they wouldn't mention his temper or any of the nasty things, just laughs and maybe even his piano playing, not too good but quietly and softly, and Mommy used to like it, and his enormous appetite for beer and laughingly how Mommy could always tell how much the old boy had sneaked, by just looking at his eyes. Then something happens and his presence becomes embarrassing, maybe she falls in love again, so young, pretty, and atttractive, or maybe there is just too much of him around. Then he dies, really dies, and he goes away, forever.

Footnote: I want to be cremated and emptied high above the smog—high enough to join a beautiful cloud—not one that brings a storm, one that brings peace and contentment and beauty.

FILMOGRAPHY

Knickerbocker Buckaroo (1919).* Directed by Albert Parker. With
Douglas Fairbanks, Jr., and Marjorie Daw.
The Twins of Suffering Creek (1920). With Dustin Farnum.
The Man Who Won (1923). With Dustin Farnum.
Second-Hand Love (1923). With Buck Jones.
Big Dan (1923). With Buck Jones.
Cupid's Fireman (1923). With Buck Jones.
The Vagabond Trail (1924). With Buck Jones.
Not a Drum Was Heard (1924). With Buck Jones.
The Circus Cowboy (1924). With Buck Jones.
When Husbands Flirt (1925).
The Boob (1926). With Charles Murray, Gertrude Olmstead, and
Lucille LeSueur (Joan Crawford).
The Cat's Pajamas (1926). Story by Ernest Vajda.
You Never Know Women (1926). Story by Ernest Vajda. With
Florence Vidor, Clive Brook, and Lowell Sherman.
Wings (1927, Paramount). Screenplay by Hope Loring and Louis
D. Lighton, from a story by John Monk Saunders. With Clara
Bow, Charles Rogers, Richard Arlen, El Brendel, Richard
Tucker, Gary Cooper, and Jobyna Ralston.
The Legion of the Condemned (1928, Paramount). Adapted from a
story by John Monk Saunders. With Fay Wray, Gary Cooper,
Barry Norton, Lane Chandler, Francis MacDonald, Voya George,
Freeman Wood, Charlot Bird, Albert Conti, and E. H. Calvert.
Ladies of the Mob (1928, Paramount). Based on a story by Ernest
Booth. With Clara Bow, Richard Arlen, Helen Lynch, Mary
Alden, Carl Gerard, Bodil Rosing, Lorraine Rivers, and Jane
Pierce.
Beggars of Life (1928, Paramount). Based on a story by Jim Tully.
With Wallace Beery, Louise Brooks, Richard Arlen, Edgar Blue
Washington, H. A. Morgan, Andy Clark, Mike Donlin, Roscoe
Karns, Robert Perry, John Morris, George Kotsonaros, Jacques
Chapin, Robert Brower, and Frank Brownlee.

* Appeared as an Actor

Chinatown Nights (1929, Paramount). Based on Samuel Ornitz's story, "Tong War." With Wallace Beery, Florence Vidor, Warner Olan, Jack McHugh, Jack Oakie, Tetsu Komai, Frank Chew, Mrs. Wing, Peter Morrison, and Freeman Wood.

The Man I Love (1929, Paramount). Based on a story by Herman J. Mankiewicz, titles by Joseph L. Mankiewicz. With Richard Arlen, Olga Baclanova, Mary Brian, Harry Green, Jack Oakie, Pat O'Malley, and Leslie Fenton.

Woman Trap (1929, Paramount). Based on the playlet, "Brothers," by Edwin Burke. With Hal Skelly, Chester Morris, Evelyn Brent, William B. Davidson, Effie Ellsler, Gary Oliver, Leslie Fenton, Charles Giblyn, Joseph Mankiewicz, and Wilson Hammell.

Dangerous Paradise (1930, Paramount). Based on incidents from a novel by Joseph Conrad. With Nancy Carroll, Richard Arlen, Warner Oland, Gustav von Seyffertitz, Francis MacDonald, George Kotsonaros, Dorothea Woolbert, Clarence H. Wilson, Evelyn Selbie, Willie Fung, Wong Wing, and Lillian Worth.

Young Eagles (1930, Paramount). Based on Elliott White Spring's stories, "The One Who Was Clever" and "Sky-High." With Charles Rogers, Jean Arthur, Paul Lukas, Stuart Erwin, Frank Ross, Jack Luden, Freeman Wood, Gordon de Main, George Irving, and Stanley Blystone.

Maybe It's Love (1930, Warner Brothers). Screenplay by Joseph Jackson and Mark Canfield, from the story, "College Widows," by George Ade. With Joan Bennett, Joe E. Brown, James Hall, Laura Lee, Anders Randolf, Sumner Getchell, George Irving, George Bickel, Howard Jones, Bill Banker, and Russell Saunders.

Other Men's Women (1931, Warner Brothers). Screenplay by Maude Fulton and William K. Wells. With Grant Withers, Regis Toomey, Mary Astor, James Cagney, Joan Blondell, Fred Kohler, J. Farrell MacDonald, Lillian Worth, and Walter Long.

The Public Enemy (1931, Warner Brothers). Screenplay by Kubec Glasmon and John Bright. With Edward Woods, James Cagney, Donald Cook, Joan Blondell, Jean Harlow, Beryl Mercer, Ben Hendricks, Jr., Robert Emmett O'Connor, Leslie Fenton, Louise Brooks, Murray Kinnell, and Mae Clarke.

Night Nurse (1931, Warner Brothers). Story by Dora Marcy, adaptation by Oliver H. P. Garrett, dialogue by Oliver H. P. Garrett and Charles Kenyon. With Barbara Stanwyck, Ben Lyon, Joan Blondell, Clark Gable, Charles Winninger, Charlotte Merriam, Vera Lewis, Blanche Frederici, Edward Nugent, and Ralf Harolde.

Star Witness (1931, Warner Brothers). Screenplay by Lucien Hubbard. With Walter Huston, Charles "Chic" Sale, Dickie Moore, Grant Mitchell, Frances Starr, Ralph Ince, Sally Blane, Edward J. Nugent, Tom Dugan, Robert Elliott, Noel Madison, George Ernest, and Russell Hopton.

Safe in Hell (1931, Warner Brothers, First National). Story by Houston Branch, adaptation and dialogue by Maude Fulton. With Dorothy Mackaill, Donald Cook, John Wray, Ralf Harolde, Ivan Simpson, and Victor Varconi.

The Hatchet Man (1932, Warner Brothers, First National). Screenplay by J. Grubb Alexander, based on the play, "The Honorable Mr. Wong," by Achmed Abdullah and David Belasco. With Edward G. Robinson, Loretta Young, Dudley Digges, Leslie Fenton, Edmund Breese, Tully Marshall, Noel Madison, Blanche Frederici, J. Carroll Naish, Toshia Mori, Charles Middleton, Ralph Ince, Otto Yamaoka, Evelyn Selbin, Allyn Warren, Eddie Piel, Willie Fung, and Anna Chang.

So Big (1932, Warner Brothers). Screenplay by J. Grubb Alexander and Robert Lord, based on the novel by Edna Ferber. With Barbara Stanwyck, George Brent, Dickie Moore, Guy Kibbee, and Bette Davis.

Love Is a Racket (1932, Warner Brothers, First National). Screenplay by Rian James and Courtenay Terrett. With Douglas Fairbanks, Jr., Ann Dvorak, Lee Tracy, Frances Dee, Lyle Talbot, Warren Hymer, William Burress, and George Raft.

The Purchase Price (1932, Warner Brothers). Screenplay by Robert Lord, based on the story by Arthur Stringer. With Barbara Stanwyck, George Brent, Lyle Talbot, David Landau, Leila Bennett, Murray Kinnell, Crawford Kent, and Hardie Albright.

The Conquerors (1932, RKO). Based on a story by Howard Estabrook. With Richard Dix, Ann Harding, Edna May Oliver, Guy Kibbee, Julie Haydon, Donald Cook, Harry Holman, Richard Gallagher, and Walter Walker.

Frisco Jenny (1933, Warner Brothers, First National). Screenplay by Wilson Mizner and Robert Lord. With Ruth Chatterton, Donald Cook, James Murray, Louis Calhern, Hallam Cooley, Pat O'Malley, Robert Warwick, Harold Huber, and Helen Jerome Eddy.

Central Airport (1933, Warner Brothers, First National). Screenplay by Rian James and James Seymour, from the story by Jack Moffitt. With Richard Barthelmess, Sally Eilers, Tom Brown, Glenda Farrell, Harold Huber, Grant Mitchell, James Murray, Claire McDowell, Willard Robertson, Arthur Vinton, Charles Seldon, and John Wayne.

Lilly Turner (1933, Warner Brothers, First National). Screenplay by Gene Markey and Kathryn Scola, from the play by Philip Dunning and George Abbott. Produced by Hal Wallis. With Ruth Chatterton, George Brent, Frank McHugh, Guy Kibbee, Gordon Westcott, Ruth Donnelly, Marjorie Gateston, Robert Barrat, Arthur Vinton, Grant Mitchell, Margaret Seddon, Hobart Cavanaugh, Catherine Ward, Lucille Ward, and Mae Busch.

Midnight Mary (1933, MGM). Based on a story by Anita Loos. With Loretta Young, Ricardo Cortez, Franchot Tone, Andy Devine, Una Merkel, Frank Conroy, Warren Hymer, and Ivan Simpson.

Heroes for Sale (1933, Warner Brothers, First National). Screenplay by Robert Lord and Wilson Mizner. Produced by Hal Wallis. With Richard Barthelmess, Aline MacMahon, Loretta Young, Gordon Westcott, Berton Churchill, Robert Barrat, Grant Mitchell, Charles Grapewin, Robert McWade, George Pat Collins, James Murray, Edwin Maxwell, Margaret Seddon, and Arthur Vinton.

Wild Boys of the Road (1933, Warner Brothers, First National). Screenplay by Earl Baldwin, based on a story by Daniel Ahearn. Produced by Robert Presnell. With Frankie Darro, Dorothy Coonan, Rochelle Hudson, Edwin Phillips, Ann Hovey, Arthur Hohl, Grant Mitchell, Claire McDowell, Sterling Holloway, Charles Grapewin, Robert Barrat, Ward Bond, Adrian Morris, Shirley Dunsted, Minna Gombell, and Willard Robertson.

College Coach (1933, Warner Brothers). Screenplay by Niven Busch and Manuel Seff. Produced by Robert Lord. With Dick Powell, Ann Dvorak, Pat O'Brien, Arthur Byron, Lyle Talbot, Hugh Herbert, Arthur Hohl, Philip Faversham, Charles C. Wilson, Guinn Williams, Nat Pendleton, Philip Reed, Donald Meek, Berton Churchill, Harry Beresford, Herman Bing, and Joe Sauers.

Looking for Trouble (1934, 20th Century-Fox Production, United Artists). Based on a story by J. R. Bren. With Spencer Tracy, Constance Cummings, Jack Oakie, Morgan Conway, Arline Judge, Judith Wood, Paul Harvey, Joseph Sauers, Franklyn Ardell, and Paul Porcasi.

Stingaree (1934, RKO). Based on stories by E. W. Hornung. With Irene Dunne, Richard Dix, Mary Boland, Conway Tearle, Andy Devine, Henry Stephenson, Una O'Connor, George Barraud, Reginald Owen, and Snub Pollard.

The President Vanishes (1934, Paramount). Screenplay by Lynn Starling from the novel by an anonymous author. Produced by Walter Wanger. With Arthur Byron, Janet Beecher, Paul Kelly, Peggy Conklin, Rosalind Russell, Sidney Blackmer, Douglas Wood, Walter Kingsford, De Witt Jennings, Charles Grapewin, Charles Richman, Jason Robards, Paul Harvey, Robert McWade, Edward Arnold, Osgood Perkins, Edward Ellis, Andy Devine, and Harry Woods.

Call of the Wild (1935, 20th Century-Fox). Screenplay by Gene Fowler and Leonard Brackins, based on the novel by Jack London. A Darryl F. Zanuck Production, presented by Joseph Schenk. With Clark Gable, Loretta Young, Jack Oakie, Frank Conroy, Reginald Owen, Sidney Tyler, Katherine DeMille, Lalo Encinas, Charles Stevens, James Burke, and Duke Green.

The Robin Hood of El Dorado (1936, MGM). Screenplay by William A. Wellman, Joseph Calleia, and Melvin Levy, based on the biography by Walter Noble Burns. Produced by John W. Considine, Jr. With Warner Baxter, Ann Loring, Bruce Cabot, Margo, J. Carroll Naish, Soledad Jimenez, Carlos de Valdez, Eric Linden, Edgar Kennedy, Charles Trowbridge, Harvey Stephens, Ralph Remley, George Regas Howard, and Harry Woods.

Small Town Girl (1936, MGM). Screenplay by John Lee Mahin and Edith Fitzgerald, based on the novel by Ben Ames Williams. Produced by Hunt Stromberg. With Janet Gaynor, Robert Taylor, Binnie Barnes, Lewis Stone, Andy Devine, Elizabeth Patterson, Frank Craven, James Stewart, Douglas Fowley, Isabel Jewell, Charles Grapewin, Nella Waller, Robert Greig, Edgar Kennedy, and Willie Fung.

A Star Is Born (1937, United Artists). Screenplay by Dorothy Parker, Alan Campbell, and Robert Carson (with Ring Lardner, Jr., and Budd Schulberg uncredited), based on a story by William A. Wellman and Robert Carson. Produced by David O. Selznick. With Janet Gaynor, Fredric March, Adolphe Menjou, Andy Devine, May Robson, and Lionel Stander.

Nothing Sacred (1937, United Artists). Screenplay by Ben Hecht (with Ring Lardner, Jr., and George Oppenheimer uncredited), from the story, "Letter to the Editor," by James A. Street. Produced by David O. Selznick. With Carole Lombard, Fredric March, Charles Winninger, Walter Connolly, Sig Ruman, Frank Fay, Maxie Rosenblum, Margaret Hamilton, Troy Brown, Hattie McDaniel, Olin Howland, George Chandler, Clair Du Brey, John Qualen, and Charles Richman.

Men With Wings (1938, Paramount). Screenplay by Robert Carson. Produced by William A. Wellman. With Fred MacMurray, Ray Milland, Louise Campbell, Andy Devine, Lynne Overman, Porter Hall, Walter Abel, Kitty Kelly, James Burke, Willard Robertson, Virginia Weidler, Donald O'Connor, Billy Cook, Dorothy Tennant, Juanita Quigley, and Marilyn Knowlden.

Beau Geste (1939, Paramount). Screenplay by Robert Carson, based on a novel by Percival Christopher Wren. Produced by William A. Wellman. With Gary Cooper, Ray Milland, Robert Preston, Brian Donlevy, Susan Hayward, J. Carroll Naish, Donald O'Connor, James Stevenson, Harry Woods, James Burke, Albert Dekker, and Broderick Crawford.

The Light That Failed (1939, Paramount). Screenplay by Robert Carson, based on the novel by Rudyard Kipling. Produced by William A. Wellman. With Ronald Colman, Walter Huston, Muriel Angelus, Ida Lupino, Dudley Digges, Ernest Cossart, Ferike Boros, Pedro de Cordoba, Colin Tapley, Fay Helm, Ronald Sinclair, Sarita, Wooton, Halliwell Hobbes, Charles Irwin, Francis MacDonald, George Regas, and Wilfred Roberts.

Reaching for the Sun (1941, Paramount). Screenplay by W. L. River, based on a story by Wessel Smitter. Produced by William A. Wellman. With Joel McCrea, Ellen Drew, Eddie Bracken, Albert Dekker, Billy Gilbert, George Chandler, Bodil Ann Rosing, James Burke, Charles D. Brown, and Regis Toomey.

Roxie Hart (1942, 20th Century-Fox). Screenplay by Nunnally Johnson, based on the play, *Chicago,* by Maurine Watkins. Produced by Nunnally Johnson. With Ginger Rogers, Adolphe Menjou, George Montgomery, Lynne Overman, Nigel Bruce, Phil Silvers, Sara Allgood, William Frawley, Spring Byington, Helene Reynolds, George Chandler, George Lessey, Iris Adrian, and Milton Parsons.

The Great Man's Lady (1942, Paramount). Screenplay by W. L. River, original story by Adela Rogers St. John and Seena Owen, based on a short story by Viña Delmar. Produced by William A. Wellman. With Barbara Stanwyck, Joel McCrea, Brian Donlevy, Katherine Stevens, Thurston Hall, Lloyd Corrigan, Lillian Yarbo, Damian O'Flynn, Charles Lane, George Chandler, Anna Q. Nilsson, George P. Huntley, Milton Parsons, Etta McDaniel, Mary Treen, and Helen Lynd.

Thunder Birds (1942, 20th Century-Fox). Screenplay by Lamar Trotti, from an original story by Melville Crossman. Produced by Lamar Trotti. With Gene Tierney, Preston Foster, John Sutton, Jack Holt, Dame May Whitty, George Barbier, Richard Haydn, Reginald Denny, Ted North, Janis Carter, Archie Got, Lawrence Ung, Montague Shaw, Nana Bryant, Iris Adrian, Viola Moore, Connie Leon, Walter Tetley, Billy McGuire, and Richard Woodruff.

The Ox-Bow Incident (1943, 20th Century-Fox). Screenplay by Lamar Trotti, from a novel by Walter Van Tilburg Clark. Produced by Lamar Trotti. With Henry Fonda, Dana Andrews, Mary Beth Hughes, Anthony Quinn, William Eythe, Henry Morgan, Jane Darwell, Matt Briggs, Harry Davenport, Frank Conroy, Marc Lawrence, Paul Hurst, Victor Kilian, Chris-Pin Martin, Frank Orth, Ted North, Dick Rich, Francis Ford, Rondo Hatton, and Leigh Whippen.

Lady of Burlesque (1943, United Artists). Screenplay by James Gunn, based on the novel, *The G String Murder,* by Gypsy Rose Lee. Produced by Hunt Stromberg. With Barbara Stanwyck, Michael O'Shea, J. Edward Bromberg, Iris Adrian, Gloria Dickson, Victoria Faust, Stephanie Bachelor, Charles Dingle, Marion Martin, Eddie Gordon, Frank Fenton, Pinky Lee, and Frank Conroy.

Buffalo Bill (1944, 20th Century-Fox). Screenplay by Aeneas MacKenzie, Clements Ripley, and Cecile Kramer, based on a story by Frank Winch. Produced by Harry A. Sherman. With Joel McCrea, Maureen O'Hara, Linda Darnell, Thomas Mitchell,

Edgar Buchanan, Anthony Quinn, Moroni Olsen, Frank Fenton, Matt Briggs, George Lessey, Frank Orth, George Chandler, Chief Many Treaties, Nick Thompson, Chief Thundercloud, and Sidney Blackmer.

This Man's Navy (1945, MGM). Story and screenplay by Borden Chase, based on an idea by Comdr. Herman E. Holland, USN Retired. Produced by Samuel Marx. With Wallace Beery, Tom Drake, James Gleason, Jan Clayton, Selena Royle, Noah Beery, Sr., Henry O'Neill, Steve Brodie, George Chandler, Donald Curtis, Arthur Walsh, Will Fowler, and Richard Crockett.

Story of G.I. Joe (1945, United Artists). Screenplay by Leopold Atlas, Guy Endore, and Philip Stevenson, based on Ernie Pyle's books, *Here Is Your War* and *Brave Men*. Produced by Lester Cowan. With Burgess Meredith, Robert Mitchum, Freddie Steele, Wally Cassell, Jimmy Lloyd, Jack Reilly, Bill Murphy, and combat veterans of the campaigns in Africa, Sicily, and Italy.

Gallant Journey (1946, Columbia). Screenplay by Byron Morgan and William A. Wellman. Produced by William A. Wellman. With Glenn Ford, Janet Blair, Charles Kemper, Jimmy Lloyd, Henry Travers, Arthur Shields, Willard Robertson, Selena Royle, Robert DeHaven, and Charles Ruggles.

Magic Town (1947, RKO). Screenplay by Robert Riskin, based on a story by Robert Riskin and Joseph Krumgold. Produced by Robert Riskin. With James Stewart, Jane Wyman, Kent Smith, Ned Sparks, Wallace Ford, Regis Toomey, Ann Doran, Donald Meek, E. J. Ballentine, Ann Shoemaker, Mickey Kuhn, Howard Freeman, Harry Holman, Mary Currier, Mickey Roth, Frank Fenton, George Irving, Selmer Jackson, Robert Dudley, and Julia Dean.

The Iron Curtain (1948, 20th Century-Fox). Screenplay by Milton Krims, based on the personal story of Igor Gouzenko. Produced by Sol C. Siegel. With Dana Andrews, Gene Tierney, June Havoc, Berry Kroeger, Edna Best, Stefan Schnabel, Nicholas Joy, Eduard Franz, Frederick Tozere, Noel Cravat, Christopher Robin Olsen, Peter Whitney, Leslie Barrie, Mauritz Hugo, John Shay, Victor Wood, and John Ridgeley.

Yellow Sky (1949, 20th Century-Fox). Screenplay by Lamar Trotti, based on a story by W. R. Burnett. Produced by Lamar Trotti. With Gregory Peck, Anne Baxter, Richard Widmark, Robert Arthur, John Russell, Henry Morgan, James Barton, Charles Kemper, Robert Adler, Harry Carter, Victor Kilian, Paul Hurst, Hank Worden, Jay Silverheels, and William Gould.

Battleground (1949, MGM). Screenplay by Robert Pirosh. Produced by Dore Schary. With Van Johnson, Ricardo Montalban, John Hodiak, George Murphy, Marshall Thompson, Jerome Courtland, Don Taylor, Bruce Cowling, James Whitmore, Douglas Fowley, Leon Ames, Guy Anderson, Thomas E. Breen, Denise

Darcel, Richard Jaeckel, Jim Arness, Scotty Beckett, and Brett King.

The Next Voice You Hear (1950, MGM). Screenplay by Charles Schnee, based on a story by George Sumner Albee. Produced by Dore Schary. With James Whitmore, Nancy Davis, Gary Gray, Lillian Bronson, Art Smith, Tom D'Andrea, and Jeff Corey.

Across the Wide Missouri (1951, MGM). Screenplay by Talbot Jennings, based on a story by Talbot Jennings, Frank Cavett, and a book by Bernard de Voto. Produced by Robert Sisk. With Clark Gable, Ricardo Montalban, John Hodiak, Adolphe Menjou, Maria Elena Marques, J. Carroll Naish, Jack Holt, Alan Napier, George Chandler, Richard Anderson, Henri Letondal, Douglas Fowley, Louis Nicoletti, Ben Watson, Russell Simpson, and Frankie Darro.

Westward the Women (1952, MGM). Screenplay by Charles Schnee, based on a story by Frank Capra. Produced by Dore Schary. With Robert Taylor, Denise Darcel, Henry Nakamura, Lenore Lonergan, Marilyn Erskine, Hope Emerson, Julie Bishop, John McIntire, Renata Vanni, and Beverly Dennis.

It's a Big Country (1952, MGM). Screenplay by William Ludwig, Helen Deutsch, Ray Chordes, Isobel Tennant, Allen Pinkin, Dorothy Kingsley, Dore Schary, and George Wells. Directed by Richard Thorpe, John Sturges, Charles Vidor, Don Weis, Clarence Brown, William A. Wellman, and Don Hartman. With Ethel Barrymore, Keefe Brasselle, Gary Cooper, Nancy Davis, Van Johnson, Gene Kelly, Janet Leigh, Majorie Main, Fredric March, George Murphy, William Powell, S. Z. Sakall, Lewis Stone, James Whitmore, Keenan Wynn, Leon Ames, Angela Clarke, Bobby Hyatt, and Sharon McManus.

My Man and I (1952, MGM). Screenplay by John Fante and Jack Leonard. Produced by Stephen Ames. With Shelley Winters, Ricardo Montalban, Wendell Corey, Claire Trevor, Jose Torvay, Jack Elam, Pascual Garcia Pena, George Chandler, Juan Torena, and Carlos Conde.

Island in the Sky (1953, Warner Brothers). Screenplay by Ernest K. Gann, based on his novel. A Wayne-Fellows Production. With John Wayne, Lloyd Nolan, Walter Abel, James Arness, Andy Devine, Allyn Joslyn, James Lydon, Harry Carey, Jr., Hal Baylor, Sean McClory, and Wally Cassell.

The High and the Mighty (1954, Warner Brothers). Screenplay by Ernest K. Gann, based on his novel. A Wayne-Fellows Production. With John Wayne, Claire Trevor, Laraine Day, Robert Stack, Jan Sterling, Phil Harris, Robert Newton, David Brian, Paul Kelly, Sidney Blackmer, Julie Bishop, Gonzalez-Gonzalez, John Howard, Wally Brown, William Campbell, Ann Doran, John Qualen, Paul Fix, George Chandler, Joy Kim, Michael Wellman, Douglas Fowley, and Regis Toomey.

Track of the Cat (1954, Warner Brothers). Screenplay by A. Bezzerides, based on a novel by Walter Van Tilburg Clark. A Wayne-Fellows Production. With Robert Mitchum, Teresa Wright, Diana Lynn, Tab Hunter, Beulah Bondi, Philip Tonge, William Hopper, and Carl Switzer.

Blood Alley (1955, Warner Brothers). Screenplay by A. S. Fleischman, based on his novel. A Batjac Production. With John Wayne, Lauren Bacall, Paul Fix, Joy Kim, Mike Mazurki, Henry Nakamura, Berry Kroeger, W. T. Chang, George Chan, Anita Ekberg, and Victor Sen Yung.

Darby's Rangers (1958, Warner Brothers). Screenplay by Guy Trosper, based on a book by Maj. James Altieri. Produced by Martin Rackin. With James Garner, Etchika Choureau, Jack Warden, Edward Byrnes, Venetia Stevenson, Torin Thatcher, Peter Brown, Joan Elan, Corey Allen, Stuart Whitman, Murray Hamilton, Bill Wellman, Jr., Andrea King, and Adam Williams.

Lafayette Escadrille (1958, Warner Brothers). Screenplay by A. I. Fleischman, based on a story by William A. Wellman. Produced by William A. Wellman. With Tab Hunter, Etchika Choureau, Marcel Dalio, David Janssen, Paul Fix, Veola Vonn, Will Hutchins, Clint Eastwood, Bob Hover, Tom Laughlin, Brett Halsey, Henry Nakamura, Maurice Marsac, Raymond Bailey, George Nardelli, William A. Wellman, Jr., Jody McCrea, and Dennis Devine.

INDEX